A set of original essays by original thinkers on crime and war. This insightful volume takes a large new step toward establishing the study of war as a field that increasingly attracts many of the best of the next generation of criminologists.

John Braithwaite, *Distinguished Professor,*
Australian National University, Australia.

Walklate and McGarry have produced a wide-ranging and inclusive collection of essays on criminology and war. This book is necessary reading for anyone interested in the study of war, resistance, state violence, and criminology.

David Kauzlarich, *Professor,*
Southern Illinois University Edwardsville, USA.

Criminology and War

It is widely observed that the study of war has been paid limited attention within criminology. This is intellectually curious given that acts of war have occurred persistently throughout history and perpetuate criminal acts, victimisation and human rights violations on a scale unprecedented relative to domestic levels of crime. However, there are authoritative voices within criminology who have been studying war from the borders of the discipline.

This book contains a selection of criminological authors who have been authoritatively engaged in studying criminology and war. Following an introduction that 'places war within criminology', the collection is arranged across three themed sections including: *Theorising War, Law and Crime; Linking War and Criminal Justice;* and *War, Sexual Violence and Visual Trauma.* Each chapter takes substantive topics within criminology and victimology (i.e. corporate crime, history, imprisonment, criminal justice, sexual violence, trauma, security and crime control to name but a few) and invites the reader to engage in critical discussions relating to wars both past and present.

The chapters within this collection are theoretically rich and empirically diverse, and come together to create the first authoritative published collection of original essays specifically dedicated to criminology and war. Students and researchers alike interested in war, critical criminology and victimology will find this an accessible study companion that centres the disparate criminological attention to war into one comprehensive collection.

Sandra Walklate is Eleanor Rathbone Chair of Sociology at the University of Liverpool and is internationally recognised for her work in and around criminal victimisation, particularly the fear of crime. She has written extensively with Ross McGarry and Gabe Mythen on risk, resilience and cultural victimology and in 2014 received the British Society of Criminology's award for outstanding achievement.

Ross McGarry is Lecturer in Criminology within the Department of Sociology, Social Policy and Criminology at the University of Liverpool. He has previously conducted research with British soldiers from the war in Iraq and is currently engaged in research on British military repatriations. He is the author and co-author (with Sandra Walklate) of other forthcoming texts, including *Victims: Trauma, Testimony and Justice* from Routledge and the *Palgrave Handbook on Criminology and War.*

Routledge Studies in Crime and Society

Criminology and War

Transgressing the borders

Edited by
Sandra Walklate and Ross McGarry

LONDON AND NEW YORK

First published 2015
by Routledge
2 Park Square, Milton Park, Abingdon, Oxfordshire OX14 4RN

and by Routledge
711 Third Avenue, New York, NY 10017

First issued in paperback 2016

Routledge is an imprint of the Taylor & Francis Group, an informa business

British Library Cataloguing in Publication Data
A catalogue record for this book is available from the British Library

Library of Congress Cataloging in Publication Data
Criminology and war : transgressing the borders / edited by Sandra Walklate and Ross McGarry.
    pages cm. – (Routledge studies in crime and society)
    Includes bibliographical references and index.
    1. War and crime. 2. Criminology. 3. War crimes. I. Walklate, Sandra. II. McGarry, Ross.
    HV6189.C74 2015
    364–dc23
                    2014030950

ISBN 13: 978-1-138-28865-2 (pbk)
ISBN 13: 978-0-415-72215-5 (hbk)

Typeset in Times New Roman
by Taylor & Francis Books

Contents

List of illustrations

Figures

Contributors

Zoe Alker recently completed her doctoral thesis on street violence in mid-Victorian Liverpool. She is currently a postdoctoral researcher on a project called After Care: Youth justice and its long term impacts 1850–1945 which examines the ways in which juvenile justice impacted upon the lives of young offenders.

William B. Brown is the Research Director for the Pacific Policy and Research Institute and Pacific Sentencing Initiative. He is also Professor of Criminal Justice at Western Oregon University. He has published recently on the problems faced by Iraq and Afghanistan veterans in their entanglement in the criminal justice system and the issues they face reintegrating back into civilian culture.

Barry Godfrey has over 20 years of experience in researching comparative criminology and international crime history. His latest co- or sole-authored books include *Policing the Factory; Crime in England 1880–1945*; and *Crime and Justice, 1750 to the Present* (all published in 2014). He currently leads a large Arts & Humanities Research Council-funded project (www.digitalpanopticon.com).

Ruth Jamieson is an honorary Lecturer in the School of Law, Queen's University Belfast. Her current research interests are in the criminology of war, the politics of victimhood, and ageing and social exclusion among politically-motivated former prisoners in Northern Ireland.

John Lea is Visiting Professor of Criminology at the University of Leicester. He is one of the founders of the Left Realist school of criminology and has written widely on criminological theory and criminal justice. His publications include *What Is To Be Done About Law and Order?* (with Jock Young, 1984) and *Crime and Modernity* (2002).

Ross McGarry is Lecturer in Criminology within the Department of Sociology, Social Policy and Criminology at the University of Liverpool. He has previously conducted research with British soldiers from the war in Iraq and is currently engaged in research on British military repatriations. He is the author and co-author (with Sandra Walklate) of other forthcoming texts, including *Victims: Trauma, Testimony and Justice* from Routledge and the *Palgrave Handbook on Criminology and War.*

Wayne Morrison is a Professor in the School of Law at Queen Mary's University College London. He has published extensively on the role of art, poetry and photography in war and genocide.

Christopher Mullins, PhD is an Associate Professor of Criminology and Criminal Justice at Southern Illinois University, Carbondale. His work focuses on violence, both street violence and armed conflict atrocities, and international criminal justice.

Emma Murray is a Senior Lecturer in Criminal Justice at Liverpool John Moores University. Emma's principle research interests and doctoral research are rooted in the development of the criminology of war. She is currently working with military veterans in probation settings in the North West. Throughout her research she aims to reposition the issues and challenges faced by returning military within a criminological and political setting through the coming together of criminology and international relations as disciplines and socio-political analytical knowledge.

Vincenzo Ruggiero is Professor of Sociology and Director of the Crime and Conflict Research Centre at Middlesex University in London. He has conducted research on behalf of national and international agencies, including the European Commission and the United Nations. Among his many sole-authored books are: *Crime and Markets* (2000), *Crime in Literature* (2003), *Understanding Political Violence* (2006), *Penal Abolitionism* (2010) and *The Crimes of the Economy* (2013).

Nishanth Visagaratnam MNS, MS is a doctoral candidate in sociology with a specialisation in criminology and criminal justice at Southern Illinois University, Carbondale. Her primary areas of research focus on war crimes, victimology and criminology, while her secondary areas include sociology of immigration, diaspora, social movements and gender.

Sandra Walklate is Eleanor Rathbone Chair of Sociology at the University of Liverpool and is internationally recognised for her work in and around criminal victimisation, particularly the fear of crime. She has written extensively with Ross McGarry and Gabe Mythen on risk, resilience and cultural victimology and in 2014 received the British Society of Criminology's award for outstanding achievement.

David Whyte is a Reader in Sociology at the University of Liverpool, where he teaches and conducts research on state-corporate crime. In 2008 he was awarded the Leon Radzinowicz Prize for his work on the role of corporations in the occupation of Iraq. He is currently finishing a long-term research project on corporate human rights violations.

Preface and acknowledgements

This edited collection brings together for the first time a selection of original essays specifically dedicated to the academic study of criminology and war. For those involved in writing and researching within this area, the suitability of criminology to engage with the subject matter of war and conflict is self-evident. However, over the years, experience has shown that, when attempting to publish work of this nature, the borders of the discipline present themselves sharply. Admittedly this has led to many frustrated conversations regarding the short-sightedness of the intellectual endeavours of criminology, the difficulties of publishing our ideas, forcing us to battle with the nuances of other disciplines. With the centenary of the First World War fast approaching we had both felt compelled to draw criminological attention to this event to ensure that the discipline made a critical mark on this significant point in history. This collection originally took the form of a proposal for a Special Issue of an international journal. We were disappointed when the proposal was rejected. Part of the feedback from the journal suggested an edited collection as an alternative avenue. On reflection we are thankful for this and the rejection since this merely made us more determined to ensure that our efforts and those of our contributors bore fruit. So if we had not found ourselves at the borders of the discipline, this book would not have come into being. However, there is more to be thankful for than the stubbornness of mainstream criminology.

We would first like to offer our thanks and appreciation to each of the contributors of this edited collection who have produced chapters that are both theoretically rich and empirically diverse. Although working independently of one another, each has managed to make contributions that are complementary and sit side by side coherently. All authors have had to work to tight deadlines, but particular thanks go to John Lea and Emma Murray, who each stepped in at the last minute to produce excellent individual chapters at very short notice. We would of course like to acknowledge the work of another of our authors, Ruth Jamieson, whose intellectual insights first coined the phrase the 'criminology of war' back in 1998. Ruth has recently published an excellent selection of earlier works in the long awaited *Criminology of War* from Ashgate. We thank Ruth for setting the groundwork within the discipline and we consider ourselves privileged to have her make a contribution here.

It is also fitting to acknowledge the sad passing of Jock Young in late 2013. Both Jock and his partner Jayne Mooney were due to make a co-authored contribution to this edited collection, but for obvious reasons this was no longer possible. Rest assured that Jock's intellectual influences are still to be found within this collection, as they can in every corner of the discipline.

The ideas for this book have, however, not been created in a vacuum. We offer our gratitude to both Tom Sutton and Heidi Lee at Routledge. Tom provided the opportunity for this book to be commissioned and Heidi has worked tirelessly to ensure it has been delivered on time. During this process we have affectionately come to refer to Heidi as 'the one who wears the stripes' for her 'military' precision and organisation: the irony of this when preparing a book of this nature is not lost on us. We would also specifically like to thank our colleague and good friend Gabe Mythen for his encouragement and intellectual input in the broader development of our criminological interests with war, security, resilience and the military, which began long before this book came into print. Gabe: we are pleased to say that there are indeed 'at least two papers here'!

Thanks also go to Expac, Seesyu Press, Daniel Heyman, an artist collective from Pakistan and the USA, the Ghetto Fighters' House Museum, The Beate Klarsfeld Foundation, the United States Holocaust Memorial Museum and Pam Feil, the Museum of Jewish Heritage, Emanuel Ringelblum Jewish Historical Institute and Anvil Press Poetry for allowing us to reproduce various materials in this book.

Finally we would like to offer thanks to our friend and colleague Stuart Griffiths (www.stuartgriffiths.net) who has been kind enough to allow us to use his photography of British soldiers and military repatriations at Royal Wootton Bassett in other work we have published. Stuart has once again generously allowed us to use his photography in Chapter 9, but more importantly he has provided the mesmerising cover image of this book. The photograph is of the silhouetted shapes of British Parachute Regiment soldiers training in the UK for a deployment to Afghanistan. To finish, we would like to offer some thoughts on why we have chosen this particular image and what it should encourage us to consider in the context of criminology and war.

Taking the soldier as our muse, war is nothing but destructive to all involved, and the overtones of this image connect wars past and present. In the context of the 'war against terror' we have come to learn of the vulnerabilities of soldiers deployed to distant lands, returning with myriad physical, psychological and social problems. However the presence of the Parachute Regiment in this image also stand to remind us of the brutality of war and the atrocities which this can bring to civilian populations, notably experienced at the behest of the British military on the streets of Northern Ireland during Bloody Sunday. You will notice that the soldiers in this image are not individually identifiable, but their silhouettes are instantly recognisable. As such they represent both the presence and the absence of the state at war. Those who leave families and loved ones behind to bloody their uniforms at close quarters are quite different from those who bloody their suits orchestrating violence at a distance. Criminological attention to war has frequently defaulted to studying soldiers and their crimes, represented by the silhouetted soldiers scattered throughout this image in the foreground and the distance. Soldiers do indeed appear in chapters throughout this book, but if we wish to move criminological knowledge forward, we need to leave some well trodden issues behind and carry some imaginative ideas along with us: taking steps down an intellectual path flanked by the conventional in order to transgress the borders of criminology and war.

Ross McGarry and Sandra Walklate
Department of Sociology, Social Policy and Criminology
University of Liverpool, May 2014

Introduction

Placing war within criminology

Ross McGarry and Sandra Walklate

Introduction

There is something to be said for the timing of this book: 2014 was the centenary year of the First World War. The social and cultural significance of this is to be marked until 2018 by the First World War Centenary Programme (see www.1914.org) in a series of global events to remember the loss of over 16 million people. Alongside events to remember the deaths of 5 million Allied forces there will also no doubt be gestures to commemorate the deaths of the 7 million civilians who lost their lives during the war. For the popular imagination this centenary not only serves to 'mark, commemorate and remember' the sacrifices that were made during this period (as the First World War Centenary Programme suggests), but it also urges us to be reflective of the impact that this war has had in shaping the contemporary social world.

Since 1918 the world has remained tainted by violence through warfare in a variety of contexts that have touched every continent. Marked most significantly by the atrocities of the Holocaust, further wars have followed with varying public expediency, (in)coherent political narratives and (questionable) justifications for their purpose. Some wars have had fractious and ambiguous relationships with the public. There have been wars that have been allowed to lapse in and out of the public consciousness. There have also been genocidal conflicts from which powerful nations have conveniently remained absent. Contemporarily, arguably one of the most significant acts of war in the twenty-first century occurred in the protracted US-led war in Iraq lasting almost 7 years. This war became a key focal point carved into the aftermath of the attacks on the World Trade Center in New York on 11 September 2001 (9/11), with post-war 2013 marked as the most violent year for civilian deaths since sectarian and political violence reached its peak there in 2008. Across the Middle East subsequent wars in Syria and Libya erupted as part of the centrifuge of the Arab Spring, seeing chemical weapons deployed against civilians and public executions conducted as a proxy for summary justice. Elsewhere, Russia has experienced acts of violence influenced by Islamic Fundamentalism from the former war-torn Caucasus territory, a region implicated in the only other terrorist attack in North America since 9/11, exemplifying for Young (2007) the confluence between terrorism and war. As 2013 drew to a close, ethnic murders began to emerge in tribal and religious clashes in the Central African Republic reminiscent of the Rwandan and Kosovan Genocides; political-ethnic violence erupted in the world's newest state, South Sudan; and sectarian violence loomed large once again in Iraq, with Fallujah coming under the control of militant groups for the first time since US forces withdrew from the country in 2011. Stepping into the present day, as we write this introduction Russian forces have deployed military personnel into Ukraine against the advice of the international community. Moreover, the centenary of the First World War incongruously charts the withdrawal of Western military forces from Afghanistan, having participated in over a decade of fighting in the 'War on Terrorism'. Taken collectively, we would suggest that pausing to observe the focal point of the First World War should instead urge us – as criminologists and victimologists – to employ our sociological imaginations (Mills, 1959): to see a violent past firmly reflected in the present and instead recognise the First World War as marking the end of a long, ambiguous and bloody period of the twenty-first century. Within this book we do not look to provide a comprehensive overview of war, nor do we lay claim to providing an expert social, cultural or historical analysis of warfare. Instead we look to remove some inertia noted by Ruth Jamieson (2014) as being present within the discipline of criminology; to pay fuller attention to war as one of the 'ten ironies' of a critical criminology (Young, 2011).

Starting at the borders

Despite emerging against a backcloth of the First and Second World Wars, criminology, and indeed its sub-discipline victimology, have yet to address war in the substantive ways demonstrated by other disciplines. This is intellectually curious given that criminology is widely concerned with subject matter that addresses violence, crime and victimisation, all of which are consistent features of war-fighting and war-making (Jamieson, 1998). Within mainstream criminology, the unreflexive approaches of positivist and 'administrative criminology', concerned with promoting effective methods of crime control and measuring and reducing 'street crime', have long since been put to use by state criminal justice institutions for the purposes of bolstering social control and maintaining social order (Hudson, 1997). These 'footprints in the sand' were outlined some time ago by Stan Cohen (1981) mapping the contours and boundaries of the academic discipline of British criminology in particular within both state and university institutions. It is the interstitial space between the state and the academy that draws our attention in this introduction, encouraging us to look for where war is addressed within criminology and to identify a space to situate it more firmly.

In recognition of the colonial impacts of war both past and present, and in looking to identify borders for us to transgress, we acknowledge that although 'The expansion of criminology in Britain has been especially striking ... it is by no means a British phenomenon' (Loader and Sparks, 2012: 9). By first casting our criminological net further afield to areas not unaccustomed to the vagaries, experiences and threat of war we can begin to draw attention to the mainstream elements of the discipline that reflect the (Western) centrefolds of the 'criminological enterprise' (Bottoms, 1987).

Let us consider Asia as an example of one of the intellectual borders within the discipline; these are not borders that we intend to shape as a binary between the Orient and the Occident, but instead they offer us our own 'footprints' to trace some of the boundaries within criminology. Within Pakistan – a region both historically connected to the Cold War and contemporarily impacted by the 'War on Terror' (see Shaikh, 2011) – the benefits of criminology lay claim to its 'administrative' values and usefulness for state penal policy. For Fasihuddin (2008: i),

> Criminology education improves our understanding of law and more firmly embeds the notion of the rule of law into the body politic ... efforts for promoting the scientific and analytical criminological studies are conspicuously absent in Pakistan, where weak rule of law traditions and popularly disparaged legal infrastructures demand such studies, perhaps more than any other social sciences.

Similar applications of criminology can be found elsewhere in Taiwan, Korea, Cambodia and Vietnam (see Hebenton and Jou, 2005; Kang, 1980; Broadhurst and Keo, 2011; Cox, 2012 respectively), where criminological positivism has found a home in state centred institutions; bolstering penal policy and enhancing social control. For academic criminology the newly published Asian Handbook on Criminology (see Liu *et al.*, 2013) is testament to the development of criminology at these intellectual borders. China in particular is prototypical of criminological positivism (see Hebenton and Jou, 2010; Cao *et al.*, 2014) symptomatic of the socio-political climate in this part of the world offering clear recognition of the 'institutional' (Loader and Sparks, 2012) purposes of criminology in ways that have put constraints on the theoretical and methodological growth of the discipline. These institutional 'footprints' are also evident within the former British colonies of Australia[1] (see Australian Institute of Criminology, 2014; Putt and Lindley, 2011), Hong Kong (Xu, 2011) and – less successfully – India (see Poornachandra, 2011). Here 'crime science' has been inherited (or at least encouraged) by state justice institutions. The former colonial state of Singapore has similarly employed criminology outwith the academy by adopting a social control agenda of right realism, administrative criminology and social control theories (Narayanan, 2005). The exception to the rule in this institutional development of criminology[2] appears to have taken place in Japan (see Yokoyama, 2013). Here labelling theories, and Howard Becker's (1963) *Outsiders* in particular, were once popularised in sociology departments, although these interests in symbolic interactionism are said to have now disappeared.

Broadly speaking, then, we can propose that the ways in which the 'field of criminology' (Loader and Sparks, 2012) has established itself in these regions is through being adopted within state criminal justice institutions interested in its functional and administrative uses for the purposes of state building and reducing 'crime' (Lee and Laidler, 2013). Looking beyond metropole knowledge within criminology in this way helps to inform us differently about the discipline (Willis, *et al.*, 1999) and, as Morrison (2006) has observed, does indicate a sense of imperialism within the discipline that is disguised as a 'global criminology'. However, rather than providing us with borders to cross between the Orient and the Occident (Cain, 2000), it presents an evolution of criminology whose 'footprints' appear to have the tread of state criminal justice institutions and penal policy. However, in what way does this assist us in locating war within criminology?

Returning to the centrefold

As a discipline, criminology has been influenced by positivism from the outset and is undergirded by a conservative outlook on 'crime', social control and social order. Following the early Classicist formation of criminological thinking concerned with punishment (see Beccaria, 1804/1983; Bentham, 1879), biological and sociological approaches influenced by positivism emerged during the nineteenth century, first observing biological aetiologies (see Lombroso, 1876/2006) and later macro sociological functions of crime and punishment (see Durkheim, 1893). Moving from its philosophical and empirical birthplace in Western Europe to the US, criminology retained its positivist and empirical roots (see Haen-Marshall, 2001) as it began to flourish within sociology departments at the turn of the twentieth century, most famously amongst sociologists and anthropologists in the Chicago School of Sociology (see Park *et al.*, 1925). Here the sociological elements of the discipline began to take shape, engaging ethnographic work with more micro sociological approaches to crime and criminal behaviour (see Shaw and McKay, 1942). A key figure emerging from this school of thought was Edwin Sutherland, whose work not only contributed to the growth of ethnography (Sutherland, 1937) but also offered criminology its own defining borders. For Sutherland *et al.* (1934: 3),

> Criminology is the body of knowledge regarding delinquency and crime as a social phenomena. It includes within its scope the process of making laws, breaking laws, and of reacting toward the breaking of laws. These processes are three aspects of a somewhat unified sequence of interactions. Certain acts which are regarded as undesirable are defined by the political society as crimes. In spite of this definition some people persist in the behavior and thus commit crimes; the political society reacts by punishment, treatment, or prevention. This sequence of interactions is the subject matter of criminology.

Evident within this definition are the intellectual boundaries of an early criminological imagination. The restrictions of this imagination, influenced by the empirical positivist roots of criminology, remained a present influence within the Chicago School. Outwith the academy it became common for criminologists, particularly in the UK, to become 'institutionally based', putting criminology to work as a technocratic tool of state criminal justice (Loader and Sparks, 2012). With this shift to state institutions came a growing suspicion of sociologically informed criminological analysis on both sides of the Atlantic (Loader and Sparks, 2012) with practitioners and policy-makers preferring the practical uses of criminology over its emerging critical application. This preference for a positivist criminological analysis is perhaps best observed in the development and lasting influence of national criminal victimisation surveys from within the US Bureau of Justice Statistics (2013), and the Home Office in England and Wales (see Hough and Mayhew, 1983). The influences of 'crime science' can also be found lurking within the Cambridge Institute of Criminology in the UK: from the early critical focus directed by Sir Leon Radzinowicz (1999), to the mainstream values of 'experimental criminology' under the direction of Lawrence Sherman (see University of Cambridge, 2013). Recognising these developments as being concurrent with the development of criminology in other parts of the world we begin to see that criminology has, to a great extent, been popularly founded and developed within state institutions or with state interests in mind. As such we aver that criminology has had its borders set from its conception. These borders have not curtailed the discipline, but they have instead anchored it to a core set of concerns and prevailing ways of thinking, fixed with a specific mainstream context: 'crime' and criminal justice.

All of this, however, is not to suggest that criminology is uncritical. The critical edge within criminology can be drawn from a variety of perspectives, including symbolic interactionism (see Becker, 1963), post-structuralism (see Foucault, 1977), feminism (see Smart, 1977), left realism (see Lea and Young, 1984) and – more recently – cultural criminology (see Presdee, 2000). Although informed by these influences, the evolution of critical criminology more readily owes its early direction to the Chicago School which stimulated the discipline in ways that departed from positivism. In addition to defining the boundaries of mainstream criminology, Edwin Sutherland (1940, 1945) also turned the criminological gaze away from crimes of the powerless to consider the perpetuation of crime within 'respectable' echelons of society. For Sutherland (1940: 5),

> White-collar crime is real crime. It is not ordinarily called crime, and calling it by this name does not make it worse, just as refraining from calling it crime does not make it better than it otherwise would be. It is called crime here in order to bring it within the scope of criminology, which is justified because it is in violation of the criminal law. The crucial question in this analysis is the criterion of violation of the criminal law.

These critical features transgressing common understandings of crime and offending were further developed during the late twentieth century.

Although commenting little on crime, the work of Karl Marx influenced radical criminology (see Quinney, 1972) in the US and the 'new criminology' (see Taylor *et al.*, 1973; Schichor, 1980) in the UK. Understood broadly as critical criminology, the discipline began drawing attention to the criminal nature of the state, taking 'sides' – as Becker (1967) urged us to do – with those either constructed as 'deviants' (Cohen, 1972), the focus of ideological social control and order maintenance (Hall, *et al.*, 1978), or perpetually in positions of relative deprivation and social injustices perpetrated by state actors (see Lea and Young, 1984). In doing so, the discipline was provided with an opportunity to transcend the borders set around it by mainstream criminological positivism and to make a formal challenge to state authority. Critical criminology has since evolved into a vociferous but marginal part of the discipline focusing on a wide variety of 'crimes of the powerful' (see Whyte, 2008), extending the criminological imagination (Young, 2011) to include human rights violations (Schwendinger and Schwendinger, 1980; Green and Ward, 2000), corporate harms (Slapper and Tombs, 1999) and violence on a 'continuum' connecting the 'street' to the state (Young, 2007). Citing Sutherland's first observations almost 70 years later, Ruggiero (2005) urged for war to be perceived as synonymous to state and corporate crime, and for criminologists to be active in putting an end to warfare.

There are of course various reasons why criminology has paid little formal attention to war, but our particular proposition is threefold. We would first suggest that the routine practice of critically engaged research is restricted at the coalface of university-led research activities (see Squires, 2013). This is particularly pertinent to criminology. It has been suggested that those working within the discipline often lack the requisite analytical skills and resources to contemplate violence and victimisation perpetrated by state and corporate actors (Tombs and Whyte, 2002). Next, we would concur with the unease expressed by Walters (2003: 22) who has previously raised related concerns about the commodification of 'market-led' criminology within universities that compromise the critical pedagogy of the discipline making it 'wedded or subordinate to the politics of existing governing rationalities'. Finally, we wonder if criminology has – as part of its routine interests – a 'hierarchy of credibility' (Becker, 1967) that discourages a critical analysis of state-based violence, particularly relating to war, rendering the influential centre of mainstream criminology largely deferential to state interests and practices. These tensions and restrictions have previously been echoed by Hagan and Greer (2002: 260) when seeking to question the inability of criminology to study war,

> The obstacles posed by the power politics of the Cold War formed a great barrier to the study of war crimes and crimes against humanity as did, for example, the more widely recognised restrictions posed by class to the

early study of white-collar crime by Sutherland and others. The ongoing events in the Balkans and more recently, Afghanistan, extend the lesson that international and domestic politics influence not only the way in which war is made, but also the way in which war is understood and studied as crime.

Put more bluntly, we question if the 'criminological enterprise' is perhaps reluctant to bite the hand that feeds it.

Locating war within criminology

Despite the suggestion by Mullins (2011: 919) that war has been 'all but avoided' by theoretical criminological analysis it would, of course, be inaccurate to suggest that criminology has had a complete disengagement with 'war'. During the course of the First and Second World Wars the characteristics of warfare were noted in similar ways from across Europe, the UK and within the Chicago School. For Bonger (1916) the use of 'militarism' served the interests of a hegemonic capitalist economy to either control domestic populations, protect sovereign borders, or exploit 'foreign' territory for capital gain. Park (1941) conceived of war as serving the purposes of nation-building, competing for geographical borders and resources, and engendering difference within society. Being able to identify a state by its ability to commit violence with 'legitimacy' (Weber, 1919), for Park (1941: 568) war outlined the interests of the state and afforded it purpose,

> As states have come into existence by war, it has seemed to certain writers that they are forever condemned to continue their conquests in order to maintain their existence. Nothing is more demoralizing to an army or to a military state than peace, and nations to survive must act. There must always be some great collective enterprise on the national agenda in which all classes can actively participate.

At the same time Hermann Mannheim (1941) had begun making transgressions of his own. In *War and Crime* we are guided through the problems and possibilities of using the preserve of the criminologist (e.g. individualised crime and criminal justice) to understand war as not simply a matter for international humanitarian law, but as a means of conceiving the perpetration of war as a crime when conducted without just cause (Mannheim, 1941). Returning to the Chicago School following the Second World War Edwin Sutherland (1949) extended this critical interpretation of 'war crimes' to include corporate acts of deviance that resulted in profiteering from the war effort, tax evasion and treason. During this post-war period – at a time when criminology had a prime opportunity to build upon these critical observations – criminological interests rested instead on the effects of war on domestic crimes (see for example Cornil, 1951) and the prosecution of individual war crimes under international humanitarian law during the Nuremberg and Tokyo Trials. Tackling war in this way provided an account of either criminal or 'victors' justice' (Zolo, 2009) that obscured rather than implicated the role of the state in the violence of war (see Morrison, 2006).

Sometime later the hegemonic, patriarchal and masculine 'metaphor of war' (see Steinert, 2003) became a key part of the criminological lexicon during the 1970s, seeing wars frequently waged against nouns, including: the 'War on Drugs' under the Nixon Administration; the 'War on Crime' typified by the zero tolerance policies of former New York Police Commissioner Bill Bratton during the mid-1990s; and the 'War on Terror' instigated by the second Bush Administration in the wake of 9/11. However, as Jamieson (2003: 260) observes,

> In spite of the pervasiveness of war metaphors in crime discourse, criminologists often fail to explore the potentially pertinent literatures that deal directly with the reality of war and its sequellae.

Such 'war-crime' metaphors have been counteracted with a move towards a humanistic view of peacemaking criminology (Pepinsky and Quinney, 1991), with different interpretations of this approach developed into the domain of warfare, political violence and human rights (see McEvoy, 2003). Other discussions concerning disarmament (see Etzioni, 1966), peace activism (Kauzlarich, 2007) genocide (see Alverez, 1997; Jamieson, 1999; Hagan and Greer, 2002; Morrison, 2006; Hagan and Rymond-Richmond, 2009; Cameron, 2012; Rafter and Walklate, 2012) and sexual violence (Mullins, 2009a, 2009b) have also formed part of criminological interest in war both past and present. The main centre point for a criminological analysis of war falls to Ruth Jamieson's (1998, 1999, 2014) 'criminology of war'.

This edited collection is influenced by Jamieson's (1998, 2014) critique of criminology. She suggests that it is focused on how war affects 'routine' crimes and avoids broader issues relating to the state. To counter this narrow view, Jamieson (1998) proposed that criminological analysis has the capacity to conceive of war in a variety of critically engaged ways: as having an influence on the moral reasoning for violence; operating as a 'school of crime' or an exaggeration of the 'gender order'; causing anomic social conditions resulting in accelerated states of emergency and the generation of new crimes, criminalised behaviours and broader social control; and causing mass victimisation at the hands of state action, frequently resulting in human rights violations. Although employed within some corners of the discipline (Young, 1999, 2003, 2007, 2011; Ruggiero, 2006), the mobilisation of Jamieson's (1998) criminology of war is an area largely un-referenced by criminologists. Nevertheless, by offering this frame of analysis, Jamieson (1998) conceptualised a space wherein war is tantamount to state crime and squarely within the concern of a critical criminology (see also the 2003 Special Issue of *Theoretical Criminology*, and the edited collection by Jamieson, 2014).

Following Jamieson's (1998) initial framing of this issue criminological interest in war clustered most coherently around the '9/11 moment' (McMillan, 2004: 383). These events fractured global ontological insecurities and became the skewed rationale for over 10 years of war in the Middle East, with the asymmetry of the 'War on Terror' facilitating the blurring of boundaries between crimes at war and crimes at 'home' (Aas, 2013). Despite the previous disparate interests in war, 9/11 appeared to focus criminological attention, displaying a particular penchant for the criminogenic nature of the 2003 invasion of Iraq (see Kramer and Michalowski, 2005; Enemark and Michaelsen, 2005; Winston, 2005). Further contributions claimed that such acts had not only escalated the sectarian violence within Iraq (see Green and Ward, 2009), but also failed to be meaningfully addressed by the British state (see Whyte, 2010). Other literature joined the conversation, providing different inflections on these emerging critical debates including neo-liberal capitalism profiteering from the Iraq War (see Whyte, 2007) and the abuse and human rights violations of Iraqi civilians by US and UK military forces (see Hamm, 2007 and Shiner, 2008, respectively). Other contributions noted the wider glocal ramifications of the wars in Afghanistan and Iraq, particularly the destructiveness of aggressive foreign policies for those who experienced the violence of these wars first hand (Hudson, 2009), and the essentialism of domestic immigration policies for minority ethnic and immigrant communities in the US and UK (Young, 2007; Evans, 2011). We later added our own contributions outlining the potential for understanding soldiers who served in the Iraq war as being victimological 'others' (see McGarry and Walklate, 2011) or placed in exception of human rights mechanisms via the denial techniques (Cohen, 2001) of the state (see McGarry et al., 2012). Taken together, these discussions merely exemplify the early criminological thought of Bonger (1916): identifying war as exacerbating the dominance of hegemonic capitalism and advancing the oppressive consequences of militarism on economic and social life. Yet, despite the high profile nature of the range of issues being raised by critical criminology in the decade after 9/11, and their clear connection with the historical application of crime and war, they remained on the fringes of the criminological imagination.

Concentrating on the troubled and troublesome

However, criminological attention on war during this period was not all critically focused. Much like the period following the Second World War, the 'War on Terror' also invoked the interests of mainstream criminology, creating a populist debate about more conventional concepts of offending, and employing routine analysis of domestic criminal justice processes symptomatic of the criminological enterprise. Willbach's (1948) study of US military veterans returning from the Second World War had indicated that returning service personnel were 'too concerned' with reintegrating themselves back into civilian life to participate in criminal activity. Much later Jamieson (1996) noted the role of the British state in maintaining the masculinity of British soldiers during the Second World War in the interests of the war effort. Although some years apart, both of these papers critically observe two sides of the same coin: military veterans are not in themselves predisposed to crime, and the gendered, violent, masculine role of soldiering is very much a part of a hegemonic state apparatus. However, following 9/11, and precisely 60 years after Willbach's (1948) observations, institutionally situated criminology began focusing considerable attention on military veterans within the domestic criminal justice system in the UK with a different view. As we go on to note later in Chapter 9, the National Association of Probation Officers (Napo) (reporting on data produced by the Veterans in Prison Association) found that the prison population (Napo, 2008) and those under the supervision of the Probation Service (Napo, 2009) in England and Wales are heavily populated by British military veterans (see also Pritchard, 2010; Willett, 2010; Prison Reform Trust, 2010). This was followed soon after by an inquiry from the Howard League for Penal Reform to investigate the extent of the British veteran-prisoner population. The Howard League (2011a, 2011b) reported that, although some British soldiers find themselves in the criminal justice process, it would be difficult to directly attribute their custody to service life. These issues have since been castigated elsewhere (see MacManus, *et al.*, 2013; Lord Ashcroft, 2014), but at the time they neatly diverted attention away from the role of the state in engendering violence in young males and neglecting to reintegrate them successfully back into society. Despite critical discussions relating to the Iraq War having been ongoing within criminology for some time before these reports, here we perhaps see evidence of a 'hierarchy of credibility' at work within criminology, with institutionally formed narratives relating to the criminal nature of those participating in the wars in Afghanistan and Iraq receiving widespread public attention (see for example McVeigh, 2011), sidelining those responsible for waging war without the agreement of the international community. Mindful of both Park (1941) and Hagan and Greer's (2002) earlier observations, this 'credibility' was achieved by removing the state from the centre of its analysis, and replacing it with a troubled and troublesome veteran 'offender', despite suggestions to do otherwise (Treadwell, 2010).

Transgressing the borders

Having moved between the centrefold and borders of the discipline, we now look to make a firmer transgression within criminology (O'Neill and Seal, 2012) towards the study of war. We do so mindful of the suggestion that 'Criminology is only beginning to consider the mass violence associated with war, armed conflict, and political repression' (Hagan, *et al.*, 2012: 489). Although some recent efforts have begun to critically challenge the boundaries of war and criminal justice policy (see Murray, 2013), others exemplify a crudeness within criminology that is tethered to base associations with 'crime'. Closer observation of work produced in this way (see Braithwaite, 2012; Braithwaite and Wardak, 2013) appears to have transposed the concepts of restorative justice, reintegrative shaming and 'hot spots' onto the problematic, violent environments of war. Such approaches to war identify that criminology truly can be 'self-referential' (Barton *et al.*, 2007), particularly when set against the backdrop of other critical developments in the discipline endeavouring to take account of war. Resurfacing criminological knowledge of the kind illustrated above prohibits how far you can approach the boundaries of the discipline, and certainly inhibits how far you can transcend its borders.[3]

So the final question that needs to be asked here is, How do we intend to take this argument forward? Cohen (1988) suggested, some time ago, that criminology is parasitic; as an inter-disciplinary subject it takes its influences from a range of sources not of its own making, adapting and slowly absorbing them into a swollen discipline. Although producing this book perhaps adds to this swelling in a small way, venturing into a criminological analysis of war, we are similarly minded that such discussions need to be considered from a wider range of thought both integral to and outwith the discipline. What follows in this book are various attempts to do this, drawing upon cross-cultural and interdisciplinary authors engaging criminology and war from a variety of critical, cultural and historical perspectives. We recognise at the outset that, although excellent, this original selection of essays have their own limitations and boundaries in how far they can take our present discussion. Nevertheless we hope that what is detailed in the following pages may be considered as a critical, more forthright criminological engagement with war, prompted by the world getting set to commemorate 100 years of violence.

What lies ahead

This book contains a selection of ten chapters arranged over three consecutive themes: Part I draws on cultural influences within criminology in 'Theorising war, law and crime'. This section begins in Chapter 1 with 'War and the death of Achilles' by Ruggiero. In this chapter Vincenzo takes up the reins of our discussion within this introduction and looks to develop the problematic connection between war and crime further by aligning them with corporate crime and crimes of the powerful. In Chapter 2 'Civilising the corporate war' Whyte explores whether the criminalisation of particular modes and techniques of warfare can be justified as part of a general aim of making war more civilised. In Chapter 3 'Criminology and war: Can violent veterans see blurred lines clearly?' Murray engages the reader in a conversation between international relations and criminology using military veterans as a muse to explore the limits of violence and morality in war and peace.

Following this, Part II provides a critical insight into war and criminal justice by 'Linking war and criminal justice'. In Chapter 4 Adler and Godfrey present 'War as an opportunity for divergence and desistence from crime, 1750–1945'. Here they explore how enforced military service was an alternative to custody in the eighteenth century and only in the First World War was service explicitly seen as the means by which criminals (particularly juveniles) could be re-moralised, or made good. The chapter concludes by re-examining predominant concepts of what reform or re-moralisation meant within the wartime and peacetime context. In Chapter 5 'Through the lens of war: Political imprisonment in Northern Ireland' Jamieson explores the experiences of IRA prisoners as mediated through the lens of war and shaped by the culture and discipline of the paramilitary organisation to which they belonged, taking the analysis beyond the established boundaries of criminology in the space between the literature on military psychiatry and welfare, and criminological work on the effects of long-term imprisonment. In Chapter 6 'Veteran coming-home obstacles: Short and long-term consequences of the Iraq and Afghanistan wars' Brown centres on pre-military, military and post-military histories of veterans with a specific emphasis on the influence of the military total institution and the level of combat exposure on the veteran's civilian reintegration process, recognising that veterans who have been exposed to war will experience similar reintegration problems regardless of geographic boundaries.

The final section, Part III, explores the vulnerability that can be caused by warfare, investigating 'War, sexual violence and visual trauma'. In Chapter 7 'Sexual and sexualized violence in armed conflicts' Mullins and Visagaratnam examine the prevalence and contemporary explanations for sexual violence during armed conflicts, specifically emphasising the need for medical, human rights and tribunal researchers to collaborate with criminologists in collecting data that will be the greatest use to all. In Chapter 8 'Normative visibility and artistic resistance to war' Morrison looks to argue that art can bring out a normative visibility within crimninology and can bring the human cost of war to a global audience. In Chapter 9 'Competing for the "trace"; the legacies of war's violence(s)' we look to the contested wars in Iraq and Afghanistan to questions the competition for resources and expertise that underpin them; bringing to the fore a demand that the state has not been exposed to before. Using photographic material in support of this analysis we suggest that the truth extracted from the trace of power on the bodies of war poses questions about the meaning of 'mere' life.

In conclusion, Lea provides us with some thoughts in a 'Postscript: From the criminalisation of war to the militarisation of crime control'. Here he outlines the interconnectedness between policing 'new wars' and domestic crime, criminal justice and welfare policies, conflated by paradigms of risk, security 'management' and counter-terrorism. In bringing these authors together we hope to regenerate a debate about criminology and war. As Jamieson (1999, 2003) has iterated, there is indeed more to be said, and much to be done.

Notes

1 We acknowledge that these institutional 'footprints' are contested in the Australian context. See Finnane (2006, 2008) for a more nuanced historical commentary on the 'intuitional' growth and divergence of criminology within Australia during the post-war era. These developments evidence the origins of criminology in the Antipodes as being twofold: first critically engaged with the policy and systems of criminal justice at the University of Melbourne; later more closely aligned with government interests and police training initiatives stemming from the Institute of Criminology at the University of Sydney, resulting in the eventual government formation of the Australian Institute of Criminology in the mid-1970s.
2 See also Smith *et al.* (2011) chapters 28–48 for individual overviews of other developments of criminology from a broader range of global perspectives; what we have offered here are for expedience.
3 For an extended elaboration of the borders present within the intellectual work of criminology, see Morrison (2006).

References

Aas, K.F. (2013) *Globalisation and Crime*. London: Sage.

Adorjan, M. and Chui, W.H. (2013) 'Colonial responses to youth crime in Hong Kong: Penal elitism, legitimacy and citizenship', *Theoretical Criminology*, 17(2): 159–177.

Alvarez, A. (1997) 'Adjusting to Genocide: The techniques of neutralization and the Holocaust', *Social Science History*, 21(2): 139–178.

Ashcroft, M. (2014) 'The veterans' transition review'. Available: www.veteranstransi tion.co.uk/vtrreport.pdf.

Australian Institute of Criminology. (2014) 'Australian crime: facts and figures'. Available: www.aic.gov.au/publications/current%20series/facts.html.

Barton, A., Corteen, K., Scott, D. and Whyte, D. (eds) (2007) *Expanding the Criminological Imagination: Critical Readings in Criminology*. Devon: Willan.

Beccaria, C. (1804/1983) *An Essay on Crimes and Punishments*. Brookline Village, MA: Branden Publishing.

Becker, H.S. (1963) *Outsiders: Studies in the Sociology of Deviance*. New York: The Free Press.

Becker, H.S. (1967) 'Whose side are we on?', *Social Problems*, 14(3): 239–247.

Bentham, J. (1879), *An Introduction to the Principles of Morals and Legislation*. Oxford: Clarendon Press.

Bonger, W.A. (1916) *Criminality and Economic Conditions*. Boston, MA: Little, Brown, and Company.

Bottoms, A.E. (1987) 'Reflections on the criminological enterprise', *The Cambridge Law Journal*, 46(2): 240–263.

Braithwaite, J. and Wardak, A. (2012) 'Crime and war in Afghanistan: Part I: The Hobbesian solution', *The British Journal of Criminology*, 53(2): 179–196.

Broadhurst, R. and Keo, C. (2011) 'Cambodia: A criminal justice system in transition', in C.J. Smith, S.X. Zhang and R. Barberet (eds) *Routledge Handbook of International Criminology*. Oxon: Routledge.

Bureau of Justice Statistics. (2013) 'National Crime Victimization Survey (NCVS) API'. Available: www.bjs.gov/developer/ncvs/index.cfm.

Cain, M. (2000) 'Orientalism, occidentalism and the sociology of crime', *British Journal of Criminology*, 40: 239–260.

Cameron, H. (2012) *Britain's Hidden Role in the Rwandan Genocide: The Cat's Paw*. Oxon: Routledge.

Cao, L., Sun, I.Y. and Hebenton, B. (2014) 'Discovering and making criminology in China', in L. Cao., I.Y. Sun. and B. Hebenton (eds) *The Routledge Handbook of Chinese Criminology*. Oxon: Routledge.

Cohen, S. (1972) *Folk Devils and Moral Panics*. London: Paladin.

Cohen, S. (1981) 'Footprints in the sand: A further report on criminology and the sociology of deviance in Britain', in M. Fitzgerald. G. McLennan and J. Pawson (eds) *Crime and Society: Readings in History and Theory*. London: Routledge and Kegan Paul.

Cohen, S. (1988) *Against Criminology*. New Brunswick: Transaction Books.

Cohen, S. (2001) *States of Denial: Knowing About Atrocities and Suffering*. Cambridge: Polity.

Cornil, P. (ed.) (1951) 'The effects of the War on criminality', *Select Papers on Penal and Penitentiary Affairs*, XV(411).

Cox, P. (2012) 'History and global criminology: (Re)inventing delinquency in Vietnam', *British Journal of Criminology*, 52: 12–31.

Durkheim, E. (1893) 'Crime and punishment', in S. Lukes and A. Skull (2013) (eds) *Durkheim and the Law* (2nd edition). Basingstoke: Palgrave.

Enemark, C. and Michaelsen, C. (2005) 'Just war doctrine and the invasion of Iraq', *Australian Journal of Politics and History*, 51(4): 545–563.

Etzioni, E. (1966) 'War and disarmament', in R.K. Merton and R.A. Nisbet (eds) *Contemporary Social Problems* (2nd edition). New York: Harcourt, Brace & World, Inc.

Evans, K. (2011) *Crime Prevention: A Critical Introduction*. London: Sage.

Fasihuddin. (2008) *Expanding Criminology to Pakistan*. Peshwar: Uni – Graphics.

Finnane, M. (2006) 'The ABC of criminology: Anita Muhl, J.V. Barry, Norval Morris and the making of a discipline in Australia', *British Journal of Criminology*, 46: 399–422.

Finnane, M. (2008) 'Promoting the theory and practice of criminology: The Australian and New Zealand Society of Criminology and its founding moment', *The Australian and New Zealand Journal of Criminology*, 41(2): 199–215.

Foucault, M. (1977) *Discipline and Punish: The Birth of the Prison*. London: Penguin Books.

Gilinsky, Y. (2011) 'Russia: An overview of crime and criminology', in C.J. Smith, S.X. Zhang, and R. Barberet (eds) *Routledge Handbook of International Criminology*. Oxon: Routledge.

Green, P. and Ward, T. (2000) 'State crime, human rights, and the limits of criminology', *Social Justice: A Journal of Crime, Conflict and World Order*, 27(1): 101–115.

Green, P. and Ward, T. (2009) 'The transformation of violence in Iraq', *British Journal of Criminology*, 49(5), 609–627.

Haen-Marshall, I. (2001) 'The criminological enterprise in Europe and the United States: A contextual exploration', *European Journal on Criminal Policy and Research*, 9: 235–257.

Hagan, J. and Greer, S. (2002) 'Making war criminal', *Criminology*, 40(2): 231–264.

Hagan, J. and Rymond-Richmond, W. (2009) *Darfur and the Crime of Genocide*. Cambridge: Cambridge University Press.

Hagan, J., Kaiser, J., Rothenberg, D., Hanson, A. and Parker, P. (2012) 'Atrocity victimization and the costs of economic conflict crimes in the battle for Baghdad and Iraq', *European Journal of Criminology*, 9(5): 481–498.

Hall, S. Critcher, S., Jefferson, T., Clarke, J. and Roberts, B. (1978) *Policing the Crisis.* London: Macmillan.

Hamm, M. (2007) '"High crimes and misdemeanors": George W. Bush and the sins of Abu Ghraib', *Crime Media Culture*, 3(3): 259–284.

Hebenton, B. and Jou, S. (2005) 'In search of criminological tradition: The development of criminology in Taiwan', *Crime, Law & Social Change*, 44: 215–250.

Hebenton, B. and Jou, S. (2010) 'Criminology in and of China: Discipline and power', *Journal of Contemporary Criminal Justice*, 26(1): 7–19.

Hough, M. and Mayhew, P. (1983) *The British Crime Survey: First Report. Home Office Research Studies 76.* London: HMSO.

Hudson, B. (1997) 'Social control', in M. Maguire, R. Morgan and R. Reiner (eds) *Oxford Handbook of Criminology.* Oxford: Oxford University Press.

Hudson, B. (2009) 'Justice in a time of terror', *British Journal of Criminology*, 49: 702–717.

Jamieson, R. (1996) 'The man of Hobbes: Masculinity and wartime necessity', *Journal of Historical Sociology*, 9(1): 19–42.

Jamieson, R. (1998) 'Towards a criminology of war in Europe', in V. Ruggiero, N. South and I. Taylor (eds) *The New European Criminology: Crime and Social Order in Europe.* London: Routledge.

Jamieson, R. (1999) 'Councils of war', *Criminal Justice Matters*, 34, 25–26.

Jamieson, R. (2003) 'Introduction', *Theoretical Criminology Special Issue: War, Crime and Human Rights*, 7(3): 259–263.

Jamieson, R. (ed.) (2014) *The Criminology of War.* London: Ashgate.

Kang, K.C. (1980) 'Criminology in Korea: An introduction', *Korean Journal of Comparative Law*, 8: 59–69.

Kauzlarich, D. (2007) 'Seeing war as criminal: Peace activist views and critical criminology', *Contemporary Justice Review: Issues in Criminal, Social, and Restorative Justice*, 10(1): 67–85.

Kauzlarich, D., Matthews, R. A. and Miller, W. J. (2001) 'Towards a victimology of state crime', *Critical Criminology*, 10: 173–194.

Kramer, R. C. and Michalowski, R. J. (2005) 'War, aggression and state crime: A criminological analysis of the invasion and occupation of Iraq', *British Journal of Criminology*, 45(4): 446–469.

Lea, J. and Young, J. (1984) *What Is To Be Done about Law and Order.* London: Penguin BooksB.

Lee, M. and Laidler, K.J. (2013) 'Doing criminology from the periphery: Crime and punishment in Asia', *Theoretical Criminology*, 17(2): 141–157.

Liu, J., Hebenton, B. and Jou, S. (2013) 'Progression of Asia criminology', in J. Liu, B. Hebenton, and S. Jou (eds) *Handbook of Asian Criminology.* London: Springer.

Loader, I. and Sparks, R. (2012) 'Situating criminology: On the production and consumption of knowledge about crime and justice', in M. Maguire, R. Morgan and R. Reiner (eds) *Oxford Handbook of Criminology.* Oxford: Oxford University Press.

Lombroso, C. (1876/2006) *Criminal Man* (translated by M. Gibson and N. Rafter). USA: Duke University Press.

MacManus, D., Dean, K., Jones, M., Rona, R.J., Greenberg, N., Hull, L., Fahy, T., Wessley, S. and Fear, N.T. (2013) 'Violent offending by UK military personnel deployed to Iraq and Afghanistan: A data linkage cohort study', *The Lancet*, 381: 907–917.

McEvoy, K. (2003) 'Beyond the metaphor: Political violence, human rights and "new" peacemaking criminology', *Theoretical Criminology Special Issue: War, Crime and Human Rights*, 7(3): 319–346.

McGarry, R. and Walklate, S. (2011) 'The soldier as victim: Peering through the looking glass', *British Journal of Criminology*, 51(6): 900–917.

McGarry, R., Mythen, G. and Walklate, S. (2012) 'The soldier, human rights and the military covenant: A permissible state of exception?', *International Journal of Human Rights. Special Issue: New Directions in the Sociology of Human Rights*, 16 (8): 1183–1195.

McMillan, N. (2004) 'Beyond representation: Cultural understandings of the September 11 attacks', *The Australian and New Zealand Journal of Criminology*, 37(1): 380–400.

McVeigh, K. (2011) 'Inquiry finds link between military veterans and crime'. Available: www.theguardian.com/uk/2011/jun/22/inquiry-link-military-veterans-crime.

Mannheim, H. (1941) *War and Crime*. London: Watts & Co.

Mills, C.W. (1959) *The Sociological Imagination*. Oxford: Oxford University Press.

Morrison, W. (2006) *Criminology, Civilization and the New World Order*. Oxon: Routledge.

Mullins, C. (2009a) '"He would kill me with his penis": Rape during the Rwandan genocide as a state crime', *Critical Criminology*, 17(1): 15–33.

Mullins, C. (2009b) '"We are going to rape you and taste Tutsi women": Rape during the 1994 Rwandan genocide', *The British Journal of Criminology*, 49(6): 719–735.

Mullins, C. (2011) 'War crimes during the August 2008 Georgia–Russia conflict', *The British Journal of Criminology*, 51(6): 918–936.

Murray, E. (2013) 'Post-army trouble: Veterans in the criminal justice system', *Criminal Justice Matters*, 94(1): 20–21.

Napo. (2008) 'Ex armed forces personnel and the criminal justice system briefing paper'. Available: www.napo.org.uk/templates/asset-relay.cfm?frmAssetFileID=317.

Napo. (2009) 'Armed forces and the criminal justice system briefing paper'. Available: www.napo.org.uk/templates/asset-relay.cfm?frmAssetFileID=319.

Narayanan, G. (2005) 'Critical realist reflections on the governance of crime control in Singapore', in J. Sheptycki and A. Wardak (eds) *Transnational and Comparative Criminology*. London: Glass House Press.

Office for National Statistics. (2013) 'Statistical bulletin: Crime in England and Wales, year ending June 2013'. Available: www.ons.gov.uk/ons/rel/crime-stats/crime-statis tics/period-ending-june-2013/stb-crime-in-england-and-wales–year-end ing-june-2013.html.

O'Neill, M. and Seal, L. (2012) *Transgressive Imaginations: Crime, Deviance and Culture*. New York: Palgrave Macmillan.

Park, R.E. (1941) 'The social function of war observations and notes', *American Journal of Sociology*, 46(4): 551–570.

Park, R.E., Burgess, E.W. and McKenzie, R.D. (1925) *The City*. Chicago: The University of Chicago Press.

Pepinsky, H.E. and Quinney, R. (ed.) (1991) *Criminology as Peacemaking*. Indiana: Indiana University Press.

Poornachandra, P. (2011) 'India: The state of criminology in a developing nation', in C.J. Smith, S.X. Zhang and R. Barberet (eds) *Routledge Handbook of International Criminology*. Oxon: Routledge.

Presdee, M. (2000). *Cultural Criminology and the Carnival of Crime*. Oxon: Routledge.

Prison Reform Trust. (2010) 'Bromley briefings prison factfile'. Available: www.prison reformtrust.org.uk/Portals/0/Documents/FactfileDec10small.pdf.

Pritchard, T. (2010) 'Front line to doing time: New inquiry on veterans in prison', *Howard League of Penal Reform*, Spring: 3.

Putt, J. and Lindley, J. (2011). 'Australia: The state of criminology', in C.J. Smith, S.X. Zhang, and R. Barberet (eds) Routledge Handbook of International Criminology. Oxon: Routledge.

Quinney, R. (1972) 'Who is the victim?', *Criminology*, 10: 314–323.

Radzinowicz, L. (1999) Adventures *in Criminology*. New York: Routledge.

Rafter, N. and Walklate, S. (2012) 'Genocide and the dynamics of victimization: Some observations on Armenia', *European Journal of Criminology*, 9(5): 514–526.

Ruggiero, V. (2005) 'Criminalizing war: criminology as ceasefire', *Social & Legal Studies*, 14(2): 239–257.

Ruggiero, V. (2006) *Understanding Political Violence: a Criminological Analysis*. Maidenhead: Open University Press.

Schichor, D. (1980) 'The new criminology: some critical issues', *British Journal of Criminology*, 20(1): 1–19.

Schwendinger, H. and Schwendinger, J. (1970) 'Defenders of Order or Guardians of Human Rights', *Issues in Criminology*, 5(1): 123–157.

Shaikh, R.A (2011) 'The Pakistan and Afghan crisis', in S. Carlton-Ford and M.G. Ender (eds) *The Routledge Handbook of War and Society*. Oxon: Routledge.

Shaw, R.C. and McKay, H.D. (1942) *Juvenile Delinquency and Urban Areas: A Study of Rates of Delinquency in Relation to Differential Characteristics of Local Communities in American Cities*. Chicago: The University of Chicago Press.

Shiner, P. (2008) 'The abject failure of British military justice', *Criminal Justice Matters*, 74: 4–5.

Slapper, G. and Tombs, S. (1999) *Corporate Crime*. Harlow: Longman.

Smart, C. (1977) *Women, Crime and Criminology: A Feminist Critique*. London: Routledge.

Smith, C.J., Zhang, S.X. and Barberet, R. (ed.) (2011) *Routledge Handbook of International Criminology*. Oxon: Routledge.

Squires, P. (2013) 'Research prevention and the zombie university', *Criminal Justice Matters*, 91(1): 4–5.

Steinert, H. (2003) 'The indispensable metaphor of war: On populist politics and the contradictions of the state's monopoly of force', *Theoretical Criminology Special Issue: War, Crime and Human Rights*, 7(3): 265–291.

Sutherland, E.H. (1937) *The Professional Thief*. Chicago, IL: The University of Chicago Press.

Sutherland, E.H. (1940) 'White collar criminality', *American Sociological Review*, 5(1): 1–12.

Sutherland, E.H. (1945) 'Is "white collar crime" crime?', *American Sociological Review*, 10: 32–39.

Sutherland, E.H. (1949) *White Collar Crime*. New York: Holt, Rinehart and Winston.

Sutherland, E.H., Cressey, D.R. and Luckenbill, D.F. (1934) *Principles of Criminology*. Dix Hills, NY: General Hall.

Taylor, I., Walton, P. and Young, J. (1973) *The New Criminology: For a Social Theory of Deviance*. Routledge & Keegan Paul.

The Howard League. (2011a) 'Report of the Inquiry into Former Armed Service Personnel in Prison', London: The Howard League for Penal Reform.

The Howard League. (2011b) 'Leaving Forces Life: The Issue of Transition', London: The Howard League for Penal Reform.

Tombs, S. and Whyte, D. (2002) 'Unmasking crimes of the powerful', *Critical Criminology*, 11: 217–236.

Treadwell, J. (2010) 'COUNTERBLAST: More than casualties of war? Ex-military personnel in the criminal justice system', *Howard Journal*, 49: 73–77.University of Cambridge. (2013) 'Experimental criminology@Cambridge'. Available: www.crim. cam.ac.uk/research/experiments.

Walters, R. (2003) 'New modes of governance and the commodification of criminological knowledge', *Social & Legal Studies*, 12(1): 5–26.

Wardak, A. and Braithwaite, J. (2012) 'Crime and war in Afghanistan: Part II: A Jeffersonian alternative?', *The British Journal of Criminology*, 53(2): 197–214.

Weber, M. (1919) 'Politics as a vocation', in D. Whyte (2008) (ed.) *Crimes of the Powerful: A Reader*. Maidenhead: Open University Press.

Whyte, D. (2007) 'Crimes of the neo-liberal state in occupied Iraq', *British Journal of Criminology*, 47(2): 177–195.

Whyte, D. (ed.) (2008) *Crimes of the Powerful: A Reader*. Maidenhead: Open University Press.

Whyte, D. (2010) 'Don't mention the motive for war', *Criminal Justice Matters*, 82: 8–9.

Willbach, H. (1948) 'Recent crimes and the veterans', *Journal of Criminal Law and Criminology*, 38(5): 501–508.

Willett, S. (2010) 'Veterans in prison inquiry gathersp, *Howard League of Penal Reform*, Summer: 3.

Willis, C.L., Evans, T.D. and LaGrange, R.L. (1999) '"Down home" criminology: The place of indigenous theories of crime', *Journal of Criminal Justice*, 27(3): 227–238.

Winston, M. (2005) 'The humanitarian argument for the Iraq war', *Journal of Human Rights*, 4(1): 45–51.

Xu, J. (2011) 'Hong Kong: The state of criminology', in C.J. Smith, S.X. Zhang, and R. Barberet (eds) *Routledge Handbook of International Criminology*. Oxon: Routledge.

Yokoyama, M. (2013) 'Development of criminology in Japan from a sociological perspective', in J. Liu., B. Hebenton, and S. Jou (eds) *Handbook of Asian Criminology*. London: Springer.

Young, J. (1999), *The Exclusive Society*. London: Sage.

Young, J. (2003) 'Merton with energy, Katz with structure: The sociology of vindictiveness and the criminology of transgression', *Theoretical Criminology Special Issue: War, Crime and Human Rights*, 7(3): 389–414.

Young, J. (2007) *The Vertigo of Late Modernity*. London: Sage.

Young, J. (2011) *The Criminological Imagination*. London: Polity Press.

Zolo, A. (2009) *Victors' Justice: From Nuremberg to Baghdad*. London: Verso.

Part 1

Theorising war, law and crime

1 War and the death of Achilles

Vincenzo Ruggiero

Introduction

War does not sit comfortably among the topics attracting criminological enquiry. In the first section of this chapter an attempt is made to identify why this is so. The suggestion is then put forward that only a criminology refusing official definitions of what the object of its study should be is capable of including this extreme form of organized violence within its analytical interests. The description of some of the features making war criminologically relevant and its analysis urgent forms the second section of this contribution.

Instincts and foundational events

Common, and often unchallenged, notions of war convey positive values, making violent conflicts among states foundational events, markers of the boundaries between barbarianism and civilization. War is assumed to establish 'just' hierarchies and allocate deserved ranks: a necessary evil. It is a regenerative event nevertheless, shaping the world and triggering transformation. Moreover, war appears to belong to the divine sphere, as it generates social and institutional forms through a sort of *theomachy*, a sacred fight which brings destruction while creating something new. In brief, war is the expression of supreme forms of interaction, and a crucial factor for the constitution of identities (Curi, 2002; Ruggiero, 2006).

Religious thought is commonly referred to when the boundaries between just and unjust wars are drawn (Walzer, 2006). Thomas Aquinas, for instance, laid down three conditions guiding the *jus ad bellum*: the right to wield war had to be exercised by a legitimate authority, in the name of a just cause and with the intention of remedying an injustice. Enemies were 'just' targets because of their evil acts. In ancient Greece and Rome there was a strong link between military organization and political system: army members belonged to the political community (Wilamowitz-Moellendorff, 2011). It is, however, in Rome that the religious element left a remarkable trace, particularly in the distinction between *bellum hostile*, war between Christian knights, and *bellum romanum*, war waged against outsiders, infidels, barbarians or insurgent peasants. The former was conducted according to chivalric code and followed strict rules, while the latter was lawless, endless (Lindqvist, 2012).

In secular thinking, however, war was not only legitimized, but also at times encouraged. A prince, warned Machiavelli (1944: 111), ought to have no other aim or thought than war and its rules and discipline: 'when princes have thought more of ease than of arms they have lost their states'. The stability of political systems, in other words, depends on the capacity to accumulate armaments, whereas being unarmed brings ignominy and contempt on rulers. Even in time of peace, a prince is advised to bear nothing in mind but the rules of war: to increase 'his resources in such a way that they might be available to him in adversity, so that if fortune changes it may find him prepared to resist her blows' (Machiavelli, 1944: 114). Machiavelli was inspired by Greek philosophy, which in several respects saw war as the original principle of the state itself, an event marking the passage from the primitive 'state of pigs' to the advanced state of luxury. From that philosophy we learn that the instinct of pugnacity is a constant component of humankind, not a survival from brutal ancestry, and cannot be eradicated. In fact, its operation is far from being wholly injurious; on the contrary, it is one of the essential factors in the evolution of higher forms of social organization (McDougall, 1915).

This legacy could still be detected in the medieval city, whose crystallization was due less to trade than to war. 'The city is the result of war, at least of preparation for war', commerce came afterwards. Cities were fortified and hosted the manufacture of weaponry; the space of the city overlapped with the space of war: this was the beginning of the economy of war, 'which eventually became simply the economy' (Virilio and Lotringer, 1997: 11). Against religious arguments in support of just war as saintly triumph over infidels and heretics, medieval just war theorists treated violent conflict less as a means to punish religious deviants and social criminals than as an initiative to acquire property (Russell, 1975). War was, therefore, a form of civil litigation, a way of settling property disputes.

> Victory was a legitimate mode of natural means of acquisition, which conferred enforceable property rights on the victor: rights to territory for commanders, and rights to booty for ordinary soldiers. Just war theory was largely property law.
>
> (Whitman, 2012: 18)

Private interests, however, were concealed behind the noble principle of 'the verdict of history', whereby the outcome of war ceased to be determined by ability or fortune, entering the realm of destiny. Nobility, later, became the main characteristic of eighteenth-century war thanks to the cultural domination of duelling aristocracy, deemed courteous and inherently chivalric. As Nietzsche (1968) remarked, the noble managed to be appreciated as the truthful ones, therefore as those holding the privilege of exercising legitimate violence.

That war retains a form of human nobility was pointed out, again by Nietzsche, in his axiomatic depiction of human instincts, epitomized by the 'blonde beast', the wild animal lying inside the human race, avid of prey and victory. But also, obliquely, by Freud (1959), who saw no antimony between 'violence' and 'right', violence being the variable allowing the designation of power, therefore of the right to govern. Original violence, in his view, is the force of a state expressed in its laws. Moreover, war and violence are the result of an active instinct for hatred and destruction, an instinct cohabiting the humans together with its opposite, namely 'eros', which aims at conserving and unifying. Love and hate are akin to those eternal polarities, attraction and repulsion, which fall within the field of study of the physical sciences, and Freud concluded that both instincts are indispensable: all the phenomena of life derive from their activity; whether they work in concert or in opposition, each is blended with a certain dosage of its opposite.

Criminology has never shown an interest in the formation of the right to govern, but in its opposite, namely conduct undermining the smooth governing of social and political systems. Nor has it been attracted to the study of 'indispensable' instincts governing life itself. On the other hand, some analytical interest in war, perhaps, might have been obtained from its, at least initial, proximity to social theory and sociology.

Industrial societies and creative periods

Classical sociology adopts an optimistic, evolutionist perspective on the subject matter. War is described as a barbaric relic, a sort of relapse of civilized societies into retrograde cultural stages. Development through trade and industry, it is assumed, will cause inevitable pacifying effects (Joas and Knöbl, 2013). The example of Auguste Comte (1953) is, in this respect, significant. Military societies and industrial societies are said to represent two fundamentally different types of social organization. The predominance of the latter type is destined to diminish warfare, which is essentially connected with the predominance of the former. The argument is put forward that there is a fundamental antithesis between military civilization and the civilization of labour, between the spirit of conquest and the spirit of industry. In an ideal evolution, first, industry is seen as being in the service of war, then war is regarded as being in the service of industry and, finally, in the ultimate form of society, peace is deemed the inevitable outcome of industry (Aron, 1958). True, Comte was proved wrong in his prediction that last century would be free from war, but it is controversial whether he is equally wrong in foreseeing that the only kind of conceivable future war would aim to directly establish the material 'preponderance of more advanced over less advanced populations'. Comte resolutely condemned such potential wars, because they are likely to cause the mutual oppression of nations and to 'precipitate various countries upon one another'. It remains unclear, however, whether Comte regarded these potential wars as part of a tendency within industrial societies or whether he was convinced that the very process of industrialization would impede their occurrence. In his belief that war has no space in the evolution of 'labour civilization', however, one could detect an implicit critique of views holding the biological, innate character of war itself.

The concepts of 'collective effervescence' and that of 'creative periods' are crucial for a sociological analysis of war. Both introduced by Durkheim (1970), these concepts allude to communities experiencing magical moments, when individuals transcend themselves and prefigure a higher collective order. Collective effervescence leads individuals to integration into a superior unit, as the experience of action results in moments of communion: 'emotional effusions of selflessness are engendered automatically whenever people are put into closer and more active relations with one another' (Peterson, 2001: 57). By acting above and beyond themselves, in concrete social practices, individuals achieve a form of solidarity typifying what Durkheim termed 'creative periods'. While new values are elaborated and egotistical interests are provisionally set aside, these periods, evanescent though they may be, remain in the memory of the collectivity as periods of supreme integration. Countries at war are typical entities experiencing such creative periods, when solidarity allegedly spreads or intensifies, and when collective efforts become paramount. Such countries, indeed, will then build a vivid memory of themselves, a sense of their uniqueness and special identity which will survive well after the end of hostilities.

Durkheim's analysis echoes a Kantian idea, for even in his manifesto for a perpetual peace the German philosopher, while spiritually recoiling from the horror of war, is led by his practical reason to appreciate its functions. On the one hand, Kant points to the ills suffered by humanity due to the incessant preparations in view of future wars, which require enormous waste of economic and cultural resources. On the other hand, he argues that, without such pressure and permanent urgency, societies would equally suffer.

> In other words, it is the constant horizon of war that maintains state and social, community and cultural cohesion, and it is the same horizon that ensures a degree of freedom, in spite of restrictive laws.
>
> (Derrida, 2011: 375)

In brief, cultural achievement by the human species still finds in war an indispensable means of perfecting it, despite the 'commodification' of countries and persons that every war entails (Kant, 1970).

There is nothing, in the brief outline above, that would justify the interest of criminology in such a 'functional' phenomenon.

Development and the power elite

The contribution of the Chicago sociologists on the subject matter is ambivalent, and it remains obscure why their particular sensitivity with respect to social exclusion, along with their active intervention in communities and ghettoes, is not translated into a similar degree of sensitivity vis-à-vis international matters. Park (1941) likens war to its ancestors, namely the judicial procedure known as trial by combat or the duel, though he is unsure whether to regard it as a social institution or as a biological necessity. The latter hypothesis seems to be validated, he muses, if one considers that war has always been one of the available ways of making claims and settling disputes. War must, therefore, be an innate human enterprise, if it still constitutes a form of litigation by which states make their claims valid. Park (1941) notes, however, that limits need to be imposed on such innate behaviour and that an understanding of the consequences of unrestricted warfare should be reached. He claims to be in favour of the technical limits drawn by international agencies trying to make war more consistent with 'the requirements of humanity'. On the other hand, he argues that all attempts to regulate wars and govern military conducts may simply result in legitimizing both and conferring a respectable institutional character on them. Legitimacy, moreover, belongs to authorities and institutions whose actions and their effects are predicable, whereas 'we do not know what to expect of war any more' (Park, 1941: 562). In a further attempt to identify the nature of war and its function, Park (1941) reiterates the adage that war is politics in its original form, through which belligerent states or parties seek to extend the territorial limits of their sovereignty and establish their own political and economic order. The victorious party will, of course, impose its own racial or national interest, and will attempt to build up an ideology that rationalizes the acceptance of its superiority and of the social order imposed upon the vanquished.

Park's (1952; 1960) critical remarks express a sense of impotence and inevitability in the face of processes leading advanced social and economic orders to impose themselves on other systems. He is faced with the Comteian dilemma as to whether the potential wars waged by more mature systems, though condemnable, are perhaps destined to loom as perennial threats during the course of human evolution. Since unequal development is a permanent feature of the history of the international community, and given that aggression by more developed nations is always a possibility, does this mean that war is indeed an immutable trait of human bevahiour? War, in this way, becomes a price to be paid for global development and its alleged corollary of generalized social advancement (Ruggiero, 2006). It should be noted that similar uncritical trust in economic growth as social advancement is found in numerous fields of knowledge, including criminology, which often looks to sheer developments in the economy as a miraculous crime prevention remedy.

Wright Mills (1956: 184) focuses less on war itself than on warlords. His notion of permanent emergency is referred to in the US international posture: 'for the first time in American history men in authority are talking about emergency without a foreseeable end'. History, he remarks, was seen in the past as a peaceful continuum interrupted by war, whereas now the elite does not have any notion of peace, if not as an uneasy interlude, a tedious, precarious recess during which reasonable people and states had better spend the available time loading their pistols. During the eighteenth century civilians were able to control specialists of violence, but this ability began to falter during the following century among all industrialized countries. Wright Mills (1956) provides an initial micro-sociological explanation of this process, suggesting that neither patriotism nor pay were encouragements to undertake a military career; rather, it was the consideration and the chances of 'laurels'. 'Every man in the army is constantly aspiring to be something higher, as every citizen in the commonwealth is constantly struggling for a better rank' (Wright Mills, 1956: 174). The race for prestige, however, found obstacles of an economic nature, as, in a country centrally preoccupied by the individual acquisition of wealth, people would not favour subsidizing an organized body mostly deemed parasitical. Military force, therefore, remained relatively decentralized in state militia, a system of armed citizens 'at a time when the rifle was the key weapon and one man meant one rifle as well as one vote' (Wright Mills, 1956: 178).

Throughout the twentieth century warlords slowly began to see the economic system as a means for military expansion and large companies as badly managed military establishments. With time, their increased stature arrived by default, due to the low stature of political and economic actors. Soon military personnel became ambassadors and special envoys and, in major international decisions, professional diplomats were simply by-passed. Later, military demands shaped and dictated the pace of corporate economy, the traffic between military and corporate personnel accelerated and shifted 'American capitalism toward a permanent war economy' (Wright Mills, 1956: 215). Wright Mills' critique of classical, evolutionary approaches to war could not be more vehement: industrialism failed to relegate militarism to a minor role; on the contrary, the latter was incorporated into the higher elite and significantly determined the direction of economic initiative. This process entailed the militarization of science and knowledge, with technological development and education becoming increasingly subordinated to armament programmes. Is there a military clique, asks Wright Mills, and his reply is unequivocal:

> Yes, there is a military clique, but it is more accurately termed the power elite, for it is composed of economic, political, as well as military men whose interests have increasingly coincided.
>
> (Wright Mills, 1956: 224)

Finally, we are warned that the warlords will attempt to spread their philosophy among the population at large, to define reality in a military fashion and, therefore, to emphasize their central role and the necessity of their expansion. We will have to return later to this military invasion of the civilian mind.

Bonger unheeded

After this brief excursus through some tenets of sociological theory we can move to the criminological field. If we regard Beccaria's contribution as mainly focused on 'domestic war', namely war declared by official authorities (by means of torture and capital punishment) against their own subjects and citizens, the first significant figure addressing war among states whom we encounter in criminology is W.A. Bonger.

After rejecting innateness, Bonger (1936) centres on crime caused by war situations. In such situations, he argues, all the factors which may lead to crime are driven up: family life is ripped apart, children are neglected, destitution spreads, while scarcity of goods generates theft and begets illicit markets. Crime is also caused by the general demoralization, and violent behavior increases as a mimetic outcome of the spectacle of 'killing, maiming and terrible destruction'. Crime statistics swell despite the fact that a large part of the male population, in the age range of the most represented offenders' group, is sometimes in military service, and thereby outside the jurisdiction of the ordinary courts. The dark figure of crime, in its turn, is assumed to go up, due to the weakening of institutional agencies such as the police and the judiciary. War is, therefore, criminogenic for those who do not fight it, but, as Bonger (1936: 105) suggests, it also pushes the very individuals who fight to commit a variety of offences, though 'the figures of the crimes committed in the field will probably never be published'.

Looking at recent conflicts in the former Yugoslavia, the invasion of Iraq and organized violence elsewhere (i.e. Libya, Afghanistan, Syria), Bonger's analysis seems totally confirmed, as in all the countries mentioned it was, and is, extremely hard to distinguish crimes committed by those who fight from crimes committed by those who officially do not: paramilitary organizations, organized criminal groups, corporations, private contractors, advisor and mercenary companies (Nicolić-Ristanović, 1998; Jamieson, 1998; Hagan 2003; Ruggiero, 2007). These events, however, did not trigger extensive interest among criminologists, who at most devoted their analytical efforts to terrorism rather than war per se, leaving this area of research to the persistent virtual monopoly of political scientists and international relations experts. That the pointer provided by Bonger failed to be pursued may be associated with some if not most of the arguments presented so far, which could be reformulated and developed as follows.

Wars are foundational events, as they establish international hierarchies and domestic order. They are crucial for the constitution of identities and for the provision of collective memory in national contexts, as war efforts mobilize unselfish feelings, encourage the formation of common sensibilities and shared goals. The accumulation of armaments guarantees stability of systems, ensuring evolution towards higher forms of social organization. Wars are expressions of human instincts, as *eros* and *thanatos* are inextricably linked. Their occurrence, however, is destined to decline because industrial development makes military systems obsolete and requires solidarity and cooperation, rather than hostility. Finally, even warlords may have a positive role to play, as they encourage scientific development and lead industrial innovation, thus fostering the general economic well-being.

This idyllic panorama is unsuitable for criminological enquiry, war being associated with an array of superior values which empower rather than victimize societies. Moreover, the aura of sacredness surrounding it makes its rejection a form of atheism (Caillois, 2002). Being intertwined with a variety of evolutionary forces guiding human societies, war generates development and is one of the tools to be utilized in the name of our civilizing mission. Establishing an advanced social order in traditional societies, albeit through war, may therefore constitute an inescapable burden of developed societies, which have a duty to drag low-achieving civilizations along their path. War, in this perspective, is not only the most intense manifestation of a collective endeavour binding a national community and strengthening its identity, it is also a way of bringing the international community together and establishing cultural and material uniformity in it. In this way 'permanent massacre becomes an element of universal harmony' (Caillois, 2002: 74).

Organized violence requires justifications, technological means, structures of command: it is therefore the outcome of complex social interactions, but also the constant catalyzer of economic development and the establishment of social order. 'Whether we like it or not, violence is one of the central constituents of human subjectivity, and modern subjectivity in particular, since modernity as we know it would be unthinkable without organized violence' (Malešević, 2010: 4). Why should criminologists, normally focused on disorder, social pathologies, deviant conducts and dysfunctional acts be concerned with 'central constituents of human subjectivity'?

It is time to look at the subject matter from another perspective.

War as crime

The twentieth century is 'unnamable' for its endless chain of destructive moments. Its destructiveness appears to be thoroughly planned and scrupulously executed, with massacres, genocides, carnage and brutalities of all sorts attributable in large measure to the action of governments and states. The first decade and a half of the current century seems to announce that this will soon become unnamable in its turn. It might be remarked that 'civilization' creates the preconditions of its own decline, that modern science is in a sense bound to produce nuclear weapons, that state bureaucracies are inclined to turn 'genocide into public service', and that the holocaust is the genuine product of administrative rationality (Sofsky, 2003; Bauman, 1989; Agamben, 1999; Ruggiero, 2008). The current multiplication of wars, however, shows more clearly than ever that military action generates criminogenic situations pertaining to the domain of war and business simultaneously. Despite attempts to publicly sanitize its manifestations, contemporary wars contain a silent incitement to illegal excesses, leading to mass victimization, violation of human rights, and a wide range of state crimes. War zones become enormous illicit markets managed by organized criminal groups supplying all sorts of commodities. Wars offer a context, a behavioural framework within which everybody may act as they please: torture turns into patriotic conduct, while rape may become an act of heroism. Those who are recruited are offered a salary, but with it they are provided with a non-written licence to loot, and are promised the emotion to kill without feeling any sense of guilt. Interviews conducted during the first Gulf war revealed a sense of excitement and joy among the North American pilots, who saw the bombings as an amusing, riveting, video game (Fogarty, 2000). Examples of brutality spread, in an imitative, learning process which makes ruthlessness acceptable and, in a vicious circle, the 'deviants' are those who do not conform to the unwritten rules of brutality, not those who are brutal (Ward, 2005). Therefore, on the one hand, war is criminogenic and, on the other hand, so-called 'war crimes' are the norm and include predatory and violent acts perpetrated by the police, the armies and para-military forces. In many circumstances, it is hard indeed to distinguish between police forces, soldiers, mercenaries and criminals: they all become agents of social control and crimes are encouraged as essential components of the conflict in which they are engaged.

Aggression, on the other hand, in the form of war, contributes to the exacerbation of the inequalities and the asymmetries that commonly accompany the emergence of the crimes of the powerful. These types of crimes take place in contexts characterized by the growing importance of 'corporate actors' as opposed to the declining role occupied by 'natural actors'. In such contexts, interactions become largely asymmetrical because the former are in the condition to control the nature and modality of the relationships they establish with the latter. They possess more information about the way in which these relationships may be altered (Coleman, 1982). War, therefore, turns into state and corporate crime, as it intensifies asymmetries and further polarizes the positions occupied by powerful and ordinary actors respectively. The latter, being devoid of decision-making power, are victims even when unaware of their own victimization, and even when the ills suffered are hidden behind values such as heroism and patriotism. In brief, recent international events have transformed war into a series of episodes of crimes of the powerful. It should be reiterated that the criminogenic condition generated by war-business not only encourages conventional crime, but also and in a larger measure the crimes of the powerful, including criminality by entrepreneurs and enterprises, and all the illegality pertaining to economic activity. The direct involvement of private companies, security agencies and firms supplying military services and paramilitary consultancy, suggests the creation of a complex apparatus whose contours are vague and in which missionary militarism, predatory enterprise and corruption mingle in an unprecedented fusion.

If war manifests itself as a form of economic crime or crime of the power-ful, its very illegality transcends the economic sphere, being the result of unauthorized action adopted against the will of international agencies (Sands, 2006). Its illegality is also manifest in the very means utilized: torture, kidnapping, prohibited weapons. More than 50 countries backed the US and were involved in rendition of prisoners destined for torture. This is more than a quarter of the world's total, covertly engaged with a wide-ranging kidnap, detention and torture programme (Cobain, 2013; Cobain et al., 2013).

Processes of privatization, on the other hand, encourage experimentation, whereby corporations 'lie in ambush': forcing ethical limits, seizing novel opportunities and constructing a rationale according to which any given good or item, including collective well-being, can be subjected to negotiation, acquisition or predation. Contemporary wars are at the same time the result of, and take a leading role in these processes; they become private affairs that turn even institutional violence, once the domain of state monopolies, into a good, a commodity among others.

Detaching the criminal label from these processes and conducts requires powerful ideologies and remarkably effective techniques of neutralization. Let us examine this aspect.

Universalism and invisibility

Military victories usually strengthen people's bonds with a regime, like national myths, and normally thrive on conquest and aggressions. Victorious organized violence fosters self-infatuation and narcissism, but at the same time needs potent mechanisms of justification. Ideas such as humanity, jus-tice, progress and civilization are strong ideological devices as they allow one side to claim adherence to universalistic values while stripping the enemy of civil and human worth. Universalist moral arguments remove the barriers to the use of force, but may be insufficient to create consensus, unless they are strengthened by other processes.

Intolerance towards acts of violence leads us to invoke the authority of an external, coercive, force monopolizing its use (Malešević, 2010). Surrendering our right to violence to a designated specialist actor, however, not only allows the accumulation of coercive means that can be used against all, but it also entails the removal of all limits as to the type and intensity of violence being used. As Durkheim (1982) argued, punishment may become with time less severe. According to his 'law of penal evolution', the decline of punitive harshness is linked with the corresponding softening of mores taking place in society as a whole. Societies, he suggested, are increasingly horrified by violence, and cruelty elicits in us a growing sense of repugnance. Unfortunately, he continued, this explanation may be reversed.

For while, on the one hand, our greater humanity makes us recoil from inflicting painful punishments, it must simultaneously make the inhuman acts which these punishments repress seem more odious to us.

(Durkheim, 1982: 38)

In other words, if our more developed altruism finds the idea of making others suffer repugnant, for the very same reason the crimes which inflict suffering will seem to us just as, or even more, abominable. Consequently, we will be tempted to react with harsher penalties. Stripping the enemy of humanity is an important strategy to justify harsher punishments, including death.

Contemporary wars are forms of punishment which reflect how the 'public conscience' is affected by the inhumanity of the enemy. This inhumanity is in itself an offence against collective ideal goods, political principles, shared customs, traditions and religion. It is, moreover, inimical to democracy, in the name of which wars of aggression are carried out. Democracy, in this way, becomes 'an altar before which the West and its admirers worship, and through which divine Western imperial crusades are shaped and legitimated' (Brown, 2010: 45). Reduced to pure ideology, the democratic creed, however, 'allows a very small number of people to govern without the people' (Ross, 2010: 98). Contemporary Western societies, by making substantive equality irrelevant, reduce democracy to the sheer exercise of the right to vote. But the electoral choice can by now be equated to the choice of a brand, as 'political policies and agendas [are] sold as consumer rather than public goods' (Brown, 2010: 47). At the same time, wars against undemocratic enemies require that the very democratic principles allegedly inspiring them are jettisoned, both domestically and internationally. The several terrorism legislations drawn up in recent years, for instance, appear to imply that the defence of freedom requests the sacrifice of giving up freedom. Simultaneously, in the name of universalistic values, some humans are placed outside the universe of moral obligation, while it is ultimately the aggressors who draw the line between legitimate and illegitimate coercion. 'Basically, political endogamy obtains: a democrat loves only another democrat' (Badiou, 2010).

In brief, the West has the ability to represent its particular interests as the expression of those of humanity in general. In this way, democracies assemble in a sort of 'League of the Public Good, against a Holy Alliance of despots and crooks' and cannot see themselves as the rest of the planet does: just another such Holy Alliance (Debray, 2013: 32).

In this sense, war does not occur because moral evaluations are disregarded, but because they are mobilized, in the form of political and cultural axioms. Even genocide can be moralistic (Campbell, 2009). The fact is that all forms of aggression and annihilation take place not only when there is a considerable distance (relational, functional or simply cultural) between the parties, but also when the acts of the enemy are perceived as offences against transcendental entities or forces and collective deeply embedded beliefs. These acts possess the character of sacrilege, as the rules violated are attributed particular sanctity, thus leading to reactions which match in severity the violations addressed. But, for annihilation to be justified, the inhuman enemy has to be described as posing uncontrollable, unpredictable risk (Mythen and Walklate, 2006).

Uncontrollability is compounded by invisibility. The suffering of the enemies, their death, fail to produce reactions but spawn insensitivity and result 'in eyes turned away from a silent ethical gaze' (Bauman and Donskis, 2013: 9). The other becomes invisible because our relationships tend to evolve into 'pure relationships', that is devoid of mutual obligations, free from constraints, in a merely contingent and transitory mutuality. 'Pure relations augur not so much a mutuality of liberation, as a mutuality of moral insensitivity ... exemption from the realm of moral evaluation' (Bauman and Donskis, 2013: 15). This tendency is said to be associated with the growing predominance of individuals *qua* consumers, who may put in motion the wheels of the economy, but bring those of morality to a halt. Invisibility, on the other hand, favours the acceptance of cruelty against the invisible, regularly described as criminals, so that human sympathy slowly vanishes, while 'the routinization of violence and killing leads to a condition in which people stop responding to horrors' (Bauman and Donskis, 2013: 37–38).

To what extent this process is typical of the current time is hard to tell. The changing status of death in modernity is a central motif, for example, in Benjamin's work (2002). Over the course of the nineteenth century, he observed, bourgeois society achieved by means of medical and social, private and public institutions, something remarkable, which may have been its subconscious main purpose: to enable people to avoid the sight of the dying. What distinguishes modernity, he suggested, is the displacement of the dying from the spaces of everyday life. In the course of modern times, dying has been pushed further and further out of the perceptual world of the living (Santner, 2011). A way of hiding death in the contemporary bellicose climate consists in continuing war without this penetrating the consciousness or even the awareness of citizens (Mazzetti, 2013). Narrowing the fight guarantees that the fight will go on, while war perpetuates an endless revenge cycle: revenge against the use of drones, for instance, justifies further revenge strikes by drones (Holmes, 2013). This entails the blurring of the distinction between civilian and militant targets, the construction of a new actor, the MAM, namely the Military-Age Male. Viewed through electronic screens, civilians and combatants are mixed, and this makes them killable not for what they are or do, but for where they happen to be. These are the victims of 'signature strikes', in that they are made targets due the signature they unwittingly leave. According to a loose description, signatures are patterns of behavior that are detected through signals intercepts, human sources and aerial surveillance, that indicate the presence of insurgents or simply of someone looking remotely suspicious, whose movement is judged evidence of hostile intent (Scahill, 2013; Schwartz, 2013).

The use of unmanned missiles as a leading counterinsurgency weapon has morphed into a campaign against tribal people generally, with the aggressors claiming a Zeus-like power to hurl thunderbolts from the sky and obliterate anyone with impunity. With drone attacks, whole communities experience the constant threat of random annihilation. For a Muslim tribesman, this manner of combat is not only dishonourable but also sacrilegious, and those appropriating the powers of god are seen as blasphemous (Ahmed, 2013). The crucial role played by this type of attack, however, is that they make war invisible: our gaze is spared its cruel spectacle and we are reassured that such spectacle will never enter our private domain. As Dal Lago (2012) remarks, since 1991 Western countries led by the US have fought in Iraq, Bosnia, Somalia, Serbia, Afghanistan, Iraq again, Libya, Pakistan, and so on. Yet, we may feel that we have never been at war, a feeling of indifference unprecedented in history.

Estimates suggest that, throughout the nineteenth century, apart from the American civil war, 90 per cent of losses were among fighting troops. In World War I (WWI) deaths of civilians still accounted for 10–15 per cent, becoming around 40 per cent in World War II (WWII). 'Today the civilians account for ninety per cent of deaths. It is not an exaggeration to state that wars today are waged against civil populations' (Dal Lago, 2012: 154).

We need a precise and limited space of representation when we are called to judge on the criminal nature of an act, and our cognitive capacity loses itself when faced with very large numbers. Numbers do not inform us about specific contexts and do not display human faces inspiring empathy. 'Limited crimes attract the attention of public opinion and justice, while limitless crimes cannot be judged, therefore, they are not crimes' (Dal Lago, 2012: 160). The word 'war' is prohibited; in its place we have 'peacekeeping operations' or 'protecting civilian populations'. Soldiers are advised to present themselves as social workers.

War, in sum, is far away from our sitting rooms, it is a background noise, and while battles are being fought in remote places in the name of democracy, democratic and exhausted shoppers can finally relax in front of a dull TV programme. Consensus is no longer adequate to describe what is in fact a kind of socializing of people into silence – silence as consent.

No more heroes

It is worth attempting to explicate how silence is achieved. The argument could be made that governments using armed force are compelled to identify a 'strategic audience': that is formulate a 'strategic narrative' as a public justification for being at war at all (Simpson, 2012). The narrative may not be persuasive in rational terms, and may need dramatic overtones appealing to emotions. It may, however, attempt to seek ethical foundation, because the distance at which war is waged can allow for its public description as a humanitarian, peace-building effort. With a distant and often indifferent audience, it becomes sufficient, for example, to wave the 'lesser evil' argument. In this respect, it has been remarked that military personnel, humanitarian organizations, human rights investigators and legal scholars have constituted a 'lesser evil community' based on shared moral values. Nothing heroic, in sum, but the neutral, technical identification of mere managerial tools capable of solving human and political crises: a sheer operation of calculus determining which evils are to be considered tolerable and which not. However, lesser evils, as Weizman (2012) shows, play an essential role in the carrying out of greater evils. 'Humanitarian aids, international law and the practice of human rights may, in this way, be playing an essential role in the deployment of military violence' (Feldman, 2013: 51). The experience of Jewish Councils during WWII provides an illuminating precedent in this respect. In their attempt to alleviate pain and assist Jewish individuals by cooperating with the Nazis, members of these councils became an integral, essential part of the extermination apparatus. Humanitarian efforts go hand in hand with another lesser evil, namely the growth of the security industry, with Western companies selling abroad their instruments, allegedly favouring peace but in fact igniting war: another suitable narrative for a silent audience (Leander, 2013).

It is through this process that a military-industrial complex is developed, namely with the military becoming more diffuse, less identifiable, more insinuating, disseminated, submerged, elusive. According to Virilio and Lotringer (1997), confused within civilian society, the military class ends up involving all, including, we might add, spectators who deny that a war is being fought or who become indifferent to its spectacle.

> All of us are already civilian soldiers, without knowing it. And some of us know it. The great stroke of luck for the military class's terrorism is that no one recognizes it. People don't recognize the militarized part of their identity, of their consciousness.
>
> (Virilio and Lotringer, 1997: 26)

War disappears, becoming one and the same with peace, and, with delinquency safely hidden, heroes become redundant: 'War is national delinquency ... we can no longer even speak of wars, they are interstate delinquencies. It's state terrorism' (Virilio and Lotringer, 1997: 31).

Conclusion

We have seen the positive, sacred values with which war is associated, but also how a criminology denying itself, namely refusing to look at the narrow institutional definitions of its object of study, can unveil the delinquency of 'legitimate' organized violence. Recent events constitute violations of *jus ad bellum* as well as *jus in bello*, being illegal at the very moment in which they are declared and, afterwards, for the criminal practices they induce while they are carried out. In classical thought, wars are a pedagogical source of identity and solidarity, but if we stretch this logic too far we may reach the conclusion that even genocide, after all, is an exercise in community building (Appadurai, 2013). Justifications for recent and current wars focus on the sacred values they allegedly protect and propagate, or on the criminal nature of those they target. They also hinge on the idea that, in fact, they are not taking place at all.

Criminology is still fighting a never-ending battle to unveil the dark figure of delinquency; it is still engaged in identifying moral entrepreneurs, studying symbolic interactions leading to criminal labels, and assessing the reality of victimization. The arguments presented in the previous pages may be a timid step towards performing a similar engagement in respect of war.

Two and a half millennia ago a definition of war was proposed that may still obtain today: a form of hunting, the hunt for human rather than animal prey (Aristotle, 1995). This is what we detect in contemporary warfare: 'not heroic confrontations between armed warriors in a "fateful day" of pitched battle but the brutal hunt for human prey' (Whitman, 2012: 26). Achilles is dead, as Sophocles (2011) was well aware. Similarly, the disappearance of war as described in this chapter carries its heroes into obliteration, leaving us to contemplate a modern Aias, whose savagery is ingrained in his very being, but hidden from the people, or a contemporary Herakles, who in Sophocles' tragedy does not perform a selfless service to his fellow citizens, but engages in brutal, deceitful, selfish acts. When he dies, burned by acid, the audience finds it difficult to feel sorry for him.

References

Agamben, G. (1999) *Quel che resta di Auschwitz*, Turin: Bollati Boringhieri.

Ahmed, A. (2013) *The Thistle and the Drone: How America's War on Terror Became a Global War on Tribal Islam*, Washington DC: Brookings.

Appadurai, A. (2013) *The Future as Cultural Fact. Essays on the Global Condition*, London: Verso.

Aristotle (1995) *Politics*, Oxford: Oxford University Press.

Aron, R. (1958) *War and Industrial Society*, Oxford: Oxford University Press.

Badiou, A. (2010) 'The Democratic Emblem' in Agamben, G., Badiou, A., Bensaïd, D., Brown, W., Nancy, J-L., Ranciére, J., Ross, K. and Žižek, S. (eds) *Democracy in What State?*, New York: Columbia University Press. pp.6–15.

Bauman, Z. (1989) *Modernity and the Holocaust*, Cambridge: Polity.

Bauman, Z. and Donskis, L. (2013) *Moral Blindness: The Loss of Sensitivity in Liquid Modernity*, Cambridge: Polity.

Benjamin, W. (2002) 'The Storyteller' in *Selected Writings*, Cambridge: Cambridge University Press.

Bonger, W.A. (1936) *An Introduction to Criminology*, London: Methuen.

Brown, W. (2010) 'We Are All Democrats Now …', in Agamben, G., Badiou, A., Bensaïd, D., Brown, W., Nancy, J-L., Ranciére, J., Ross, K. and Žižek, S. (eds) *Democracy in What State?*, New York: Columbia University Press. pp.44–57.

Caillois R. (2002) *La vertigine della Guerra*, Troina: Città Aperta.

Campbell, B. (2009) 'Genocide as Social Control', *Sociological Theory*, 22: 150–172.

Cobain, I. (2013) 'More Than 50 Countries Backed US Project to Torture Terror Suspects, Report Alleges', *The Guardian*, 6th February.

Cobain, I., Norton-Taylor, R. and Hopkins, N. (2013) 'M16 Was Involved in the Rendition of Tortured detainees, Inquiry Finds', *The Guardian*, 20th December.

Coleman, J.S. (1982) *The Asymmetric Society*, Syracuse: Syracuse University Press.

Comte, A. (1953) *Cours de philosophie positive (vol. VI)*, Paris: Gallimard.

Curi, U. (2002) 'Introduzione' in Caillois, R. (ed.) *La vertigine della Guerra*, Troina: Città Aperta.

Dal Lago, A. (2012) *Carnefici e spettatori. La nostra indifferenza verso la crudeltà*, Milano: Raffaello Cortina.

Debray, R. (2013) 'Decline of the West?' *New Left Review*, 80: 29–44.

Derrida, J. (2011) *The Beast and the Sovereign (Vol. II)*, Chicago IL: University of Chicago Press.

Durkheim, E. (1970) *La science sociale et l'action*, Paris: Presses Universitaires de France.

Durkheim, E. (1982) 'Two Laws of Penal Evolution' in Gane, M. (ed) *The Radical Sociology of Durkheim and Mauss*, London: Routledge. pp.21–49.

Elliott, A. and Turner, B.S. (2012) *On Society*, Cambridge: Polity.

Feldman, Y. (2013) 'Collateral Assets'. *Radical Philosophy*, 178: 50–52.

Fogarty, B.E. (2000) *War, Peace and the Social Order*, Boulder, CO: Westview Press.

Freud, S. (1959) 'Why War?' in *Collected Papers*, New York: Basic Books.

Hagan, J. (2003) *Justice in the Balkans: Prosecuting War Crime in the Hague Tribunal*, Chicago IL: University of Chicago Press.

Holmes, S. (2013) 'What's in It for Obama?', *London Review of Books*, 18 July: 15–18.

Kant, E. (1970) *Political Writings*, Cambridge: Cambridge University Press.

Jamieson, R. (1998) 'Towards a Criminology of War in Europe' in Ruggiero, V., South, N. and Taylor, I. (eds) *The New European Criminology*, London: Routledge. pp.480–506.

Joas, H. and Knöbl, W. (2013) *War in Social Thought*, Princeton, NJ: Princeton University Press.

Leander, A. (ed.) (2013) *Commercialising Security in Europe. Political Consequences for Peace Operations*, London: Routledge.

Lindqvist, S. (2012) *A History of Bombing*, London: Granta.

McDougall, W. (1915) *An Introduction to Social Psychology*, London: Methuen.

Machiavelli, N. (1944) *The Prince*, London: J.M Dent & Sons.

Malešević, S. (2010) *The Sociology of War and Violence*, Cambridge: Cambridge University Press.

Mazzetti, M. (2013) *The Way of the Knife: The CIA, a Secret Army and a War at the Ends of the Earth*, Harmondsworth: Penguin.

Mythen, G. and Walklate, S. (2006) 'Criminology and Terrorism: Which Thesis? Risk Society or Governmentality?', *British Journal of Criminology*, 46: 379–398.

Nicolić-Ristanović, V. (1998) 'War and Crime in the Former Yugoslavia', in Ruggiero, V., South, N. and Taylor, I. (eds) *The New European Criminology*, London: Routledge. pp.462–479.

Nietzsche, F. (1968) *The Genealogy of Morals*, New York: Random House.

Park, R.E. (1941) 'The Social Function of War', *American Journal of Sociology*, XLVI: 551–570.

Park, R.E. (1952) *Human Communities*, New York: Free Press.

Park, R.E. (1960) *Race and Culture*, New York: The Free Press.

Peterson, A. (2001) *Contemporary Political Protest: Essays on Political Militancy*, Aldershot: Ashgate.

Ross, K. (2010) 'Democracy for Sale', in Agamben, G., Badiou, A., Bensaïd, D., Brown, W., Nancy, J-L., Rancière, J., Ross, K. and Žižek, S. (eds) *Democracy in What State?*, New York: Columbia University Press. pp.82–99.

Ruggiero, V. (2006) *Understanding Political Violence*, Maidenhead: Open University Press.

Ruggiero, V. (2007) 'War, Crime, Empire and Cosmopolitanism', *Critical Criminology*, 15: 211–221.

Ruggiero, V. (2008) 'Privatizing International Conflict: War as Corporate Crime', *Social Justice*, 34: 132–147.

Russell, F.H. (1975) *The Just War in the Middle Ages*, Cambridge: Cambridge University Press.

Sands, P. (2006) *Lawless World: Making and Breaking Global Rules*, Harmondsworth: Penguin.

Santner, E.L. (2011) *The Royal Remains. The People's Two Bodies and the Endgame of Sovereignty*, Chicago: University of Chicago Press.

Scahill, J. (2013) *Dirty Wars: The World is a Battlefield*, New York: Nation Books.

Schwartz, M. (2013) 'Like a Mosquito', *London Review of Books*, 4th July: 13–15.

Simpson, E. (2012) *War from the Ground Up: Twenty-First-Century Combat as Politics*, New York: Columbia University Press.

Sofsky, W. (2003) *Violence: Terrorism, Genocide, War*, London: Granta.

Sophocles (2011) *The Complete Plays*, New York: Harper Perennial.

Virilio, P. and Lotringer, S. (1997) *Pure War* (Revised edition), New York: Semiotext(e).

Walzer, M. (2006) *Just and Unjust Wars*, New York: Basic Books.

Ward, T. (2005) 'State Crime in the Heart of Darkness', *British Journal of Criminology*, 54: 434–445.

Weizman, E. (2012) *The Least of All Possible Evils: Humanitarian Violence from Arendt to Gaza*, London/New York: Verso.

Whitman, J. Q. (2012) *The Verdict of Battle. The Law of Victory and the Making of Modern War*, Cambridge: Harvard University Press.

Wilamowitz-Moellendorff, U. (2011) *Cittadini e guerrieri negli stati dell'antichità*, Gorizia: Libreria Editrice.

Wright Mills, C. (1956) *The Power Elite*, Oxford: Oxford University Press.

2 Civilising the corporate war

David Whyte

Introduction

A hundred years ago, James Connolly, the Marxist theorist and Scottish revolutionary, known for his leading role in the Easter Rising in Dublin in 1916, famously asked 'Can Warfare Be Civilised?' His question was rhetorical of course. In response to the early-twentieth-century movement to make 'dum-dum' bullets illegal at the time, Connolly (1915) argued against refining the rules of war, proposing that criminalisation of a particular type of military hardware would merely sustain the long-term, general, legitimacy of war as a mode of power. The basic co-ordinates of this very same debate can be found in post-Second World War movements to outlaw nuclear weapons, and, latterly, campaigns against landmines, white phosphorous and, most recently, the use of bombing by unmanned 'drones'.

The implication of Connolly's argument is that the civilisation/regulation of war does not merely control and place limits upon the harms produced by war, but has a much more damaging impetus. By claiming to 'civilise' war, the laws and regulations that govern war seek to present acceptable limits upon the use of military violence. In other words, the regulation of war also *legitimises* war. This chapter takes Connolly's argument as a point of departure for exploring the role of business organisations, or corporations, in war. It begins by arguing that, in order to fully grasp the implications of the state-corporate relation in war, we need to conceptualise the origins of the relationship in 'regimes of permission'; in the context of corporations that are directly implicated in armed conflicts, the process of making war more civilised rests upon a very specific regime of permission in which the business of killing is regulated and licensed. The chapter then sets out a brief history of state-corporate collaboration in war-making, before showing how various claims in relation to the 'corporate responsibility' of war-making corporations represent a key current attempt to civilise corporate involvement in war and thus open up new regimes of permission.

Regimes of permission

There is, across the critical scholarship on corporations, a tendency to focus upon what might be called 'moments of rupture' in the constitutional public/

private relation (Whyte, in press, 2014). In other words, a dominant theme in criminological work impels to look at where public authorities have either colluded in ways that breach the normal constraints of their 'public' role, or have failed to protect us, the public, from the harmful activities of the private (corporate) sector. In this sense, there is a tendency in the literature to follow classical liberal formulations of the public/private relation whereby public policy-making is insulated from the corrupting influence of private interest, the political order is based upon the formal constitutional segregation between public and private spheres that envisages an antagonistic or oppositional relationship between the two spheres. From a liberal perspective, regulatory failures occur where this constitutional segregation is ruptured. However, as the discussion in the following section will indicate, corporate involvement in war-making arises from the *common interests* that are consolidated in the relationship between those institutions, rather than a 'rupture' in an idealised notion of an antagonistic or oppositional interests.

There is good reason to argue that the neo-liberal era has both materially intensified, and has made more visible, the interconnectedness of 'public' and 'private' spheres. Because neo-liberal capitalism conceptualises the main role of government as facilitating the profitability of business, it encourages closer collaboration between government and capital at an institutional and individual level. An increasingly visible manifestation of this process is the 'revolving door' that often facilitates the movement of personnel between public and private sectors and provides the social networks that are ultimately used to concentrate power in social elites (Whyte, 2013).

The architecture of state-corporate war-making briefly sketched out in the following section will show that the lines of separation across state power and corporate power are not easily drawn. Indeed, corporate power is wholly reliant upon a series of state-organised regimes of permission (for example, the permission to trade as a separate entity; investment regimes which permit limited liability; the application of the separate entity in criminal law; the permission for corporations to act as holders of 'rights' and so on). Crucially, within those regimes of permission we also find the co-ordinates of impunity (a corporate veil which shields owners from civil liability; and a de facto corporate veil which shields both owners and managers from criminal liability; Tombs and Whyte, forthcoming 2015). The power to employ workers, to buy and sell goods and services, to deal in financial markets, or to transform future surplus value into capital on stock markets are also only possible as a result of a broader complex of regimes of permission. Together those regimes allow us to see how an understanding of the state-corporate relationship at the level of 'moments of rupture' has its limits; it does not allow us to break down the formal (liberal) separation between 'state' and 'corporation' and move towards an understanding of the relation as a symbiotic one (Whyte, in press, 2014).

The 'regimes of permission' that enable corporations to engage in commercial activity also enable corporations to engage in socially harmful activity.

The regulation of the environmental impact of industrial production, for example, is based upon the establishment of acceptable limits of pollution. In liberal democratic societies, every polluting factory has limits placed upon it that stipulate the level of permitted emissions of particular substances it produces; factories are licenced to produce an acceptable level of pollution. In other words, a regime of permission sets a tolerable level of harm that can be produced at a particular industrial site. Similarly, a regime of permission in corporate tax regimes enables a tolerable level of tax avoidance. Indeed, the practice of tolerating partial corporate tax payment has been acknowledged as normal practice by the British tax regulator, HMRC (Aldrick, 2012). The regulator has agreed a series of 'sweetheart deals' involving behind-closed-doors agreements to reach discounted tax settlements with large corporations such as Vodafone and Goldman Sachs. This practice is therefore part of a regime of permission that facilitates the avoidance of tax payments that companies are normally legally obliged to pay.

As I have noted elsewhere, the regulation of the private security industry is based upon precisely the same principle: to establish a regime of permission that legitimates the deployment of violence for profit (Whyte, 2003). Private military companies (PMCs) provide a crucial extension to states' capacity for war-making. It is therefore a regime of permission that has considerable value for both states and for private military corporations. The introduction to this chapter begins to set out the argument that the effect of laws governing war is not merely to civilise war, but at the same time to establish a regime of permissible war. Private military companies that engage in combat are in fact only part of this parallel regime. Private providers are now involved in virtually all routine military functions such as food, fuel and logistical supplies, transport, sleeping accommodation of armies, the administration of prisoner of war camps, and even the interrogation of prisoners (Schooner, 2005). Private sector involvement in all of those functions profoundly changes the basis of legitimate involvement in war, and raises fundamental questions about the process of 'civilising' war.

Merchants of death

Corporate involvement in war-making has a long history. The ruthless use of military violence was part of the core business of the very first joint-stock companies. In the earliest days of the European empires, trade routes were run and policed by corporations established for that very purpose. The English and Dutch East Indies Companies operated essentially as private trading armies, and it was openly recognised by the colonial powers that chartered those companies that profitability could only be guaranteed in two ways. Throughout two-and-a -half centuries, the English (latterly British) East India Company was implicated in countless atrocities as part of an on-going military suppression of local peoples. Its proxy colonial role on behalf of the British government enabled the company to act as a maverick corporation routinely involved in bribery and illegal trade (Lawson, 1993). The Company's private army also waged war against its French, Portuguese and Dutch counterparts to protect their access to raw materials and the factories and warehouses set up along the Indian coastline. The torture, decapitation and burning alive of corporate rivals was not unusual, in many cases merely for breaking mutual trade agreements. By the end of the company's reign, as Karl Marx (1857) observed in his *New York Daily Tribune* column of the time, 'torture formed an organic institution of [British] financial policy'.

The British government set up other joint-stock corporations on a similar model at the end of the nineteenth century – notably the British Imperial East Africa Company and the British South Africa Company – to seize land, settle colonising forces and then plunder resources. Such companies were seen as a highly effective and efficient means of colonising Africa, simply because they administered trade, conducted military operations and ran local police forces. History showed that those companies had little moral compunction and waged brutal campaigns of terror wherever they met local resistance.

For the British state there were three main advantages in chartering companies that would secure the colonial territories for British interest.

1   The first advantage was that it enabled the reduction of political risks to the British state: when colonial companies were involved in activities that provoked public condemnation or local resistance, the state could plausibly deny its knowledge or involvement.
2   Second, colonial companies were created to enable private investors to shoulder the state's burden during this period of rapid expansion in markets and trade routes. Private capital was mobilised for operations and the development of new territories that the government lacked the necessary capital to fund.
3   Third, by arming the company, the state found an efficient way of reducing the need for a constant military presence along trading routes and across remote parts of the colonies. In the seventeenth and eighteenth centuries, the former was a task way beyond the capacity of the fledgling British Navy, and the latter task would have involved a constant deployment and redeployment of regular military forces, thus stretching regular military capacities.

In many ways, precisely the same reasons are behind the recent rise in the use of private military companies by states engaged in wars. There is no shortage of analyses that point out that the use of private corporations in military operations is a grossly inefficient way of fighting a war, and in many ways a false economy (for example, Goodman, 2004; and Musah and Fayemi, 2000). Yet economic 'efficiency' is not the primary advantage to be accrued in those economies. Those advantages are precisely the same reasons for using private military force that have endured through the history of modern states.

1   First, one of the most attractive reasons for deploying private military companies is that they are relatively invisible, both in terms of the application of international law, and in terms of a visible body bag count (Sheppard, 1998).

2   Second, due to the short-term nature of the deployment, private military capital does at the same time enable some of the long-term cost burden of deploying personnel to be absorbed by business. Those jobs, in very practical terms, require private armed security; companies that can be contracted on a day-by-day basis by government institutions and corporations with contracts tailored to respond to the particular requirements of short-term deployment.

3   Third, under conditions of permanent war economy (Oakes, 1944) the need to maintain a constant presence to safeguard post-conflict areas is beyond the current capacities of even the most dominant states. In Iraq or Afghanistan for example, it would be wholly impractical for the coalition forces to guard on a company-by-company basis the huge numbers of US or British firms involved in the economy, or to guard effectively a sprawling Iraqi oil infrastructure (Whyte, 2003). Private military companies therefore provide a crucial extension to states' capacity for war-making.

Of course, this issue of private corporations being deployed to enhance the capacity of war machines goes much deeper than the operational logistics of managing armed security and the occasional military engagement *per se*. The war machines of all modern states have been predicated on major mobilisations of *private* capital. There is a now established history that shows military capacities of the German Third Reich were only made viable by both German and US corporations (Sutton, 1976). Of course, this relationship is always mutual – the capacities to grow in militarised economies are always for the mutual benefit of states and corporations. Perhaps the most notorious of such mutual relationships in the context of the Third Reich was IBM. A partnership with IBM's subsidiary Dehomag ensured that the Nazis would be supplied with the sorting machines that identified, and lead to their slaughter, the victims of the concentration camps. In fact IBM, in partnership with its German associates, modified the design of their equipment for this purpose. The Nazi's also tailored their data that identified those to be exterminated to fit the IBM machine. Without IBM's technology, it is therefore unlikely that the Nazis would have been capable of killing 6 million people with the same brutal efficiency. Without the impetus to create this technology, it is unlikely IBM would have subsequently developed such a commanding industrial position in the post-war high-tech industry (Black, 2001).

IBM was by no means the only corporation to enter into mutually beneficial deals with the Nazis. It is well know that Nazi-controlled firm I.G. Farben used slave labour from Auschwitz and supplied gas to the concentration camp, and that it was Swiss banks – including Union Bank of Switzerland, the Swiss Bank Corporation and Credit Suisse – that facilitated the theft of Jewish property. General Motors manufactured German tanks, and the sheer volume of trade and investment that was maintained in the war years was crucial to maintaining Germany's economic survival. US tele-communication giant ITT was another company that profited vastly from their collaboration. ITT ran Hitler's telecommunications systems and oper-ated aircraft factories for the Nazis on the agreement that they would be financially recognised for this after the war. They also knowingly supplied fuses to the Nazi regime for artillery used against the Allied forces and bombs that were dropped on London. In 1942 Standard Oil of New Jersey (now Exxon) entered into a huge cartel agreement with I.G. Farben which essen-tially carved up the global oil and chemical markets. Standard agreed not to develop processes for manufacturing synthetic rubber, crucial for the war effort, in exchange for I.G. Farben's agreement not to compete in the Amer-ican petroleum market. Eventually the US government were forced to seize the patents, but only after Standard had threatened to withdraw their supply of fuel to the US forces. Ethyl G.m.b.H. (now Ethyl Inc.) was a subsidiary formed by US companies Du Pont, General Motors and Standard Oil of New Jersey with I.G. Farben to build the plants that would supply the German armies with synthetic tetraethyl fuel at the request of the Third Reich. Prior to this deal, Germany's petroleum reserves did not give them the capacity to build a war-machine capable of fighting a world war; according to Nazi documents seized after the war it was confirmed that 'Without lead-tetraethyl the present method of warfare would be unthinkable' (Higham, 1983: 166).

There is a point at which this type of corporate collaboration takes on a much greater significance than simply the act of doing business with totali-tarian regimes; the point at which corporate collaboration actually determines the very existence of the regime. This is clearly how the corporate collaboration in the building of the Nazi war-machine must be conceptualised. Arguably, it is how corporate collaboration in the building of all war-machines since then must be conceptualised (Whyte, 2002/2003). The post-Second World War years are littered with similar examples of indispensable collaboration. In most of those cases, collaboration refers to the influence of both foreign and domestic capital, but it is foreign capital – often because of the scale of investment required to build heavily militarised states – that has proven most indispensable to totalitarian regimes. The racist regimes of South Africa and Rhodesia were sustained by US and European capital. British corporations notoriously worked in collaboration with British civil servants to illegally circumvent the international embargo on Rhodesia (Bailey, 1979). British businesses have been instrumental in supporting oppressive regimes in count-less cases since, including Saudi Arabia, Nigeria and Burma, and in sustaining wars in Africa, the Middle East and Latin America.

Thus, we return to the point that this chapter is framed by: none of those collaborations would be possible without established regimes of permission – both in the states that those corporations collude with, and in their domicile states – that provide corporations with infra-structural capacities that sustain their ability to act as private corporations. The success of the corporations guaranteed by those regimes of permission involve benefits for those states – or at least for elites within those states. Put simply: corporate collaboration in war-mongering states (whether they are foreign or domestic states) is always facilitated by state infrastructures. It is the benefits that accrue to those states, as measured by the three structural advantages outlined above (the minimisation of political risks; the minimisation of financial risks; and the expansion of states' military capacities) that provide clear incentives for the state facilitation of corporate war-making.

Elsewhere, I have shown how, under conditions of a 'war on terror' (no matter how contrived this 'war' might be), governments are increasingly likely to couple the national interest to the interests of particular private corporations. This phenomenon, described as 'market patriotism' (Whyte, ibid., 2013), has been mobilised to facilitate the un-interrupted accumulation of profits, to provide a basis for heightened collaboration between corporations and military institutions and to provide a more general 'common' sense basis for the mobilisation of public and private apparatuses to 'secure the imperium' at home and abroad (Whyte, 2008). Thus, following the September 2001 attacks on the World Trade Centre and the Pentagon, ideologies of market supremacy became prominent in relation to the defence of 'our' markets and 'our' market system against the 'terrorists'. Typically, such national security crises are coupled with appeals to 'consumer patriotism' (Whyte, 2003).

When Tony Blair recently argued, at a conference of the Iraq British Business Council in 2012, that British companies are obliged to take advantage of Iraq's economic opportunities because British troops fought there with 'heroism and sacrifice', he was merely articulating what many already suspected about the motivations for war (*The Telegraph*, 5th November 2012). It is known that key figures in the US and UK oil companies had been involved in the planning of the invasion and even in the capture of the oil fields (Whyte, 2008). It is also known that UK ministers intervened directly on behalf of the British oil company BP in the negotiations of the carve-up of Iraq's oil fields (Muttitt, 2011). In the current period, ruling elites are seeking to find ways of securing consent for neo-liberal policies and strategies that are increasingly pared down to a purely economic rationale. There is no sophisticated way to do this.

Neo-liberalism in the present era is reliant upon ever more vulgar means of seeking consent for ever more vulgar forms of social organisation. Moreover, despite regular overtures to 'market patriotism' in the most powerful governments, corporations can never claim that all of what they do is in the 'public' interest. This is because their legal constitution – the conditions that apply to them in legal regimes of permission – forces corporations to pursue *private* interests above *public* interests. The fiduciary duties of corporation which exist in a similar form in all liberal democracies, obliges corporate boards of directors to maximise the long-term interests of the corporation and returns for owners or shareholders. It is this feature of corporate constitution that enabled Standard Oil and IBM to claim that they were disinterested parties in the development of European fascism, and enables companies like Shell and BP to plausibly deny their political role in locations like Nigeria, Colombia and Iraq. However, most large corporations do have a public profile and, in recent years, have been highly conscious of how they project their activities to the public. This public projection can never fully articulate the public interest, but must also be resolved with the corporation's private revenue-maximising aims. Public projections that seek to do this have become known as 'corporate social responsibility' (CSR) strategies. It is to a brief discussion of those strategies and how they are applied in the context of war-making corporations that the next section turns.

Corporate social responsibility and the war machine

The central assumption in the CSR literature is that corporations can develop responsibilities and standards of 'behaviour' beyond that which the law requires and, at the same time, meet their responsibilities to investors and shareholders. In some industrial sectors, and for some firms, there clearly is a business case for corporate social responsibility, as companies can and do see CSR as a 'corporate social opportunity' (to use the title of a widely used management handbook on the subject; Grayson and Hodges, 2004). This means something, both in crude public relations terms, and in attempts to reposition external relationships with customers, and giving impetus to a renewed leadership role for corporations engaging in wider political fora (Fryzel, 2011).

Nowhere has CSR's use as a means of enhancing corporate political leadership been brought to bear more effectively than in the sphere of legal regulation. It is never stated explicitly, but the principles of voluntarism and self-regulation that sit at the core of corporate CSR strategies are always implicitly aimed at obfuscating – or indeed displacing – legal responsibilities, even if the prospect of law enforcement against corporations is generally remote (see again Grayson and Hodges, 2004). Yet, as Baars (2012) shows, firms' CSR documents and policies can and do serve the function of diverting legal process or, if it cannot be diverted, of mitigating the impact of enforcement and punishment of legal violations. CSR is a strategy that dilutes or deflects law enforcement thus allowing 'corporations to continue being harmful in a more controlled manner' (Baars, 2012: 298). An adjunct political function, as Shamir (2004a: 7) argues convincingly, is that CSR has been used as part of a more general political strategy to 'block the use of legal methods' for taming corporations. Thus, CSR is deployed as a strategy to dilute or ward off legal regulation (Shamir, 2004b) and, contemporaneously, provides arguments for the continuance of market-based forms of self-regulation.

CSR strategies are not merely aimed at preventing regulation. After all, all markets need some level of regulation – some ground rules – to operate. As argued in the preceding discussion, once we begin to explore the full architecture of regulation that gives corporations their lifeblood, the lines of separation across state power and corporate power are not easily drawn. Crucially, within regimes of permission we also find the co-ordinates of impunity (a corporate veil which shields owners from civil liability; and a de facto corporate veil which shields both owners and managers from criminal liability; Tombs and Whyte, forthcoming, 2015). The power to employ workers, to buy and sell goods and services, to deal in financial markets, to transform future surplus value into capital on stock markets are also only possible as a result of a broader complex of regimes of permission.

Thus, to position CSR as merely a counter-regulation strategy makes no sense, since corporations would not exist without some measure of regulation. Indeed, as Maltby (2005) has shown, a strategic attempt to develop the business case for CSR reporting can be identified in the public pronouncements and AGMs of key British firms between 1914 and 1919. British industry used CSR reporting during the period of the First World War as part of a political strategy to maintain profit accumulation under wartime conditions. This, she argues, was both defensive, in the sense that it provided a means of bolstering the legitimacy of businesses – even those clearly engaging in war profiteering, and allowed business to demonstrate strong moral and political leadership. It was therefore a viable 'regime of permission' that those firms sought. In many ways, this latter motivation to assert the social responsibility of business seems to reflect the strategies of war-making corporations.

Britain's largest arms manufacturer, BAE systems, has, over the past decade or so, developed a CSR strategy that similarly allowed the company to take the initiative in defining the condition of the regime of permission. In a dedicated corporate responsibility page on its website, BAE Systems proclaims that 'responsible business is embedded within the Company's Strategy and is supported across the business via our Corporate Responsibility (CR) agenda'.[1] This strategy currently focuses on four areas: ethics and governance, employee and product safety, diversity and inclusion, and environmental impact (BAE Systems, 2012).

As part of this corporate responsibility strategy, BAE Systems seeks to resolve a fairly glaring contradiction between the interests of its customers (the users of weapons systems) and those that are at the other end of the firing line. Thus it asserts in its most recent annual report:

> No complex and innovative product, whether used in defence or civilian markets or both, is without risk. It is essential that the Group achieves an appropriate balance between the benefits they provide to customers and the risks associated with their use.
>
> (BAE Systems, 2012)

Furthermore, the annual report notes: 'The Group ensures that environmental considerations are taken into account throughout a product's lifecycle from concept, design and manufacture through to use and disposal' (BAE Systems, 2012). Here, BAE Systems seems to be trying to square a circle, to produce deadly weapons systems that are a little less deadly, and take some account of the interests of the military personnel and civilian populations at the receiving end.

There is no indication in the 2012 annual report of precisely how this circle will be squared in practice. However, its current corporate responsibility strategy is shaped by a significant document that was published in 2003. It is this document that provides more of a clue as to how its deadly weapons systems are to be made less deadly without compromising the quality of the product. In this document, BAE Systems (2003: 9) notes:

> We aim to design products that are safe to handle and transport. For example, RO Defence, a BAE Systems company, has developed a range of insensitive munitions, using new explosives that are significantly less likely to explode in an accident.
>
> Lead used in ammunition can harm the environment and pose a risk to people. Our RO Defence site at Radway Green is developing lead-free ammunition which will be available in 2005.

Presumably the targets of BAE Systems weapons, whether they be targeted by the US and the UK in Afghanistan, or Israel in Palestine, can be gratified by the knowledge that they will be killed by bullets that are less likely to pollute the biosphere. Elsewhere in the same report, the company notes that it is aiming to be more responsible by making their missile-targeting systems more precise (to ensure they hit their intended target). The targets, together with the personnel who point the weapons are presumably supposed to be comforted by the assertion that they will be killed deliberately and not in 'accidents'. This report also proclaimed the company's environmental credentials by reducing the number of plants that apply depleted uranium in missile production (BAE Systems, 2003). Since the publication of this report, BAE Systems has noted that, as part of their corporate responsibility strategy, the company has ceased to produce depleted uranium.[3]

BAE's attempt to reposition itself over the past decade or so as a 'green' arms supplier also includes the development of armoured vehicles with hybrid diesel/electric engines that significantly reduce carbon emissions and the reduction of emissions of other toxic substances such as volatile organic compounds (VOCs) in its weapons systems. The gradual replacement of depleted uranium with tungsten as a material used to tip weapons was clearly presented as part of a strategy to improve the environment. The company has failed to mention in any of those statements the concerns that depleted uranium has contaminated ground water. The statements also fail to mention evidence of a sharp rise in rates of cancers, such as breast cancer and lymphoma, in parts of Iraq where those weapons were used in the 1991 and 2003 conflicts.[2]

At one level, those examples represent a familiar example of how CSR doubletalk seeks to present issues that are really about market performance and improvement in product standards as 'corporate responsibility'. Tungsten is now a cheaper substance that can be used for the purpose of tipping missiles and is equally effective. More generally, the corporate social responsibility strategy outlined in various BAE Systems' documents can be understood precisely as a process of civilising the technologies of war. Targets are killed in more efficient, less environmentally damaging ways, and the robustness of the technology means that accidental killings and 'collateral damage' can be reduced in a twisted morality that claims to guarantee a more effective machinery of war.

The civilisation of war, then, is a principle that applies, through the doctrine of CSR, to corporations involved in the business of war. Partly, as the preceding section has argued, this enables corporations such as BAE Systems to speak legitimately as a good corporate citizen that is clearly capable of shaping the 'regime of permission' that governs it. The function of CSR in this regard is of course contested, and BAE Systems' motivations for developing such a strategy are as complex and contradictory as the strategy itself. However, the argument here makes assertions, not about the intentions of BAE Systems in the framing of such a policy, but merely about its effects as a means of civilising war.

This same effect is currently visible in the development of a CSR strategy for private military companies. One of the most often cited criticisms of the use of PMCs was the apparent exclusion from the civilising confines of the law of war. The laws enshrined in the Geneva Conventions and their related treaties apply only to states and not private corporations; individuals within those corporations may theoretically be prosecuted for war crimes in the international criminal court, or in other international tribunals, but this prospect remains unlikely.

Legal vacuums and legitimacy

The Geneva Conventions and the treaties and agreements that extend them apply only to states. In the case of private military companies, in fact, it is assumed in international law that only regular forces engage in combat. Private military companies therefore stand outside the regime that aims to civilise war. Under Article 47 of the Geneva Convention, 'mercenaries' are declared illegal, and signatory states have an obligation to take necessary steps to prevent such persons and groups participating in conflicts. The International Convention Against the Recruitment, Use, Financing and Training of Mercenaries, which prohibits individuals from engaging in mercenary activities and makes illegal the recruitment of mercenaries by states for any purpose, came into force in 2001 after being ratified by the requisite 22 members, but has failed to attract much support from the majority of members and is supported by few Western governments. Consistent appeals from the UN Commission on Human Rights, condemning the toleration of the recruitment and use of private combatants, and the Secretary General's Special Rapporteur on Mercenaries, highlighting the net impact of privately employed soldiers in the undermining of state sovereignty, have been routinely ignored by the most powerful members of the UN (Whyte, 2003).

In so far as the use of particular weapons and substances is also governed by the international law, the onus is on *states* not to use particular weapons or particular substances, or to prevent their manufacture. Arms manufactures are not the object of international treaties such as the Geneva Convention. What arms manufacturers can or cannot produce and sell within a particular jurisdiction only be regulated effectively by the government within that jurisdiction. Simply put, this is a variation of what has been described as a 'space between the laws' (Michalowski and Kramer, 1987), where a lack of international standards produces gaps in the regulation of corporate activities that operate on a global level.

In the regulation of both arms companies and PMCs, this gap clearly still exists. The lack of a legal framework for corporations in international law prevents their ability to claim legitimacy in war (in the way that Connolly envisaged that law provides states with a basis for legitimate war-making). Corporations that seek legitimacy, or at least seek to present themselves plausibly as engaging in war on a 'civilised' basis, must use sources other than *law* upon which to base those claims. This is a particular issue for corporations that are directly involved in war: the arms companies that supply military hardware and private military companies. From the point of view of international law, both of those types of firms are directly implicated in military violence, yet are not bound by the same laws as states. It is this vacuum in legal standards that creates a demand for standards to be asserted in other ways. This demand for legitimacy has perhaps been most visible following the 2003 Iraq conflict, which involved several high-profile incidents and several mass killings involving the notorious Blackwater corporation (Scahill, 2007). Following Iraq, it was clear that PMCs would require some form of regulation. At the same time, a formal legal structure – and an enforcement mechanism that places limits on corporate activities – is very often regarded by companies as something to be avoided, not least because of the transaction costs associated with regulation. PMCs are therefore caught between the need for a framework that allows them to legitimately claim compliance with a standard of conduct and the need to minimise the transaction costs associated with regulation. The post-Iraq solution of the private military industry was the development of an International Code of Conduct for PMSC (private military and security companies). Codes of Conduct have a special place in the development of corporate social responsibility strategies. As this section of the chapter has already noted, CSR strategies are always implicitly aimed at obfuscating or displacing legal responsibilities. Codes of Conduct, well established in the global garment industry, have been part of such a strategy. The Code of Conduct for PMCs (hereafter, ICoC, 2010) has a similar pedigree. The ICoC has its origins in an initiative led by the International Committee of the Red Cross (ICRC) and the Swiss government, which resulted in the 'Montreux Document on Private Military and Security Companies', which reaffirmed the obligations of states to ensure compliance with international law by PMCs in armed conflicts. The ICoC was developed out of discussions around the Montreux Document, involving representatives from PMCs, industry associations and governments, including those with the largest private military industries, the US and UK, and non-governmental organisations.

The preamble to ICoC (2010: 3) notes that,

> [t]he Montreux Document On Pertinent International Legal Obligations and Good Practices for States Related to Operations of Private Military and Security Companies During Armed Conflict recognizes that well-established rules of international law apply to States in their relations with private security service providers and provides for good practices relating to PSCs.

The ICoC (2010) thus explicitly establishes that the 'rules of international law' apply to states but that international law 'provides for good practices' in relation to PMCs. It is on this basis in the Code that signatory companies affirm their responsibilities to respect human rights and fulfil humanitarian responsibilities to those affected by their business activities. The Code therefore does not create any new legal responsibilities for corporations and is not binding upon the states that recognise it. Rather, it 'affirms' the 'responsibilities' of corporations. The envisaged enforcement mechanisms are weak. First, it is noted that Signatory Companies 'intend to', along with other 'interested stakeholders' meet regularly to review progress toward compliance: a multi-stakeholder steering committee. The resultant committee comprises representatives from four PMCs (currently Triple Canopy, Drum Cussac, GardaWorld and Aegis), two from establishment NGOs (Human Rights Watch, Human Rights First), one from a security think-tank (the Geneva Centre for Security Policy) and representatives from the US, UK and Australian government (countries that together host in which about two-thirds of the industry are based). Second, the Code provides for an unspecified 'oversight mechanism' to be developed by the board before the end of March 2011. This mechanism was eventually agreed upon in February 2013 and is governed by a similar three-pillar structure of governments, 'civil society' and companies themselves. Lacking a binding system of enforcement, but instead using a listing process for compliant firms, the mechanism is for all intents and purposes based upon a form of self-regulation.

Current and previous UK government policy has been shaped by the regulatory structure around the Montreux Document in 2008 and the subsequent International Code of Conduct for Private Security Providers. The current UK government summarises its approach to the regulation of industry by:

introducing robust regulation in the UK through a trade association based on a voluntary code of conduct agreed with and monitored by the Government; using the Government's leverage as a key buyer of PMSC services to promote compliance with the code.

(Foreign and Commonwealth Office, 2011a)

The government has proposed that monitoring will be based on a system of certification; in order to be certified as a PMC, companies must comply with the standards set in the Code (Foreign and Commonwealth Office, 2012). Certification of PMCs will be scrutinised by a third-party auditor (though it has not been any more specific about the auditing process than this).

In 2011, the government 'appointed' the trade organisation Aerospace Defence and Security (ADS) as the Government's partner in developing and implementing UK national standards for PMCs (Foreign and Commonwealth Office, 2011b). If this suggests a closer formal relationship with the industry that any government had previously announced, it does not change the general self-regulatory trajectory of policy. As Labour's (then) Foreign Secretary, David Miliband asserted in 2009, the government intended to develop a 'Code of Conduct' approach in partnership with security companies themselves, building upon the Montreux initiative. This government also favoured a market regulation approach in which the government would use its status as a buyer 'to contract only those companies that demonstrate that they operate to high standards' (*Hansard*, 29th April 2009: 24th April 2009: Column 27WS).

The standards that PMCs are to comply with in the UK, then, are standards set by the industry itself, or, to use the parlance of the British government: 'Our trade association partners, the Security in Complex Environments Group, will, in consultation with Government, develop guidance to help British PSCs meet the requirements of the new standards'. The British government has further noted that '[w]e are still consulting with industry and civil society partners on what additional steps PSCs might need to take to obtain full certification by the ICoC that they are meeting the Code's principles' (Foreign and Commonwealth Office, 2012: 1). It is instructive that the British government sees PMCs as part of the defence industry, which enjoys a prominent position in the global economy. Of the 600 or so companies that have signed up to the ICOC, around a third of them are British (Foreign and Commonwealth Office, 2012).

The Code of Conduct for PMCs can be understood as an attempt to civilise corporate involvement in war. The Code enables PMCs to legitimately claim that they can apply standards of conduct that are widely agreed upon and therefore that those companies can speak legitimately as good corporate citizens. In the meantime, a more punitive or restrictive regime of permission has clearly been avoided by those companies. The outcome is a positive one PMCs themselves: this 'light touch' form of self-regulation, which is based upon soft law mechanisms rather than an external enforcement regime, will enable markets in privatised security to grow unencumbered by the transaction costs or the barriers to market entry that a stricter regime might involve.

Conclusion

Both of the CSR strategies briefly explored in the previous section aim at either shaping (in the case of BAE Systems) or even constructing (in the case of the ICoC) regimes of permission that enable entry into war markets. In this sense, the regulatory outcomes that they seek are not the kind of controlling regulatory outcomes that liberal criminologists normally envisage when they analyse corporate regulation.

Yes, the regulation of corporations in capitalist social orders is characterised by a contradictory relationship between a practical need to observe the laws that structure, and place restrictions upon, economic activity on the one hand, and, on the other, an ideological impulse and normative structure which places the values of 'free enterprise' above values of law observance. This fundamental contradiction between the promotion of law observance on one hand, and profit-seeking values on the other hand is an ever-present feature of capitalist social orders. Yet this looks less like a contradiction when regulation opens up new market spaces that provide fertile locations for commoditised military violence, or for the proliferation of demand for deadly hardware used in war.

States do not just control corporations; they empower them and at the same time control them – so there is a constant tension or interplay between state control and corporate agency in this story. Indeed, in capitalist social orders, it is not possible to have one without the other. Corporations continue, as they have done throughout history, to provide the motor force of militarism; capitalist states ensure that corporations are empowered to profit from an expansionist, war-mongering agenda.

None of this is about corporate "responsibility"; it is all about establishing regulatory regimes that give life to corporate war.

Notes

1 See: www.baesystems.com/our-company-rzz/corporate-responsibility/working-resp onsibly?_afrLoop=21531789239000&_afrWindowMode=0&_afrWindowId=jn43g0l wx_92#%40%3F_afrWindowId%3Djn43g0lwx_92%26_afrLoop%3D215317892390 00%26_afrWindowMode%3D0%26_adf.ctrl-state%3Djn43g0lwx_156, viewed 20th March, 2014.

2 For an alternative perspective on depleted uranium and a useful summary of sources of evidence relating to its health impacts, see the International Coalition to Ban Uranium Weapons briefing at: www.bandepleteduranium.org/en/overview#4, viewed 20th March, 2014.

3 See: www.baesystems.com/article/BAES_052474/depleted-uranium?_afrLoop= 105779615246000&_afrWindowMode=0&_afrWindowId=null&baeSessionId=SlbQ TspPTKQv4TF2N2JlTkQ7xphVnKh17YH1KmrYGhGWhXY1cmgT!743012858# %40%3FbaeSessionId%3DSlbQTspPTKQv4TF2N2JlTkQ7xphVnKh17YH1KmrY

GhGWhXY1cmgT%2521743012858%26_afrWindowId%3Dnull%26_afrLoop%3D
105779615246000%26_afrWindowMode%3D0%26_adf.ctrl-state%3Dp9n2biidj_4,
viewed 20th March, 2014.

References

Aldrick, P. (2012) 'HMRC Cleared of "Sweetheart" Tax Deals for Business', *The Telegraph*, 14th June.

Baars, G. (2012) 'Lawyers Congealing Capitalism: On the (im)possibility of using international criminal law to restrain business in conflict', unpublished PhD thesis, London: City University.

BAE Systems. (2003) 'Corporate Social Responsibility Report', London: BAE Systems.

BAE Systems. (2012) 'BAE Systems Annual Report 2012', London: BAE Systems.

Bailey, M. (1979) *Oilgate: The Sanctions Scandal*, London: Hodder & Stoughton.

Black, E. (2001) *IBM and the Holocaust: The strategic alliance between Nazi Germany and America's most powerful corporation*, London: Little, Brown.

Connolly, J. (1915) 'Can War Be Civilised?', *The Worker, 30th January*. Available: www.marxists.org/archive/connolly/1915/01/warfrcvl.htm.

Foreign & Commonwealth Office. (2011a) 'Promoting High Standards in the Private Military and Security Company Industry, Statement by Minister for Conflict Issues', Henry Bellingham, 10th March.

Foreign & Commonwealth Office. (2011b) 'Promoting High Standards in the Private Military and Security Company Industry, Statement by Minister for Conflict Issues', Henry Bellingham, 21st June.

Foreign & Commonwealth Office. (2012) 'Private Security Companies, statement to Parliament by Foreign Office, Statement by Minister Mark Simmonds', 17th December.

Fryzel, B. (2011) *Building Stakeholder Relationships and Corporate Social Responsibility*, Basingstoke: Palgrave.

Goodman, A. (2004) *Exception to the Rulers: Exposing oily politicians, war profiteers and the media that love them*, London: Arrow.

Grayson, D. and Hodges, A. (2004) *Corporate Social Opportunity! 7 steps to make corporate social responsibility work for you*, Sheffield: Greenleaf.

Higham, C. (1983) *Trading With the Enemy: An expose of the Nazi-American money plot, 1933–1949*, New York: Delacorte Press.

ICoC. (2010) 'The International Code of Conduct for Private Security Providers (ICoC)'. Available: www.icoc-psp.org/uploads/INTERNATIONAL_CODE_OF_CONDUCT_Final_without_Company_Names.pdf.

Lawson, P. (1993) *The East India Company: A History*, London: Routledge.

Maltby, J. (2005) 'Showing a Strong Front: Corporate social responsibility and the "'business case" in Britain', *Accounting Historians Journal*, 32(2): 145–171.

Marx, K. (1857) 'The Indian Revolt', *New York Daily Tribune*, 4th September.

Michalowski, R. and Kramer, R. (1987) 'The Space Between Laws: The problem of corporate crime in a transnational context', *Social Problems*, 34(1): 34–53.

Musah, A. and Fayemi, J. (2000) *Mercenaries: An African security dilemma*, London: Pluto.

Muttitt, G. (2011) *Fuel on the Fire: Oil and politics in occupied Iraq*, London: The Bodley Head.

Oakes, W. (1944) 'Towards a Permanent Arms Economy?', *Politics*, February.

Scahill, J. (2007) *Blackwater: The rise of the world's most powerful mercenary army*, New York: Nation Books.

Schooner, S. (2005) 'Contractor Atrocities at Abu Ghraib: Compromised accountability in a streamlined, outsourced government', *Stanford Law and Policy Review*, 16: 559–572.

Shamir, R. (2004a) 'The De-Radicalisation of Corporate Social Responsibility', *Critical Sociology*, 30(3): 1–21.

Shamir, R. (2004b) 'Between Self-Regulation and the Alien Tort Claims Act: On the contested concept of corporate social responsibility', *Law and Society Review*, 38.

Sheppard, S. (1998) 'Foot Soldiers of the New World Order: The rise of the corporate military', *New Left Review*, 228.

Sutton, A. (1976) *Wall Street and the Rise of Hitler*, New Rochelle, NY: Arlington House Publishers.

Tombs, S. and Whyte, D. (forthcoming, 2015) *The Corporate Criminal*, London: Routledge.

Whyte, D. (2002/2003) 'War is Business, Business is War', *Corporate Watch Magazine: Attack on Iraq Special Issue*, 11/12, December/January.

Whyte, D. (2003) 'Lethal Regulation: State-corporate crime and the UK government's new mercenaries', *Journal of Law and Society*, 30(4): 575–600.

Whyte, D. (2008) 'Market Patriotism and the War on Terror', *Social Justice*, 35(2–3): 111–131.

Whyte, D. (2013) 'Market Patriotism: The liberal mask slips' in Fisher, R. (ed.) *Managing Democracy, Managing Dissent*, London: Corporate Watch.

Whyte, D. (in press, 2014) 'Regimes of Permission and State-Corporate Crime', *State Crime Journal*.

3 Criminology and war

Can violent veterans see blurred lines clearly?

Emma Murray[1]

Introduction

Criminology and International Relations (IR) contribute to connected concerns and concepts – both disciplines have shared in an analysis of political violence, security, crime, risk and human rights (Aradau and van Munster, 2009) which are each engulfed in a shared analysis of the so-called 'war on terror'. In light of this shared focus and despite fewer lines being drawn between war and crime, both disciplines go on as markedly distinct fields – pre-occupied with their 'own' dilemmas (Loader and Percy, 2012). The commonality of such dilemmas allows both disciplines to straddle across concerns with national security as they concentrate their efforts on what can crudely be considered as threats to security with an inside and outside dimension. This allows for a dialogue of security scholarship that is fashioned around dichotomies of inside/outside, domestic/international or quite simply here/over there. If we continue to assume for a few moments that these divides make sense in terms of how far academic disciplines can stretch their nets of understanding, then this is illustrated by a criminology that speaks of the 'inside' (the managing of a domestic criminal threat) and an IR that concentrates for the purposes of this chapter on the 'outside' (the managing of the international threat of war and terrorism).

Discussions of crime and war are structured and discussed around and across limits or borders, both in terms of the meaning ascribed to physical state boarders but also to the epistemological construction on the inside and the outside. Walker (1993), an IR scholar, first suggested this in an exploration of his discipline that considered the 'limits' of international relations. Criminology has also faced scrutiny for some time about the limited tools it draws upon in order to understand a narrow view of the subject of crime; Standing accused of being both 'self-referential' and 'self-perpetuating' and lacking 'the ability to look outside itself' (Barton *et al.*, 2007: 2). Such criticisms are not only directed at mainstream criminology, but critical strands of the discipline have also faced reproach with suggestions that its 'heyday' is over. Van Swaaningen (1997: 7) makes this claim based upon what he perceives to be a shift 'from epistemological and socio-political questions' back to what could be described as an 'applied science ... fuelled by the political agendas of the day, and geared by the agenda of its financers'. Whilst criminology has responded in collections such as this one, and more broadly through analyses of harm that can been seen for example in Hillyard et al., (2004), these claims are worth revisiting in this discussion as a means of assessing the academic response to the 'war on terror' not least because of the timing of this discussion.

As NATO (North Atlantic Treaty Organization) coalition forces prepare to leave Afghanistan by the end of 2014 the coalition host counties have become unsurprisingly interested in the resettlement of veterans post war which will no doubt only intensify. It is now recognised that this resettlement period which is also discussed as reintegration poses challenges for some that lead to criminality. September 2013 marked five years since NAPO (National Association of Probation Officers) claimed that a significant 20,000 ex-armed forces personnel were currently embroiled in the criminal justice system in England and Wales (NAPO, 2008). Although these figures have been contested – a debate I have had elsewhere (Murray, 2014) – the criminality of veterans post-war (and often post-service) has since captured our imagination. The returned British veteran who commits a criminal offence in the domestic sphere is certainly a striking political agenda of the day – especially as research has proven that most frequently those criminal offences are violent in nature (The Howard League, 2011; MacManus *et al.*, 2013).

That agenda has encouraged a wealth of new understandings about this *new* 'troubled' identity, which are to date largely quantitative and offer statistical probabilities of behaviour and experience (Dandeker et al., 2003; Greenberg *et al.*, 2011; Iversen et al., 2005; MacManus *et al.*, 2013; van Staden *et al.*, 2007). They are positivistic in nature, discussing the challenges faced by veterans from this perspective. Such is the research produced by the psychiatry department of King's College London, which adopts a rational-actor analytic (Iversen, 2005; van Staden, 2007). The little qualitative work that has been conducted discusses the criminal veteran as a new problem to be highlighted and understood as a criminological or criminal justice issue and a subject to be analysed. In this vein, veterans who commit crime can be perceived and researched as either criminal or vulnerable, or both, in a way that, when reading between the lines, points to their position being a product of their experience of war before the research turns its gaze back upon the individual in search for answers about why they have become criminal or vulnerable as a result. It is how they have experienced war and not the war itself that comes into question. This approach fails not only to question the state's role in creating the violent veteran identity but also their role in constructing their criminality and in consequence how they then manage it.

In previous work I have begun to unpick this issue, however, in doing so I too have presented the criminal (now understood largely as violent) veteran as a problem for criminal justice practice (Murray, 2013, 2014). Through 'veteranality' I have attempted to conceptualise the criminal veteran as a crisis of identity before questioning how that identity overwhelms normative criminal justice processes. Veteranality is then in many respects a theoretical observation of the criminal justice process that places the veteran within it before attempting to critically point to ways in which it problematises the same: first it points to the polemic value of the 'veteran' identity as being something that is inherently 'good' and in doing so considers the tension between this and their new equally polemical identity of being a 'criminal', which is viewed as inherently 'bad'; second veteranality allows a glimpse at how the state's criminal justice apparatus then manages or (mis)manages that complex identity. As a conceptual starting point it is hoped that veteranality will be viewed as an invitation to engage in a more critical conversation about how representations of war (which are perceived as occurring in the international sphere) manifest themselves in domestic security issues. It is, however, still wedded to the criminal law and fails to challenge the relationship between the social construction of crime and legal parameters. As a consequence, it is a concept which speaks to the socio-political whilst remaining within the neat confines of criminological discourse upon which to make its claims.

How then can criminology begin to ask the epistemological and socio-political questions that van Swaaningen (1997) spoke of with reference to the returned veteran who commits a violent crime? How can we make better sense of this identity theoretically? How can we ensure that at this pivotal point in the 'war on terror' veterans' experiences are not only seen as a practical criminal justice problem or a new unit of analysis in administrative criminology but as a means of advancing our understandings of the complexities connecting war and crime in a way that we have not yet begun to consider? In a modest attempt to engage the reader in these very issues, this chapter is one of two halves. This first part of the chapter aims to map out some of the ways in which criminologists have engaged with IR in the past which have disrupted stable meanings between the inside and the outside. This is by no means exhaustive, but the literatures that have been selected provide the framework on which to hang the suggestions to follow. It is intended to provide some context through a brief exploration of some key perspectives and literature that have endeavoured to see the blurring of lines between the inside/outside dichotomy more clearly. The second part of the chapter utilises narrative interviews with veterans currently serving a sentence in the criminal justice system of England and Wales as a muse to suggest that the veteran is a logical extension of a debate between the inside and the outside. This has emerged from a fresh look at the wealth of data collected that demonstrates the complexities of the veteran convicted of a violent offence. These narratives demonstrate that these individuals who once managed 'criminal' groups and the risk that they posed internationally are now managed as risky for their criminal status in the domestic sphere.

Taking stock

The lack of engagement with war in criminological literatures is well documented elsewhere (Jamieson, 1998; Ruggierio, 2005) and throughout this book. It is important, however, to just briefly map out the landscape here before looking outside the discipline. Jamieson's (1998) efforts are often taken as a starting point; this is not to dismiss or to treat previous less connected efforts as tokenism (Durkheim, 1992; Hakeem, 1946; Mannheim, 1941; Sorokin, 1944) but to afford war a clear place in criminology under the banner of a 'criminology of war'. The chapter from *The New European Criminology* (Jamieson, 1998) was less concerned with the legitimacy or illegitimacy of war as a phenomenon but rather on how exceptionally damaging engaging in such behaviours can be both during and immediately after war periods. Upon providing an overview of explanatory representations that underpin the relationship between war and crime, Jamieson (1998) calls for students of criminology to be more attentive to such complex connections. Those calls, and the calls from others, have led to a surge of interest and subsequent production of writing and research within (albeit on the fringes) of the discipline (Ruggiero, 2010).

The dominant focus has been the extent to which criminology can look beyond legalistic and narrow definitions of state crime in a way that affords war a place amongst state crime literature (Green and Ward, 2004; Jamieson and McEvoy, 2005; Kramer and Michalowski, 2005; White, 2008). This included drawing on states of exception – where the legal and illegal co-exist (Agamben, 2005), infringements of human rights legislations (Gearty, 2006), dual-purpose violence (Green and Ward, 2009) and 'legality' arguments (Hudson, 2009). These works question the conditions upon which the parameters of crime could be extended and reworked to encompass the waging of war and go as far as to suggest that a 'sociological-criminological analysis of war today may lead to its unconditional criminalisation' (Ruggiero, 2005: 239). This is of course a theoretical criminalisation (Mandel 2004; Ruggerio 2005, 2006) and Degenhardt (2010) proposes these new offerings as idealistic. It is argued that these influences call for 'exceptional practices' to emerge to call states to account in a way that 'dissolves the issues to a super-national institution ... instead of solving the problem of illegitimate violence by liberal regimes' (Degenhardt, 2010: 344). It is further limited, she claims, by imagining the state as a source of power at a time when power can no longer be limited to an understanding of the state as a set of institutions that are accompanied by private agencies in both war and criminal justice – the monopoly of force is now a commodity.

This emergence, however, gives rise to a challenging of the legitimacy of war, and its development allows theoretical criminological analysis to demonstrate the criminogenic properties of war whilst aiming to tease out the many complexities that connect war and crime. Such developments explore both war conflicts and post-conflict conditions (Bouffard, 2005; Green and Ward, 2009;

Hudson, 2009; Jeffery, 2007; McGarry, 2010; Ruggiero, 2006; Treadwell, 2010). The advances in the literature since can be described as moving in four directions: war as inherently criminal or as having criminological properties (as has been discussed); the complexities that link military operations with policing functions (Kraska, 1993, 2001, 2007; Sparks, 2006; Krasman, 2007); war as a site of victimisation (Kauzlarich *et al.*, 2001; McGarry and Walklate, 2011); and lastly how post-war situations frequently challenges the boundaries of war and domestic criminal justice process (Murray, 2013; 2014). This not only engages criminology in discussions of war but complements growing concerns with the international. They highlight macro-structural changes of physical state borders and our understandings of those boundaries through an analysis of the relationship between technology, governance, risk and politics – all of which not only transcend national borders but also disciplinary borders. The 'war on terror' is a 'global war' and hence by its very nature exceeds conventional understandings of space (Jabri, 2006: 49).

Taking a look outside

Through a series of articles in a special issue of *Global Crime* (2012) it is argued that globalising processes render the inside and outside divide visible only in academia – impossible to draw outside university walls (Aas, 2012; Holmqvist, 2012). Whilst this is not the space to discuss the contributions found in that issue in turn, it highlights that fostering and feeding the link between criminology and IR is both a challenging and a rewarding enterprise. Thus, it is important to remain mindful that although there is now a small body of work that reduces the lines drawn between both disciplines, such lines are nonetheless very real in terms of the literature and our understandings of common problems. The special issue can be and should be taken as invitation for more efforts to engage with international security problems from an interdisciplinary perspective. It calls for 'approaches to criminology and international relations which engage thoroughly and thoughtfully with the literature of the other field' (Loader and Percy, 2012: 218). Previously Aradau and van Munster (2009) and Degenhardt (2010) had highlighted the worth of such actions. It is anticipated that a project such as this may of course lead to what will be considered an 'interesting but not perfect criminology' whilst discussing an 'important but not flawless IR'; even so, the insights gleaned from an engagement such as this create new opportunities that have the capacity to overcome current 'obstacles to understanding' (Loader and Percy, 2012: 214).

In light of this potential for a less than perfect dialogue, two cautionary notes are essential before continuing to embark on this endeavour. It may of course seem ironic to map out limits in an argument based on challenging limits (both the physical and epistemological). To clarify the 'limits' about to be discussed concerns how far this argument can claim to engage with international relations, whereas the limits discussed beyond this point refer to the points at which both disciplines appear to pass the problem over to the other. With respect to the former, it is the intention here to engage with international relations in the lower case. That is not to engage directly with the discipline or a thorough exploration of its understandings (both novel and contested) but rather to highlight the worth of exploring alternative discourses centred in and around common problems. As part of this exercise appreciations can surface that are at the least inclusive rather than exclusive of one another, and at the most can point to problems that almost occur between disciplines. The second point is that erosions of lines in security are much broader than the inside and outside (Loader and Percy, 2012) and efforts to disrupt understandings between the inside and outside are much broader than an unpicking of the relationship between war and crime – for example public vs. private security are omitted here but can be found elsewhere (Avant and Haulfer, 2012).

That said, let us now turn to the ways in which lines between war and crime are now blurred. This blurring (and the literature that exposes it) has developed in three ways: the metaphorical; the merging of military and police policy and practice; and lastly matters of spatially. At the outset there is blurring of language through the sharing of metaphors. It is well documented that one cannot escape the war metaphor in criminological discourse (Garland, 1996; Ruggiero, 2005; Steinert, 2003 to name but a few). It is a rhetorical trope that speaks of ways in which to manage social problems, namely crime, in a way that assumes for 'them' an 'enemy' status. Warfare is understood in populist politics as a 'process of civilisation' (Steinert, 2003: 265); so, too, is the punishment framework. As a result, 'the war on drugs', 'war on trafficking' and of course the 'war on terror' allow a governing of apparent social ills in such a way that serves to reiterate sovereignty at the point of crisis (Garland 1996) in a curious way. Once the 'enemy' is identified, so too is something to be fearful of, an elusive 'other' and deviant group that must be governed and its risk managed. What is perhaps not so well documented in criminology is that warfare relies more and more frequently upon metaphors of criminal justice – waged through a language that situates and perceives insurgents not as actors of war but rather as criminals. This did not start with the 'war on terror'; earlier examples can be found in a language constructed around the need to 'punish' or react to the illegal in the first Gulf war, Kosovo (Degenhardt 2010) and Northern Ireland. It is perhaps now increasingly obvious, however, through public and political rhetoric entrenched with notions to 'bring terrorists to justice' and 'eliminate the threat that they pose' (Blair, 2001). Inviting once more an elusive 'other' that must be governed and its risk managed.

Distinctions are problematised then also by a process of labelling, as the 'named' terrorists perceive their acts as those of war, whilst counter-terror discourses perceive them as criminal. The counter-strategies that have emerged as a result do so then with criminals in mind leading to a war that merges military provision with police provision and practices of war with law enforcement in a bid to protect the domestic through international designs (Kraska, 1993, 2001, 2007; Sparks, 2006; Krasman, 2007; Loader and Percy, 2012). This blurring has seen NATO coalition forces train Afghan Police as part of their role in occupying Afghanistan (Loader and Percy, 2012); the military employing policing tasks such as going on 'patrol'; and even the military having an increasing role in securing the domestic arena, of which the Olympics in London 2012 is testament. Such strategies are constructed around the 'inside' going 'out', a 'fascination with turning limits into links' through a methodology that operates 'to secure the expansion of global governance' from police power (Ryan 2013: 21). But, in the example of the Olympics in London 2012, the 'outside' is also brought 'in' as the military are utilised to provide domestic security against the imagined terror threat. Ryan (2013: 437) explores the work of Walter Benjamin (2006) to claim that 'policing displays an intrinsic will to transcend limits' it is 'a limit unto itself'.

Essentially, then, when war and terrorism intersect, action is based on the management of dangerous populations and the risk that they pose, such is the aim of the criminal justice system. This brings into question relations between 'punishment' and 'defence mechanisms' (Degenhardt, 2010: 343). This problematises discourses that perceive war and punishment systems as separate, exclusive of one another in post-modernity. As systems they are instead intertwined in a complex way that allow 'punishment to represent violence' (Degenhardt, 2010: 343). That violence is a response to the violence of 'others'. War grants its combatants an authority to engage in behaviours such as murder and destruction of property in the name of 'duty' and 'military necessity' (Jamieson, 1998). Individuals are taken from predominately ordinary homes and communities and are taught to be aggressive, to hate and to kill (Hakeem, 1946). Violent behaviour, which is largely concealed in civil society 'is provided with a public and legitimate object' (Jamieson, 1998: 483). A new perception of brutality promotes and legitimises violence *per se* as the solution to social problems (Jamieson, 1998: 484) and allows for a destructive violence to be seen rather as 'heroic folly' (Durkheim, 1974). Benjamin (1928) suggests that a critical interrogation of violence must start by setting out the relationship it has to law and justice. This is because violence (in its subjective sense) is only achieved when the reason for that violence interferes with moral associations. The scope of such associations is defined by designs of law and justice. Violence is then a point upon a legal compass that measures morality through ends and means. Our response to that interaction is subjective (ranging from triumph to horror) and shaped by a range of societal and cultural influences that outline in which circumstances we attribute culpability to individuals whose actions have caused harm (Levi and Maguire, 2002).

One final and briefer point concerning the third theme should also be made: that of spatiality and physical space. Without intending to over-labour the point that understandings of war and crime are both discussed across distinctions between the inside/outside, and noting once more that this is about physical space as well as constructions of knowledge, it is important to consider the issue of spatiality as it is this moving from once place to another that will be essential in understanding the dialogue on veterans to follow. Globalising processes have eroded territory-based states, which has led to discrepancies between the epistemology of war which almost takes for granted that engaging in warfare is a linear motion based upon territory and how the practices of modern war disrupts those understandings through new realities of the modern state (Holmqvist, 2012). Aas (2012) discusses this as a process: when international and domestic security are blurred, risks no longer have a territory or point of origin.

From this point the chapter now turns to explore the ways in which the experience of the returned veteran who commits a violent crime can be used as a muse to see those blurred lines more clearly. Put simply, what happens to our new understandings of the inside and outside of security when those who have been the security provider on the outside become a threat to security on the inside? The remainder of this chapter now turns to empirical data collected to highlight a new problem – a new debate about those who have been instrumental in managing the risk posed by enemy groups in 'war on terror' and have become a group to be managed because of the risk they pose to domestic security as a result of their crimes.

Veterans and risk – beyond what we can 'know'

Hillyard et al., (2004: 25) contend that, although Foucault is a recurrent reference in criminology, 'the epistemological significance of much of Foucault's work seems to have passed criminology by'. The epistemological assumptions of the data presented here, and the socio-political analyses to follow, are based upon Foucault's understanding of discourse. Foucault (1974) invited his books to be used a 'toolbox' instead of simply being read: a source that can be rummaged through and, if a tool will help in an area, then to use it. Foucault's offerings on discourse can then be *used* as a tool from which the narratives generated, and the wider socio-political context in which they were constructed, can be better understood.

Central to this analysis is the view that discourse and power cannot be separated, and that meaning is constantly agreed and realised within complex power relations (King and Horrocks, 2010). Dominant discourse become accounts of reality, for example a veteran may be the hero, the victim or the dangerous through discursive frames pre-existing long before their experience of such an identity. Thus exploring the way in which individual biographies are narrated and consequently framed tells us something about knowledge and power. To pose epistemology in this way is to accept Foucault's description of self-constitution, that 'a regime of truth offers the terms that make self-recognition possible' (Butler, 2005: 22). The 'regime of truth' is historically specific – sustained by discursive formation and functioning to provide discourses of 'truth' in definite temporal spaces (Foucault, 1980).

Accordingly, the veteran's identity is shaped by a regime of truth that suggests who will be recognised as a subject and who will not. Hall (1997) advises that Foucault approached each population by asking six questions. What follows in this section is the application of these six questions to the study of violent veterans.

The first task is to question the set of accounts/statements that provide us with knowledge about violent veterans. There is always more than one way of thinking about a subject within the *discursive formation*, providing us with ways to understand or articulate violent veterans at any particular time – this is what Foucault (1970) termed the *episteme*. The hero, the victim and the beast are all ways of understanding the veteran – they are all part of the episteme. These accounts need not be confined to a 'top-down' approach upheld by the state. Accounts of what it means to be a violent veteran can also take shape from the 'bottom-up' through resistance, conformity and acceptance (Van Dijk, 1993). Being a veteran who becomes violent and criminal is perhaps evidence of resistance – their narratives subordinate and their status untold.

The second concern is the way in which understanding is organised so as to exclude ways of thinking about the topic, governing the 'sayable' or 'think-able' about soldiering and veterans at any given historical moment (Hall, 1997). An example of this is the urgency to attribute a veteran's criminality to their often socially deprived background, and not to their time spent in combat. The Howard League (2011) has claimed that their time in the forces will have actually delayed their criminality and not caused it. Blaming social deprivation pre-combat for their behaviour above the combat experience in itself encourages an understanding of violent veterans as people vulnerable to committing crime as opposed to the belief that war has damaged them.

The third is to question the subject of the discourse itself – what constitutes the violent veteran. I use the term subject and not individual intentionally, as it aids in our understanding that the human experience of reality is a con-struction. A Foucauldian subject then undergoes a self-crafting process within the context of the regime of truth that provides what a recognisable subject can be. Butler (2005: 22) points out that this,

> does not mean that any given regime of truth sets an invariable frame-work for recognition; it means only that it is in relation to this framework that recognition takes place or the norms that govern recognition are challenged and transformed.

I will return to this shortly. What is important to understand here, however, is that *being* a subject is not merely the product of discourse, but discourse represents us 'at a cost' (Butler, 2005: 121).

The fourth problem is to ask how knowledge gains authority. What con-stitutes the 'truth' about violent veterans in a particular space and time (Hall, 1997)? Foucault considers 'truth' to be a historical event. Truth is then pro-duced and not in permanent existence (waiting to be found). This production of truth is bound to associations with power, knowledge and the subject. An analysis of this kind aims to show the 'real as polemical' (O'Farrell, 2005).

The fifth concern is with the ways in which we deal with the 'subjects'; the criminal justice system is charged with regulating the conduct of the violent veteran. The sixth, however, is more of an acknowledgement than a question, that the contingent nature of truth provides an ever changing *episteme* of war. As Foucault (1970: 168) observes, 'in any given culture and at any given moment, there is always only one episteme that defines the conditions of possibility of all knowledge'.

Socio-political analysis assumes an analysis of the arrangement of discourse, power and dominance – and the place of the researcher in such social relationships (Van Dijk, 1993). Meaning is produced by discourse and, although subjects may and will produce texts, they are always functioning within the *regime of truth*, which governs the *discursive formation* that provides the *episteme* (Hall, 2001). In consequence, the data used in this chapter were part of a project that explored those six problems through the use of narrative interviews.[2] The project was concerned with the investigation into crimes (in particular violence) committed by Iraq and Afghanistan veterans post-war and -service with the purpose of developing our understanding of *being* a violent veteran and their experiences of punishment in the criminal justice system in England and Wales.[3]

The Western veteran: a new risk in the 'war on terror'?

The discourse representing the veteran is rich and expansive, stretching across oral histories (Martin, 2014; Sarkar, 2012), personal accounts (Beattie, 2008; Cawthorne 2007; Rayment, 2008), psychiatric studies (Lifton, 1974; Sherman, 2010) and sociological readings (Hill, 1949; Turner and Rennell, 1995) to popular culture in what has been called 'militainment' (Stahl, 2010). This literature provides a source of reflection (from soul-searching accounts to sensationalist (re)interpretations) as both veterans and their authors strive to attribute meaning to the veteran's position in society. The meaning provided is largely of pride or vulnerability both of which are constructed around understandings of what is good. In a study titled *Heroic anxieties: the figure of the British solider in contemporary print media* Woodward *et al.*, (2009: 5) suggest the function of the discourse in the media (at least) was to 'smooth out the complexities of the conflicts they purport to represent ... and the moral frameworks that the stories purport to engage with'. During a war, and for many years afterwards, the nation is proud; a collective approval of the power to fight and win masks the sacrifice of men (Edkins, 2003). Trauma and, more specifically, 'the memory of politics' is constructed post-war around national frames that omit individual experience (Edkins, 2003). It is also possible that individual experience can speak to conflicting national frames of risk, such as *being* a veteran and then *becoming* criminal.

When military personnel are discharged from their military service they assume this veteran status. At first, this label has modest personal meaning to the veteran; the worth of their new position is decided on by existing discourses. Throughout the reintegration process veterans can begin to attach meaning to the label (Brown, 2011). As the veteran learns to live as an individual again the collective memory lives on to mask the suffering of having been to war with a sense of pride. This individual often does not question the statecraft that created the war. Ruggirio (2006: 188) explains a collective memory as like a cancer that causes 'damage beyond the functional threshold'. The violent veteran could be viewed as evidence of this damage. To assume this identity is to identify with the symbolic and subjective function of the armed forces, but also with the glorification of war that cements nationalism. It is a proud position that recognises the powerful yet precarious nature of life at war (Butler, 2009).

We have already seen that war and crime are now both the management of an 'enemy'. In Foucault's (2007) lectures, *Society must be defended*, it is proposed that both crime and war work through the identification of a selected group of 'others', whether that be a dangerous class or group or those outside of the nation state. Based upon those stark differences, social order can be organised and maintained. Degenhardt (2013: 38) explains that it is on these very constructions that 'the continuum between war and crime rests as the facilitator of the processes of governance'. Through discourses concerning 'the enemy within' we have seen that discourses that assume a simple us/them or good/bad binary are unsettled. This unsettling is also demonstrated through the Afghan civilian that is both an identity to protect, and provide security for, whilst at the same time being an identity of threat (Loader and Percy, 2012). The discussion that the veteran may also unsettle these meanings is yet to be addressed in these terms. The narratives that they offer about their life embody both the national defender and national offender. It is to these narratives that this chapter now turns.

If risk is imagined on a continuum from high risk to those who manage it, then the trajectory of a veteran's life cuts right across it. The participants' data offer stories about times in their lives when they were 'good', when their key role was to manage the 'bad' in the world:

> Some people just have to die and should die, they are bad people, not like the bad people you see in here, I mean really bad and it was my job to deal with that. That is what I was trained to do, that is exactly what I should be doing now stuck in here for some daft fight, there is a real fight to be had and now I won't be part of it.
>
> (Veteran Participant 2012)

> See what these loons in here don't understand is I am not the risk here, the risk is out there, and it is everywhere. I got into trouble I will admit that, it got messy; I will admit that, I am the most dangerous thing in the

UK? [Laughter]. Should they be spending god knows how much money assessing my risk and paying you no doubt to do the same? I don't think so, I tell you what I think for what it is worth – I think that you all should be paying me to get back to it, get back to protecting you all and not protecting people from me. It's frustrating!

(Veteran Participant 2012)

The returned soldier provides a meaningful metaphor for the domestic effects of a 'war on terror' that is portrayed as existing in the international sphere. This representation invalidates the distinction between the local and global, state and inter-state violence, as the returned soldier often cannot recognise the arbitrary limits of political space, carrying the themes and the morality learned at war back to the site of that war. The returned solider, then, more than anything materialises the impossibility of there being a dividing line between the inside and outside.

I walk down the street and want to blow the windows out of the buildings, why is everything so normal? We are at war and I want the street to look like that, like it is never about the war here it is about learning to live in Civvy Street again.

(Veteran Participant 2011)

Why are they all laughing? I remember thinking that a lot when I got back, I couldn't speak to anyone about what I had been through, that was my job and I was cool not to tell anyone anything, I actually didn't want to. What really wound me up though was the lack of recognition from everyone. To them I had been to a bad place and might be a bit strange for a while, no acknowledgement whatsoever that I had been there for them and that actually their country was at war, they are at war, they are at risk.

(Veteran Participant 2013)

The troubled veteran then illustrates vividly the presence of the war in our apparently peaceful and prosperous world – threatening the narrative that upholds boundaries between the inside and outside, between us and them and amid peace and war. But also between positivist epistemology that maintains separate spheres on the inside and the outside:

What we are dealing with here are men who have been rewarded for violent behavior, yet punished for not turning up to work. They have lived under different rules to the rest of us, we must expect crime and when dealing with it be more understanding. I am not saying they should get away with it but I am suggesting a different justice system for ex-armed forces, similar to the system that operates in the military.

(Veteran Treatment Manager 2012)

These lads have been to war; fought for their country, we were proud of them then. They have been trained to kill and celebrated for extreme violence. They come from a culture that promotes 'suffering in silence' and often the first time they get the support they deserve is when they end up in the criminal justice system.

(Offender Manager 2013)

Categorising the actions of the returned solider as criminal, or rehabilitating the veteran to an apparently civilian environment, highlights the militarisation of society which wages a 'distant' war and the morality of there being a site where violence is just and necessary and others where violence is unjust and must be brought to justice. Accordingly, this investigation of the returned soldier permits an interrogation of the limits of violence and morality in war and peace:

I got a medal for killing people and a jail sentence for throwing a punch, because I'm dangerous [laughter].

(Veteran Participant 2010)

The judge said that because I was a veteran that I would receive a custodial sentence because I was dangerous like and couldn't control my temper. I only pushed her but it was seen as a lack of control.

(Veteran Participant 2012)

He will stay on weekly reporting for the remainder of his sentence because of his military past he must be seen as high risk.

(Offender Manager 2013)

Elsewhere I have suggested that 'risk' in the context of criminal justice practice and processes should be explored further on the basis of evidence that illustrates that veterans are perceived as 'risky' by criminal justice professionals; that assessment is frequently becoming based upon their occupational status and not the more traditional approach that makes such assessments based upon offending status (Murray, 2013, 2014). Assessing the risk posed by individuals, and then managing that risk is the priority throughout the criminal justice process (Canton 2011): an assessment that is based upon individuals' predicted capability to cause serious harm – we know that veterans display that capability just from who they are. There is clear evidence, however, that this conversation can be extended to notions of a 'world risk society' proposed by Beck (1999). This is not to propose extending this conversation to a full exploration of the Risk Society thesis which is both supported (Giddens, 1998; Strydom, 2002), contested (Dingwall, 2000; Scott, 2000) and explored (Mythen, 2007), but to suggest that how the veteran represents both the risk and management of it is an issue worthy of much further examination. Beck (2002) himself has in the wake of what he calls a 'collapse of language' since 9/11 invited the 'war on terror' to his Risk Society thesis. It has been demonstrated here that the veteran of the 'war on terror' invites a new dimension to studies that seek to evaluate the worth of the 'world risk society' in the future.

Can the violent veteran see blurred lines more clearly?

What then can be taken from the analysis above? Can the violent veteran indeed see blurred lines more clearly? This chapter has argued that the violent veteran's position can progress our understandings of the muddy waters between the inside and the outside of security scholarship through a new reading of data that invites a new conversation between criminology and IR. Research on the military and its place in society has grown considerably in academia. Since the Cold War these studies have grown in impact and size in the field of military studies and military sociology. Drawing upon political science, sociology, international relations and psychology these studies have offered a progressive understanding of the military as an institution and most recently its masculine culture (Higate, 2003; Higate and Cameron, 2006). Most of these are, however, quantitative, with the few that are qualitative in nature rarely turning to in-depth methods (Carreras and Castro, 2012). Such has been the case in criminology. Research such as this, however, can not only expand the criminological imagination further, to consider what it means to *be* a violent veteran in the criminological sense, but qualitative narrative methodology can also be used to entrench each participant's biography in a socio-political setting.

In doing so a case can be established that the violent veteran is socially constructed and that this construction is assembled through tropes (styles of discourse). This epistemological position poses problems for previous studies that fail to question the frames that they adopt in their analysis. In doing so, discursive frames can be no more than polemical. Research must consider the relationship that analytical frames have with the social reality they represent (Shapiro, 2001). To respect the agency of each participant above the intellectual abstractions of particular psychological or political theories, this chapter has made a modest attempt to offer an analysis both within and beyond such frames of understanding. The real skill of interpretive research is to sift through the data produced to identify these frames and to find where and when they correlate with what we know already, but more importantly where and when they show themselves to be in excess of 'what we know'.

This is not only to look beyond 'what we know' within the discipline of criminology but also to look beyond discursive frames of knowledge about our own subject matter. The advantages of bringing the inside and outside together in an analytical approach is, as Loader and Percy (2012: 216) suggest, a process which 'allows scholars to capture better the types of security provision that cut across traditional security divides' and thus 'grasp the intellectual and practical challenges that such boundary crossing generates'.

We have seen that the inside/outside dichotomy is at best blurred, if not wholly artificial, as modern practices of war, coupled with a new understanding of the state, obscure epistemological teachings that claim clear-cut differences between war and crime, between internal and external security provision, between the military and the police and between warfare and punishment. It was emphasised in the introduction that the arguments contained here will be considered an 'interesting but not perfect criminology' whilst discussing an 'important but not flawless IR'. It was also stressed that the insights gleaned from an engagement such as this create new opportunities that have the capacity to overcome current 'obstacles to understanding' (Loader and Percy, 2012: 214). In a time when risk discourses are being revisited in a 'war on terror' – with the concern that risk no longer has spatial or temporal confines – it is crucial not to understand the solider deployed to manage risk and the veteran managed for their risk upon their return as separate concerns for separate disciplines.

Notes

1 The author would like to acknowledge Justin Moorhead of Merseyside Probation and Wessley Doyle Foulkes of the University of Liverpool for their informal discussions about the content of this chapter.
2 Narrative interviews took place across four probation areas and the data used for the purposes of this chapter are drawn from nine narrative interviews, with each participant being interviewed twice. The interview technique employed is based upon the Free-Association Narrative Interview method but, at the point of analysis a critical discourse analysis was employed to shift the focus from the psycho-social to the socio-political in line with the interdisciplinary aims of the project. Brockmier and Carbaugh (2001) inform us that the narrative shifts our focus from that of inner mechanism of the mind to the 'discursive arena'.
3 Participants of the study were combat veterans of either Afghanistan or Iraq (or both) and had been subsequently convicted of a violent offence post-deployment and were still serving their sentence. Men were chosen because at the time and still at the time of writing female veterans have not yet been perceived as a criminal justice 'problem'. The conflicts were selected as an acknowledgment of time which is crucial when considering the contingent nature of truth which, by its very nature, provides an ever changing episteme of war. As Foucault (1970: 168) observes, 'in any given culture and at any given moment, there is always only one episteme that defines the conditions of possibility of all knowledge'.

References

Aas, K.F. (2012) '(In)Security-at-a-Distance: Rescaling Justice, Risk and Warfare in a Transnational Age', *Global Crime*, 13(4): 235–253.
Agamben, G. (2005) *States of Exception*, translated by Attell, K. London: The University of Chicago Press.
Aradau, C. and van Munster, R. (2009) 'Exeptionalism and the "War on Terror" Criminology meets IR', *British Journal of Criminology*, 49(5): 686–701.
Avant, D. and Haulfer, V. (2012) 'Transnational Organisations and Security', *Global Crime*, 13(4): 254–275.

Barton, A., Corteen, K., Scott, D. and Whyte, D. (2007) 'Introduction: Developing a Criminological Imagination' in Barton, A., Corteen, K., Scott, D. and Whyte, D. (eds) *Expanding the Criminological Imagination: Critical Readings in Criminology,.* Oxon: Willan Publishing.

Beattie, D. (2008) *An Ordinary Solider: Afghanistan: A Ferocious Enemy: A Bloody Conflict: One Man's Impossible Mission.* London: Pocket Books.

Beck, U. (1999) *World Risk Society.* Cambridge: Polity Press.

Beck, U. (2002) 'The Terrorist Threat: World Risk Society Revisited', *Theory, Culture & Society,* 19: 39–55.

Benjamin, W. (1928) 'On the Critique of Violence' in Benjamin, W. (ed.) *One-Way Street and Other Writings.* London: Penguin.

Benjamin, W. (2006) 'Critique of Violence', in Benjamin, W. (ed.). *One-Way Street.* London: Verso.

Blair, T. (2001) 'Prime Minister Statement to Parliament on the War on Terror'. Available: http://news.bbc.co.uk/1/hi/3536131.stm last accessed 02.05.14.

Bouffard, L.A. (2005) 'The Military as a Bridging Environment in Criminal Careers: Differential Outcomes of the Military Experience', *Armed Forces and Society,* 31(2): 273–295.

Brockmeier, J. and Carbaugh, D. (2001) 'Introduction' in Brockmeier, J. and Carbaugh, D. (eds) *Narrative and Identity: Studies in Autobiography, Self and Culture.* Amsterdam and Philadelphia: John Benjamins Publishing Company.

Brown, W. (2011) 'From War Zones to Jail: Veteran Reintegration Problems', *Justice Policy Journal,* 8(1): 1–32.

Butler, J. (2005) *Frames of War: When is Life Grievable.* London: Verso.

Butler, J. (2009) *Frames of War: When is Life Grievable.* London: Verso.

Canton, R. (2011) *Probation, Working with Offenders.* London: Routledge.

Carreras, H. and Castro, C. (eds) (2012) *Qualitative Methods in Military Studies.* London: Routledge (Taylor & Francis Group).

Cawthorne, N. (2007) *On The Frontline.* London: John Blake Publishing.

Dandeker, C., Wessely, S., Iversen, A. and Ross, J. (2003) *Improving the Delivery of Cross Departmental Support and Services for Veterans,* London: The Institute of Psychiatry: King's College.

Degenhardt, T. (2010) 'Representing War as Punishment in the War on Terror', *International Journal of Criminology and Sociological Theory,* 3(1): 343–358.

Degenhardt, T. (2013) 'The Overlap between War and Crime: Unpacking Foucault and Agamben's Studies within the Context of the War on Terror', *Journal of Philosophical and Theoretical Criminology,* 5(2): 29–58.

Dingwall, R. (2000) 'Risk Society: The Cult of Theory and the Millennium' in Manning, N. and Shaw, I. (eds) *New Risks, New Welfare: Signposts for Social Policy.* London: Blackwell. pp. 137–154.

Durkheim, E. (1974) *Sociology and Philosophy.* New York: New Press.

Durkheim, E. (1992) *Professional Ethics and Civic Morals,* London: Routledge.

Edkins, J. (2003) *Trauma and the Memory of Politics Cambridge.* Cambridge University Press.

Foucault, M. (1970) *The Order of Things: An Archaeology of the Human Sciences.* London and New York: Routledge Classics.

Foucault, M. (1974) 'Prisons et asiles dans le mécanisme du pouvoir' in *Dits et Ecrits, t.II,* Paris: Gallimard. pp. 523–524.

Foucault, M. (1980) *Power/Knowledge.* Brighton: Harvester.

Foucault, M. (2007) 'Society Must Be Defended', *Lectures at the Collège de France, 1975–1976*. St Martin's Press.

Garland, D. (1996) 'The Limits of the Sovereign State: Strategies of Crime Control in Contemporary Society', *British Journal of Criminology*, 36(4): 445–471.

Gearty, C. (2006) *Can Human Right Survive? The Hamlyn Lectures 2005*. Cambridge: Cambridge University Press.

Giddens, A. (1998) 'Risk Society: The Context of British Politics' in Franklin, J. (ed.) *The Politics of Risk Society*, Cambridge: Polity Press. pp. 23–35.

Green, P. and Ward, T. (2004) *State Crime, Governments, Violence and Corruption*, London: Pluto Press.

Green, P. and Ward, T. (2009) 'The Transformation of Violence in Iraq', *British Journal of Criminology*, 49: 609–627.

Greenberg, N., Jones, E., Jones, N. and Fear, N.T. (2011) 'The Injured Mind in the UK Armed Forces', *Philosophical Transactions of the Royal Society*, 366, 261–267.

Hakeem, M. (1946) 'Service in the Armed Forces and Criminality', *Journal of Criminal Law and Criminality*, 37(2): 120–131.

Hall, S. (1992) 'The West and the Rest' in Hall, S. and Gieben, B. (ed.) *Formations of Modernity*, Cambridge: Polity Press.

Hall, S. (1997) 'The Work of Representation' in Hall, S. (ed.) *Representation: cultural representations and signifying practices*. London: in association with the Open University.

Hall, A. (2001) 'Foucault: Power, Knowledge and Discourse' in Wetherell, M., Taylor, S. and Yates, S. (ed.) *Discourse Theory and Practice: A Reader*. London: Sage.

Higate, P. (2003) *Military Masculinities: Identity and the State*. Praeger.

Higate, P. and Cameron, A. (2006) 'Reflexivity and Researching the Military', *Armed Forces and Society*, 32(2): 219–233.

Hill, R. (1949) *Families under Stress*. New York: Harper and Row.

Hillyard, P., Pantazis, C., Gordon, D. and Tombs, S. (ed.) (2004) *Beyond Criminology: Taking Harm Seriously*. London: Pluto Press.

Holmqvist, C. (2012) 'War/Space: Shifting Spatialities and the Absence of Politics in Contemporary Accounts of War', *Global Crime*, 13(4): 219–234.

Hudson, B. (2009) 'Justice in a Time of Terror', *British Journal of Criminology*, 49(5): 701–717.

Iversen, A., Nikolaou, V., Greenberg, N., Unwon, C., Hull, L., Hotopf, M., Danderker, C., Ross, J. and Wessley, S. (2005) 'What Happens to British Veterans When They Leave the Armed Forces', *European Journal of Public Health*, 15(2): 175–184.

Jabri, V. (2006) 'War, Security and the Liberal State', *Security Dialogue*, 37(1): 47–64.

Jamieson, R. (1998) 'Towards a Criminology of War' in Ruggiero, V., South, N. and Taylor, I. (eds) *The New European Criminology, Crime and Social Order in Europe*. London: Routledge.

Jamieson, R. and McEvoy, K. (2005) 'State Crime by Proxy and Juridical Othering', *British Journal of Criminology*, 45(4): 504–527.

Jeffery, A. (2007) 'The Geopolitical Framing of Localized Struggles: NGOs in Bosnia and Herzegovina', *Development and Change*, 38(2): 251–274.

King, N. and Horrocks, C. (2010) *Interviews in Qualitative Research*. London: Sage.

Kramer, R.C. and Michalowski, R.J. (2005) 'War, Aggression and State Crime: A Criminological Analysis of the Invasion and Occupation of Iraq', *British Journal of Criminology*, 45(4): 446–469.

Kraska, P.B. (1993) 'Militarising the Drug War: A Sign of the Times' in Kraska, P.B. (ed.) *Altered States if Mind: Critical Observations of the Drug War*. New York: Garland Publishing.

Kraska, P.B. (2001) 'Crime Control as Warfare: Language Matters' in Kraska, P.B. (ed.) *Militarising the American Criminal Justice System: The Changing Roles of The Armed Forces*, Boston: Northeastern University Press.

Kraska, P.B. (2007) 'Militarization and Policing – Its relevance to 21st Century Police', *Policing*, 1(4): 501–513.

Krasman, S. (2007) 'The Enemy Boarder', *Punishment and Sentencing*, 9: 301–318.

Levi, M. and Maguire, M. (2002) 'Violent Crime' in Maguire, M., Morgan, R. and Reiner, R. (eds.) *The Oxford Handbook of Criminology*. Oxford: Oxford University Press.

Lifton, R.J. (1974) *Home from the War*. London: Wildwood House Publishing.

Loader, I. and Percy, S. (2012) 'Bringing the "Outside" In and the "Inside" Out: Crossing the Criminology/IR Divide', *Global Crime*, 13(4): 213–218.

McGarry, R. (2010) 'Accept It and Forget It: Demobilization, Reintegration and the Military Homecomer' in Ferguson, N. (ed.) *Post-Conflict Reconstruction*. Cambridge: Cambridge Scholars Publishing.

McGarry, R. and Walklate, S. (2011) 'The Soldier as Victim: Peering Through the Looking Glass', *British Journal of Criminology*, 51(6): 900–917.

MacManus, D., Dean, K., Jones, M., Rona, R.J., Greenberg, N., Hull, L., Fahy, T., Wessley, S. and Fear, N.T. (2013) 'Violent Offending by UK Military Personnel Deployed to Iraq and Afghanistan: a data linkage cohort study', *The Lancet*, 381: 907–917.

Mandel, M. (2004) *How America Gets Away with Murder: Illegal Wars, Collateral Damage and Crimes Against Humanity*. London: Pluto Press.

Mannheim, H. (1941) *War and Crime*. London: Watts & Co.

Martin, M. (2014) *An Intimate War: An Oral History of the Helmand Conflict*. London: Hurst Publishers.

Murray, E. (2013) 'Post-army Trouble: Veterans in the Criminal Justice System', *Criminal Justice Matters*, 94(1): 20–21.

Murray, E. (2014 forthcoming) 'Veteran Offenders in Cheshire: Making Sense of the "Noise"', *Probation Journal*.

Mythen, G. (2007) 'Reappraising the Risk Society Thesis: Telescopic Sight or Myopic Vision?', *Current Sociology*, 55(6): 793–813.

Napo. (2008) 'Ex Armed Forces Personnel and the Criminal Justice System', Briefing Paper. Available: www.napo.org.uk/templates/assetrelay.afm?frmAssetFileID=317.

O'Farrell, C. (2005) *Michel Foucault*. London: Sage.

Rayment, S. (2008) *Into the Killing Zone*. London: Constable.

Ruggiero, V. (2005) 'Criminalizing War: Criminology as Ceasefire', *Social and Legal Studies*, 14: 239–257.Ruggiero, V. (2006) *Understanding Political Violence: A Criminological Analysis*. Berkshire: Open University Press.Ruggiero, V. (2010) 'Armed Struggle in Italy: The Limits to Criminology in the Study of Political Violence', *British Journal of Criminology*, 50: 708–724.

Ryan, B. (2013) 'Reasonable Force: The Emergence of Global Policing', *Review of International Studies*, 39(2): 435–457.

Sarkar, D. (2012) *Spitfire Voices*. Amberly Publishing.

Scott, A. (2000) 'Risk Society or Angst Society? Two Views of Risk, Consciousness and Community' in Adam, B., Beck, U. and van Loon, J. (ed.) *The Risk Society and Beyond: Critical Issues for Social Theory*. London: Sage. pp. 33–46.

Shapiro, M. (2001) 'Textualising Global Politics' in Wetherell, M., Taylor, S. and Yates, S.J. (eds) *Discourse Theory and Practice: A Reader*. London: Sage, in association with the Open University.

Sherman, N. (2010) *The Untold War: Inside the Hearts, Minds, and Souls of Our Soldiers*. London: Norton and Co.

Sorokin, P. (1944) *Russia and the United States*. New York: Dutton.

Sparks, R. (2006) 'Ordinary Anxieties and States of Emergency: Statecraft and Spectatorship in the New Politics of Insecurity' in Armstrong, A. and McAra, L. (ed.) *Perspectives of Punishment*. Oxford: Oxford University Press.

Stahl, R. (2010) *Militainment Inc: War, Media and Popular Culture*. New York: Routledge.

Steinert, H. (2003) 'The Indispensable Metaphor of War: On Populist Politics and the Contradictions of the State's Monopoly of Force', *Theoretical Criminology Special Issue: War, Crime and Human Rights*, 7(3): 265–291.

Strydom, P. (2002) *Risk, Environment and Modernity*. Buckingham: Open University Press.

The Howard League. (2011) 'Report of the Inquiry into Former Armed Service Personnel in Prison. London: The Howard League for Penal Reform.

Treadwell, J. (2010) 'COUNTERBLAST: More than Casualties of War? Ex-military Personnel in the Criminal Justice System', *The Howard Journal*, 49(1): 73–77.

Turner, B. and Rennell, T. (1995) *When Daddy Came Home: How War Changed Family Life Forever*. London: Arrow Books.

Van Dijk, T.A. (1993) 'Principles of Critical Discourse Analysis', *Discourse and Society*, 4(2): 249–283.

van Staden, L. (2007) 'Transition Back into Civilian Life: A Study of Personnel Leaving the UK Armed Forces via "Military Prison"', *Military Medicine*, 172(9): 925–930.

van Staden, L., Fear, N.T., Iversen, A.C., French, C.E., Dandeker, C. and Wessely, S. (2007) 'Transition Back into Civilian Life: A Study of Personnel Leaving the U.K. Armed Forces via "Military Prison"', *Military Medicine*, 172(9): 925–930.

van Swaaningen, R. (1997) *Critical Criminology: Visions from Europe*. London. Sage.

Walker, R.B.J. (1993) *Inside/Outside: International Relations and Political Theory*. Cambridge: Cambridge University Press.

White, R. (2008) 'Depleted Uranium, State Crime and the Politics of Knowing', *Theoretical Criminology*, 12(1): 31–54.

Woodward, R., Winter, T. and Jenkings, K.N. (2009) 'Heroic Anxieties: The Figure of the British Soldier in Contemporary Print Media', *Journal of War and Culture Studies*, 2(2): 211– 223.

Part 2

Linking war and criminal justice

4 War as an opportunity for divergence and desistance from crime, 1750–1945

Zoe Alker and Barry Godfrey

Introduction

This chapter attempts to capture the spirit of probation theory immediately before and during World War I (WWI). It will first explore the opportunity for pre-trial divergence that war offered to sentencers from the eighteenth century onwards; then it will consider whether military service can be said to encourage offenders to cease their criminal career; and last it will discuss in depth the theories of one influential probation officer, Robert Holmes, and other contemporary theorists writing around the WWI period. Their theories of re-moralisation will be examined, and we will draw heavily upon the experiences of those boys who had been held by institutions of reform and punishment, and then entered into military service, in order to reveal what happened to some of the boys that Holmes arranged for the armed forces to recruit during World War I. It was these young boys who bore the hopes of probation officers as well as the expectations of a public who called on them to serve their country.

Diverted into uniform?

In the eighteenth and nineteenth centuries, professional soldiers had a reputation for revelry, drunkenness and fighting (Sharpe, 1984), but they were, of course, vital to the nation's military capacity. The British State could not fight wars without soldiers; and, at times, there were problems in filling the army barracks and the Royal Navy with enough men to keep up the war effort. Arrested men held more value as soldiers than prisoners, and sentencers may have been aware that the armed forces needed young men and been willing to divert them into military service. There has been a long-standing, but of late little discussed, historical debate about the additional sentencing option that periods of warfare offered to magistrates and judges. Studies of the relationship between war/peace transitions and recorded crime rates have been dominated by histories of the eighteenth century. Hay and Beattie's research found that there was a tangible reduction in indictments at the onset of war which later increased during peacetime (Hay, 1982; Beattie, 1986). This pattern was also uncovered in a number of local county studies (Beattie, 1974; Beattie, 1977; Beattie, 1986; Hay, 1982; Williams, 1985; King, 2000), and King estimated that, on average, peacetime indictments were approximately a third higher than in wartime, 'a pattern only broken in a few years of either peacetime recruitment (e.g. 1770–1771) or in exceptionally bad wartime harvests (e.g. 1740–1741, 1800–1801)' (King, 2002: 98). However, historians have attempted to explain why there were higher levels of prosecution in peacetime and lower in wartime in different ways.

Hay and Beattie both argued that increases in the prosecution of indictable property crimes, such as theft and burglary, were a result of the impact of demobilisation. They concluded that saturated post-war labour markets combined with fluctuations in prices of basic foodstuffs resulted in a marked increase in property offences. Hay utilised the Schumpeter-Gilfoy index of consumer goods to argue that there had been a 'strong connection' between a rise in the cost of consumer goods and increases in property offences during the transition to peacetime in eighteenth-century Staffordshire (Hay, 1982). Interestingly, this relationship does not appear to have been geographically uniform. Beattie's study of London showed that, despite discernible increases in property crime during periods of peace, the capital was far less vulnerable to the combination of rising prices and demobilisation than were less urban areas.

For Hay (1982: 145), 'the greater pressure on the poor could be expected when dearth and the disaster of demobilisation coincided'. He argued that, 'We might conclude that indictment levels reflect important changes in the experience and behaviour of the poor' (Hay, 1982: 145). In addition, Palk's (2006) study of war/peace transitions and indictment levels in the Old Bailey between 1780 and 1830 reiterated the quantitative pattern uncovered by Hay and Beattie's research. She focused on the gendered dimension of crime levels during war/peace transitions and found that women featured more heavily for theft indictments during wartime. Palk (2006) argued that this was largely due to the fact that war removed men from society, and she also concluded that men's absence during wartime placed increasing pressure on poor and labouring women's ability to survive financially. But, the conclusion that shifts in indictment levels were largely a result of changes in the criminal activities of the poor, means that such work treats criminal statistics as a reflection of actual crime rates, and fails to acknowledge the wider causes of fluctuating prosecutions. In particular, by focusing on the aftermath of war and arguing that crime increased in periods of economic hardship, these histories fail to consider the role that judicial discretion and military recruitment drives played in shifting indictment rates during transitions between war and peace. It does seem to be the case that prosecutors were dissuaded from pursuing cases, and also that the courts sent offenders into the army rather than the prison, during times of war. Prosecutions then rose when the war ended, when the young men returned home.

The scarcity of research in this area, however, means that it is impossible to know the extent of these practices, or the impact they had on prosecution rates. For example, whilst Radzinowicz (1968: 96) suggests that pre-trial enlistment was used extensively by magistrates in periods of mobilisation, arguing that, 'robberies were daily compounded [informally settled] before the magistrates, on condition the thief would be handed over' to the army. Beattie is more sceptical. He argues that it is impossible to know the extent to which pre-trial enlistment was used due to the paucity of surviving criminal records (Beattie, 1986). In fact, King's (2002) study remains the only systematic study of the ways in which the courts used war as an alternative to imprisonment or transportation. King's (2002) study focused on Assize and Quarter sessions returns from Lancashire, Bristol and Gloucestershire (1740–1830) and found that, during the onset of war, enlistment was used as an alternative prosecution strategy which thus explained the decline in indictable offences. Enlistment was an attractive option for magistrates in eighteenth-century England. King's (2002) examination of the age-structure of offenders uncovered that it was young, unmarried men who were the most affected by impressment (forced enlistment into the army). Enlistment removed men most vulnerable to committing crimes, in particular, young unmarried men and vagrants. By examining age structures of male and female offenders, he found that 'war removed young men from the clutches of the courts' (King, 2002). Due to heightened concern amongst the propertied classes about the dangerous poor, military service was viewed as an effective way of dealing with the criminal population (Hay, 1982).

The nature and extent of pre-trial enlistment cannot be fully explained by quantitative analyses of indictment levels. King (2002: 111) uncovered anecdotal evidence from 'letters, diaries, magistrates notebooks, newspapers, petty sessions records, parliamentary papers, criminal autobiography, and gaol calendars' to examine the ways in which victims and magistrates utilised the armed forces as an alternative to indictment at court. During the eighteenth century, it was not uncommon for disputes to be settled informally without the intervention of a magistrate. Fragmentary evidence from private papers such as the Oakes and Williamson letters demonstrated that victims of property crime were willing to use enlistment as an alternative to punishment. This material showed that, 'a number of victims clearly ensured that in wartime young male offenders were either taken directly to a local recruiting party with very little choice, or coerced into agreeing to enlist by the threat of prosecution' (King, 2002: 107). King's (2002) study also revealed that serious offenders chose enlistment over a formal trial. As it was noted,

> In every wartime period, and in the final quarter of 1787, the Essex gaol records contain references to property offenders avoiding formal trial by being 'sent on board his majesties tender' or 'discharged by entering on board on of his majesties' ships'.
>
> (King, 2002: 111)

Offenders also appeared to have preferred enlistment to imprisonment or (more understandably) capital punishment. Griffiths contended that men sought war as an escape route rather than face the gallows (Devereux and Griffiths, 2004).

For perpetrators of indictable offences who faced harsh punishment in the form of transportation or even death, enlistment was 'clearly a better option than facing a public trial for an offence that frequently led convicts to the gallows' (King, 2002: 112). Enlistment was not, however, so attractive for those convicted of lesser offences such as minor theft. King (2002: 112) noted that those accused of minor theft, who if convicted were most likely to be either imprisoned or whipped, 'did not necessarily see enlistment as such an attractive option'. Desertion rates were high and the threat of enlistment was so greatly felt amongst offenders who were able men likely to be sent to war that there is evidence of them cutting off their fingers so that they could not perform military duties (King, 2002).

Nevertheless, magistrates' far reaching discretionary powers meant that those convicted for non-indictable offences were sent to war. Munsche's (1981) study of English game laws (1671–1831) discovered several examples where impressment was used for petty offenders, such as vegetable thieves. Similarly, King's (2002) research found that enlistment was used in the City of London summary court, which prevented men from receiving indictment at trial. Thus, as King (2002: 113) concludes,

> for a broad spectrum of property offenders, but more especially for those accused of indictable property crimes, there is considerable evidence that war, and the possibility of impressments or semi-compulsory enlistment, created a parallel sanctioning system, an alternative judicial resource for both victims and magistrates.

In the context of military recruitment drives, as the army and navy sought to increase their forces, 'Most of the offenders who were brought before the magistrates were adolescent or young adult males whose physical fitness was sufficient to meet the fairly basic requirements of the armed forces' (King, 2002: 115). King (2002: 105) continued that, 'It was probably mobilisation rather than demobilisation that created the key distortion – a unique collapse in the proportion of young adult males among recorded offenders'. Thus:

> Given their wide powers in relation to vagrants, unruly apprentices and servants, and the disorderly poor – precisely the groups which recruitment policies and impressments acts mainly targeted – the magistracy could and did use their discretion to shape criminal justice policy in ways that made informal pre-trial enlistment a potentially important plank of penal policy in the eighteenth century.
>
> (King, 2002: 115)

When England went to war, the government had to recruit a large number of men very quickly. 'No task was more central to the role assumed by eighteenth-century central government than the provision of the means and forces necessary for fighting its wars, and that task was highly demanding' (Landau, 2002: 9). Rodger's (1986: 386) study of the eighteenth-century Navy found that, during the Seven Years War, 'the central government had to speedily enlarge its peacetime navy of 9797 men to a force of 81, 929'. Richard Williams's (1985: 254) study of rural crime in eighteenth-century Berkshire noted that voluntary recruitment was a constant challenge for the military. Barnett's (1974: 140–141) broad history of the British military contended that:

> Recruitment was supposedly based on voluntary enlistment. Regiments sent round recruiting parties to recruit by 'Beat of Drum', on 'beating orders' from the sovereign or Commander in Chief. If the King's shilling could be somehow got into the hands or pockets of some yokel, drunk or sober, an enlistment had been made (and often) men were virtually kidnapped.

In addition, the forcible enlistment of offenders during wartime, 'was a cheap alternative to starting a prosecution' and a common condition of pardons from transportation, imprisonment and even death (Hay, 1982: 141–142). In the context of military recruitment drives at the onset of war, enlistment into the armed and naval forces was an established form of discretionary justice in the late eighteenth and early nineteenth century.

The twentieth century is not so well served with research studies, but some fragmentary evidence indicates that magistrates and judges between 1900 and 1940 were at least occasionally willing to allow military service to 'trump' normal punishments for offences. For example, notes made by South Staffordshire Discharged Prisoners' Aid officers reveal that on 1st July 1914, Fred Kirby, a 43-year-old man, who had been convicted of a minor crime (loitering), stated that he 'wanted to go to Duty on Discharge'. In October that year William Cooper, aged 27, was 'Back from Mons – wounded – discharged medically unfit – States that he is fit, and has made application to go back'. The same month, James Young, and Henry Hunt, both men in their 20s and 30s were released in order to enlist. John Bryant, a deserter from the Royal Navy, was remanded on a serious charge, but was released in order to join the Devonshire Regiment. Stephen G. Avery escaped with a reduced prison sentence for drunkenness due to his willingness to enlist. Over the border in Cheshire, a local lad, Henry Rickard, was convicted of illegal gambling on 8th September 1914 in the Crewe Juvenile Court and was released in order to enlist. At 16 years of age he was eligible to join the war effort. Fellow resident, James McGowan of 34a Market St, Crewe, convicted of being drunk and disorderly in April 1916, also escaped punishment by being willing to go back to fight in France; Frank Percival in August 1916 was released from court, despite being convicted of larceny, on promising to enlist. In Crewe, as presumably everywhere, the magistrates did not necessarily rely on the discharged offenders doing what they promised, and they were marched directly from court to the local enlisting office. They went from court, to police officer, to enlisting sergeant, to the trenches.

These defendants added to thousands of men that the First and Second World Wars took out of civil society, men who otherwise would have perhaps committed a measure of crime? Echoing debates about the eighteenth- and nineteenth-century levels of crime and their relationship to periods of war and peace, the Prison Commissioner at the time, Evelyn Ruggles-Brise (1916), argued that a fall in petty crimes was linked to enlistment: 'There is every reason to believe that the country's call for men appealed as strongly to the criminal as to other classes'. However, since Emsley (2013) showed that crime statistics fell during World War I but rose during World War II, simple links between low crime and the absence of men should be treated with caution – the creation of new laws (e.g. stealing, looting, hoarding food and rations coupons, etc.), the willingness of the criminal justice system or victims to proceed with cases and so on, all make axiomatic links difficult to establish. However, it is indisputable that the prison population fell during World War I. As Figure 4.1 shows, the prison population approximately halved between 1910 and 1920, from 114,283 to 64,160 – a decrease of 50,123, and the prison estate became available for other forms of use. Some prisons, such as Stafford, were emptied of adult prisoners, some juvenile institutions were converted to hold foreign aliens, and so on (Rose 1954; see Jewkes and Johnston, 2011).

The war and the reduction in carceral capacity may have again provided an opportunity for sentencers to divert some offenders away from the prison gate and into uniform, but it appears that only a small percentage of convicted men (and of course, no women) were diverted in this way. It would be impossible to make a strong claim for World Wars I and II engendering significant opportunities for divergence. However, as the following section makes clear, some have argued that the real benefit of military service was not meant

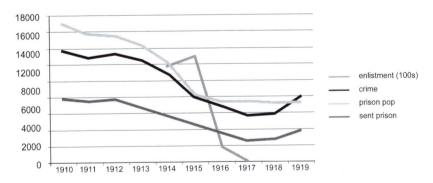

Figure 4.1 Rates of enlistment, crime, prison population and committals to prison 1910–1920[1]

for pre-trial defendants, but for providing post-conviction support for reforming offenders.

Desistance from offending and military service

The part that wartime conditions played in diverting defendants away from the courts at the pre-sentencing stage (or even as convicted offenders) has received a little attention, as noted above. The part that military service played in helping offenders to curtail their criminal career has also received some limited attention too, but from a different set of researchers, and with different concerns. Whilst desistance studies have grown in importance and prominence within criminology, little has been written about the impact of wartime service on those who had begun a criminal career. However, scholars have pointed to a wide range of possible social and economic factors that encouraged desistance, including finding employment, gaining strong social bonds and forming meaningful relationships, having children, and so on; and it is conceivable that military service, too, could play a part. Association with pro-social peer-groups, gaining a purpose in life, re-skilling with relevant training, strong routine and discipline, might all have aided military personnel to develop a useful life and non-offending habits. Existing studies of desistance tend to focus on the modern period, or at least the mid-to-late twentieth century (Meisenhelder, 1977; Mischkowitz, 1994; Shover, 1983; Farrall, 2002; Laub and Sampson, 2003; Laub et al.,1998; Irwin, 1970; Sampson and Laub, 1993; Jamieson *et al.*, 1999; Warr, 1998; Laub and Sampson, 2003). Godfrey et al.'s study (2007) is one of the few studies that bridges that gap between historical and criminological approaches and which includes a significant period of warfare (the First and Second Boer Wars, as well as World War I). Their research drew upon criminal registers, newspaper reports and census material to explore what factors encouraged desistance and persistence in crime in late nineteenth- and early twentieth-century Crewe. However, the fact that railway work was a reserved occupation during the two World Wars means that their focus was also restricted to informal social controls such as marriage, family ties and employment. So, despite much work on desistance and the life course, very little research has explored the impact that war and military service had upon rates of reoffending. Laub and Sampson (2003) still remains the most systematic study of the links between the military and criminal desistance in the early twentieth century. The study utilised the Glueck's data of 1,000 juvenile offenders from Boston that had been collated between 1939 and 1965. The study compared 500 juvenile delinquents and 500 non-delinquents and considered what factors during the offenders' life courses impacted on their desistance from crime.

Sampson and Laub's earlier work (1993) utilised the age-graded theory of informal social control to argue that individuals commit crimes when their bonds to social capital are weak. The authors argued that certain turning points in the life course including marriage, employment, and enlistment in the military were crucial in offenders' desistance from crime. The presence of these integrating factors could increase offenders' social capital and therefore increase their integration into conventional society. A decade later, Laub and Sampson (2003) highlighted the role that the war played on male desistance levels. In particular, they considered the ways in which military service in World War II gave these men more opportunities through better employment prospects, such as through the GI Bill (1944) in the United States, alongside an increase in living standards. The GI Bill (1944) gave men the opportunity to learn skilled trades and attend university, and ensured that millions of ex-servicemen did not overwhelm the already saturated post-war labour market. Laub and Sampson (2003) concluded that war encouraged desistance. Inter-views that featured in the dataset highlighted men's perceptions that military involvement was a major turning point in their life. The interviewees reported that service during World War II provided them with supervision, removed them from delinquent peer groups and gave them a rigid schedule. Their military success and their positive interactions with other members of the military helped remove the stigma of their criminal pasts and allowed them to create a successful life for themselves upon their return. The men that fea-tured in Laub and Sampson's (2003: 164) data claimed that war had changed their subjective world-views to be more accepting (Elder's, 1986 study of enlistees in World War II and the Korean war generated similar results).

However, Laub and Sampson's (2003) study has not gone unchallenged. Critics of their approach have argued that it was the opportunity for ex-servicemen to continue their education after the war rather than military ser-vice itself which encouraged desistance. Laub himself acknowledged that military service teaches 'bad' behaviours such as aggressive responses, the interruption of social roles and the use of dangerous weapons, and considered the damage to mental and physical health that was triggered by war such as post-war traumatic stress syndrome (Bouffard and Laub, 2004). In a separate study, Bouffard (2005) found that military service actually led to an increase in violent attitudes amongst AVF (All-Volunteer Force) veterans and, as a result of that, AVF veterans encountered the criminal justice system far more often than their non-serving counterparts.

Recent research suggests that the relationship between military service and desistance is not uniform in time and place. Wright et al. (2005) argued that Vietnam veterans suffered longer periods of unemployment in the post-war labour markets than the World War II servicemen that had featured in Laub and Sampson's (2003) study. Craig and Connell's (2013) recent survey of the AVF in the Middle East found that contemporary military experience is sig-nificantly different today compared with the 1940s and '50s and found that military participation did not necessarily result in desistance due to the lack of protective factors in post-war contemporary society. However, when World War I broke out, notions of protective factors and desistance were unknown. Although there were various theories about the causes of crime, and why people, particularly young people, initiated criminal careers, very few commentators discussed why people stopped offending. Only the Police Court Missionaries (who acted as informal friends and advisors to defendants in local courts) and early pioneers of probation gave that any serious thought.

The state of probation 1908–1914

Probation officers, and before them the police-court missionaries, provided moral support for defendants appearing before magistrates (and often for their partners, usually wives). They encouraged defendants to sign the temperance pledge to stop drinking and they also provided some practical support: finding homes or care institutions for juvenile offenders to stay in when they had been abandoned by their parents (some police court missionaries even placed offenders temporarily in their own homes); obtaining jobs for those who could be found work with local sympathetic employers; and, in some cases, providing boots with which to go 'on the tramp' for work. They did not, of course, employ modern theories of cognitive therapy, but they did spend time talking and listening to defendants, even if their dialogue was heavy with religious overtones. As researchers make clear, the police court missionaries and early probation officers tried to imprint a moral framework upon young offenders, drunks, would-be suicides, habitual low-level offenders and the poor of the inner cities. They offered valuable service to the magistrate (in giving information about family circumstances) and practical aid to those whom the magistrate delivered into their hands (Page, 1992; Bochel, 1976; Vanstone, 2007; Gard, 2007). No doubt the military appeared to be just one more piece of the jigsaw, a different kind of employment for young offenders, but one that perhaps offered a different and better prospect of 'making good'.

The 'laundering' of troubled youths through military service

At the time war that broke out in 1914, and certainly when conscription in 1916 engendered a citizenry in uniform, the military were enjoying a reputation for discipline and resolute bravery. Newspapers were full of stories about the courage of soldiers at the front, and there were frequent stories about individual acts of valour that were designed to improve morale on the home front and encourage new recruits. Indeed, the initial training performed by these new recruits was seen as a mechanism for transforming slovenly or rebellious youths into well-drilled polite representatives of a military ethos that promoted good manners, self-discipline, and (in short) 'manly' attributes. If it worked this well for the normal decent young men who signed up, how much better would it be to send juvenile offenders through this system?

In 1915 the probation officer and former Police Court Missionary, Robert Holmes, published *My Police Court Friends With The Colours*. Of the nearly 17,000 (16,738) offenders whom the courts had entrusted to Holmes, nearly 2,000 (1,715) had joined the armed forces when the First World War broke out in 1914. Holmes alleged that a further 7,205 convicted offenders had been ineligible to serve due to age or infirmity, but laboured in the munitions factories in order to support the war effort. His book produced 72 vignettes of lightly convicted young men who had left crime behind some time before they 'picked up the colours'. The stories valorised the efforts of the soldiers and sailors who had managed to put aside a troubled upbringing to serve their country. Holmes's (1915) point was that these boys were already reformed, and were now making a further contribution over and above that made by others. He seemed to have then considered the lives of boys who had very recently passed through his hands. These were offenders who had just been convicted, but who might have a valuable part to play in fighting for their country.

His second volume on this theme was *Walter Greenway, Spy, and Others Sometime Criminal*, published in 1916. The namesake of the title was a 'cat-burglar' who was well educated, intelligent, a bit bored and looking for excitement. When Holmes (1916) came across him before WWI he was pretending to be 'deaf and dumb' much to the confusion of the police and the exasperation of the deaf-signer/interpreter whom the court had called in to help. Usefully, he was not only 'swarthy-looking', but also spoke German. Despatched to wander around the Turkish/German occupied parts of the Middle East as a Bedouin, he was able to glean intelligence on troop movements, which he passed back to the British Expeditionary Force. Despite being tortured to ensure that he was truly voiceless, he maintained his charade with thorough British pluck. Holmes sought out his parents to inform them of his former charge's heroics, but they had died without knowing the honour that their son had brought onto them and his country. The War had suited Walter Greenwood's particular (even peculiar) set of skills and inclinations. More than that, they had laundered them into something desirable and honourable (Holmes, 1916). This book was not just a collection of tales of derring-do, then, but a reminder to modern probation officers that the old values of duty, religious adherence, and personal sacrifice were still valid; and also a clarion call to those who found themselves in the dock or being released from prison that they could make good in a military enterprise:

> The wonderful rebirth of the old spirit of Britain within many a breast where untoward circumstances of birth and upbringing might have crushed out the spark of patriotism …. Throughout August 1914 youths who had 'been down' … poured into my rooms daily to tell me that the cry 'Your King and Country need you' had come home to them.

Holmes did his best to ensure that the army became their new home in the belief that military discipline might help them to reform, and that participating in a moral (almost) crusade certainly would.

As studies of the twentieth century have shown, wartime conditions could be criminogenic for both the civilian population (Roodhouse, 2013; Thomas,

2003) and for serving personnel (Allport, 2009; Emsley, 2013; Galiani et al., 2010).[2] A London magistrate in the 1920s described an ex-serviceman who had indulged his love of fast motorbikes as a dispatch rider during the war and had adopted a practical 'can-do' soldier's attitude which he had taken into civilian life – unfortunately this had resulted in a 'can-do robbery' attitude when he was demobilised (Wiggin, 1948: 115–117). Nevertheless, the calls for youths to be straightened out through military service seem as strong as they were when Holmes (1915, 1916) was writing. For example, Major Jim Panton, chief executive of military charity *Erskine*, has stated that:

> It's understandable how many of the older generation believe the return of National Service is the answer to many of the country's problems. Many feel the strict regime would knock the rough edges off many troublesome youngsters, and we have found in the past that this view is shared across society because people believe re-introducing National Service would reduce crime levels.
>
> (*Daily Telegraph*, 29th July 2009)

The Director General of Saga agreed, and both were quoted by conservative-leaning newspapers (*Express* 12th May 2011; *Daily Telegraph* 16th July 2013). We might expect the right-wing press to call for national service to be resumed (having ended in 1960), but the leftist *New Statesman* also suggested that the government should 'Bring Back Square Bashing!' (27th August 2008); and a letter to *The Magistrate*, (December 2010) depressingly alleged that it was better for young people to be 'employed on the streets of Kabul, than unemployed on the streets of Leeds'. We can counter these arguments by noting again that there is an almost complete lack of evidence to suggest that military service encourages desistance (although see Albæk et al. Tranæs 2013).[3] However, for Holmes (1915; 1916) and others, desistance was actually just a by-product of a process of military service that served a higher purpose – winning a just war and re-moralising Britain's young men. Fighting in a war was constantly presented as heroic in contemporary literature, but heroism comes with dangers: what happened to the boys that Holmes discussed, or the others that were mentioned in contemporary records?

What did re-moralising really involve?

One of the boys under Holmes's charge, George, a neglected child who had been convicted of stealing food for himself and for his younger brother, subsequently became a sailor on a minesweeper when war broke out. Like others, he sent home letters whenever he was able. In January 1915 he complained that

> It is lonely, and I don't know how we live through the cold. I never seem to get used to the danger. I'm so frightened that I can't sleep proper. I

never prayed much before, but I say many prayers now, and I should be glad if you'd pray for me now and then'.

A fortnight later, this letter was followed by another, this time from George's skipper, with tragic news.

George was only one lost, and he gave up the bit of board that would have saved him so as to let a chap have it who could not swim. He never made any shout about his pluck, and we most of us thought him a bit of a coward, but he showed us, after all, he was a game 'un, and no mistake'.

The captain of the ship, like Holmes, considered that George had paid his debt to society with his selfless act. Holmes also related the tale of two sons of a persistently offending father who Holmes arranged to join the navy without their parents' knowledge. The father was soon reconvicted and sent to prison, and the mother became very ill. Holmes noted that on her deathbed she confirmed Holmes's views of redemption: 'Oh it is beautiful – beautiful – my sons doing their duty as good, brave men should: daring to die like men!'

The lives of the other men that Holmes described in his vignettes had mixed but generally poor outcomes: Erhaget (made atonement for his past crimes and survived the war), Ward (died in the trenches), Buxton (shell-burst, dead), Macdonald (dead), Brand (blinded but survived), Gibbs (drowned after submarine attack), Sims (wounded but survived), Peary (wounded but survived), Barrow (blown up by mine), Garrett (shot by sniper whilst trying to rescue his superior officer), Reaney (survived), James (died in ambush), Williams (captured, survived in German POW camp) and Gillies (died of wounds at home). Infantryman Stephen G. Avery (mentioned in the South Staffordshire Discharged Prisoners Aid Society records) of 'O' Company, 23rd Battalion Middlesex Regiment (Football) was killed on 11th September 1916 at the Battle of the Somme. He had been in France for just over three months. The local Minister told his mother, Catherine Avery, the sad news, and in 1919 she received Stephen's British War Medal, which was issued to all men who served in the War. He had served a month in a military detention centre (the glasshouse) for separate offences whilst on training in England (being dirty on parade; having dirty kit; being absent without leave; disobeying orders). He had also been hospitalised for two months in Woolwich with syphilis.

The information we have about Avery and the men Holmes valorised is not as detailed and complete as we would wish. Military records reveal details of offences committed whilst on service, periods of illness, the theatre of war in which they served and details of their pension or death (depending on whether they survived the war or not). However, new research using life-grids and whole-life methodologies[4] (Godfrey et al., 2007; Godfrey, 2011) now allows us to have a much more rounded view of the youths who joined the war after being confined on the Akbar Training Ship.[5] In the late nineteenth century children who had been convicted of a criminal offence (from Cheshire and Liverpool, but also from other areas) could be dealt with in a variety of ways, from a fine to being sent to a Reform School for a number of years. Some were sent to one of the two military training establishments on the Mersey: HMS Clarence, for Roman Catholic boys, or the HMS Akbar, established for the reform of Protestant Boys.[6] In 1907 the Akbar boys were transferred to the Heswall Nautical School, but were still known as the Akbar boys. Conditions in the naval training establishments were harsh, and investigations in 1910 found the conditions for the 200 boys on the Akbar to be brutal, and some claimed it was even fatal for some children.[7] When war was declared in 1914, military service provided immediate employment and purpose for boys leaving the Akbar/Heswall establishment.

David Harvey was born in Congleton in Cheshire. His father and his brothers (Thomas and Samuel) were both convicted of various petty offences whilst he was growing up, until David himself was convicted at Crewe Juvenile Court for stealing jewellery worth 11s. in June 1906. The victim and prosecutrix in the case was his own mother. The magistrates sent him to the Akbar Training Ship, and a detailed file was kept on his progress in the institution (Reg No. 3364; DDX824.4.12 Heswall Progress Register). On 27th January 1911 it was noted that 'he has kept very steady as houseboy and is not entirely trustworthy but has shown considerable improvements'. Indeed not, for he was accused of stealing a purse containing £8–00 in 1912. He absconded twice after he was accused, but was brought back by the police. His brothers, cousins and sister Ellen all continued to offend whilst David was on the Akbar and then the Heswall Nautical School (and some of them were sent to various penal and reform institutions). When David left the School, he joined the army, but only for a short while as he was prosecuted at Crewe magistrates Court in 1916 for desertion. The army took him back, and he was demobilised at the end of the war. He was then convicted and imprisoned for stealing a gold ring (in 1918) and gaining property by false pretences (in 1919).

Fourteen-year old Everton-born Joseph Drumgool was admitted to the Akbar in 1907 (Admission No: 3186; DDX824.4.12 Heswall Progress Register). He made excellent progress, becoming 'top of school' in 1909. The files note that he was 'very good in all ways. Honest, hardworking, clean. Particularly good in every way'. On leaving the Reformatory in 1910, he sailed on the RMS Nigeria and then as a steward on the Cunard liner RMS Lusitania. Obviously enjoying a life at sea he then signed on to serve on the Class B Torpedo Boat Destroyer HMS Kangaroo as 1st stoker. He was then transferred to the K Class Destroyer HMS Victor, the ship he died on in 1917. His body was not recovered for burial (Portsmouth memorial to WWI mariners: Peter Singlehurst; *Memorials to the Naval Ranks and Ratings of the Empire Who Fell in the Great War and Have No Other Grave than the Sea Portsmouth Memorial Part 6 1917*; roll #: *40465_291245*), but his brother and mother were sent his war medals in 1918.

Last of the trio of examples, Richard Gibbs, was aged 14 when he was sent to the Heswall Nautical School (Reg. No. 3445 DDX824.4.12 Heswall Progress Register). He came from a working-class Liverpool home; his parents had been married for 40 years and had 15 children (10 were still alive when WWI started). Richard's file noted that he had a difficult transition to the home

> An inveterate smoker. Most untruthful and cunning. Worked well but it was impossible to trust him in any way. The mother does not appear to be a good influence on him .... Is proving to be a low, ruthless ruffian type of boy ... lies in the most blatant manner. Is by far the worst and most repulsive boy .... One just at a loss to know how to appeal to a better nature in him.

Like the others, he joined the army when the war was in progress. A year later he was prosecuted at Wallasey for fraud. In 1916 he was charged with obtaining charitable institutions by false pretences and also with being an absentee from the South Wales Borderers. When he had been arrested, he had been carrying a collecting box bearing the words, 'For Wounded Soldiers'. A month's imprisonment was imposed and the magistrate ordered him afterwards to be handed over to the military authorities. He was demobilised in 1919 after being wounded (his left foot was irreparably damaged) and gassed at the battle for Salonica, just two months before the war ended.

Conclusion

So, of these three case studies, two of them survived the war and one died; two re-offended after joining the armed forces, and the boy that died was never given the chance either to re-offend or to continue a life free from crime. These cases are interesting, but a significant pattern will not become clear until a large-scale cohort study is conducted of WWI military personnel (comprising of those who had and who had not committed offences before joining up). Given the centenary anniversary of World War I this year, it may be unlikely that Research Councils would support this kind of research. In a period when the Research Councils are under increasing pressure to justify the awards they make to politicians and the media, they are unlikely to fund a study which reveals that some of the heroes of World War I already had a criminal record when they enlisted, or soon acquired one during or after active service. However, if they did, such a study might not only inform our knowledge of the links between military service, offending and desistance, but it might also help to show that the men who served in the war were not mere ciphers for jingoistic or nostalgic posturing, but were real people living difficult lives (inside and outside military life). Until they do, the Leverhulme Trust-funded study of the Akbar/Heswall Reformatory boys will at least allow us to make a start in investigating these important and fascinating matters.

Notes

1 UK Parliamentary Papers, 1921 [Cmd. 1193] *General annual reports on the British Army (including the Territorial Force) for the period from 1st October, 1913, to 30th September, 1919*: Annual Published Judicial Statistics 1910–20.
2 There are also some detailed criminological studies of criminality during wartime by the Howard League for Penal Reform (Benney, 1948) and particularly by German criminologists between WWI and II (Wetzell, 2000: 107–25).
3 Prisoners such as Wood (1932: 44–45) considered army and prison regimes to be similar, and of course Foucault (1977) later made similar comparisons, although many breached regulations in both institutions (Wood, 1932; Godfrey and Johnston, 2013).
4 This is a theoretical and methodological approach which uses a variety of official and civil records to re-create the whole life of offenders and victims of crime – or as much as can be realistically reconstructed through combining data from historical documents – because of the belief that the sequencing of events in a person's life can influence their behaviour before, during and after periods of offending and punishment.
5 This research is funded by The Leverhulme Trust and conducted by the authors of this article, Pamela Cox, and Heather Shore. We are grateful to Drs Cox and Shore for their allowing us to present some of our cases studies in this article.
6 Two other ships were moored in the Mersey for the training of young navy officers, and for the training of poor and destitute boys for naval service.
7 *John Bull* magazine published an article in 1910 entitled 'Reformatory School Horrors – How Boys at the Akbar School are Tortured – Several Deaths' which alleged that boys at the Akbar Nautical Training School at Heswall were gagged and then birched, that boys believed to be feigning illness in order to escape their duties were caned and that boys were drenched with cold water or made to stand up all night as a punishment for trivial misdemeanors. The magazine alleged that boys had died as a result of such punishments, but the subsequent Home Office investigation could not substantiate these claims. It did, however, find that there had been instances of 'irregular punishments'. Incoming Home Secretary Winston Churchill later appointed a Departmental Committee to conduct a broad review of Reformatories and Industrial Schools, which led to reforms, and the Akbar Nautical School eventually closed in 1956 (Shore, 2012).

References

Albæk, K., Leth-Petersen, S., le Maire, D. and Tranæs, T. (2013) 'Does Peacetime Military Service Affect Crime?' Available: www.lemaire.dk/CrimeMilitary_WP.pdf.

Allport, A. (2009) *Demobbed. Coming Home After the Second World War*, New Haven, CT: Yale University Press.

Barnett, C. (1974) *Britain and Her Army, 1509–1970: A Military, Political and Social Survey*, London: Pelican

Beattie, J. (1974) 'The Pattern of Crime in England, 1660–1800', *Past and Present*, 62 (1): 47–95.

Beattie, J. (1986) *Crime and the Courts in England, 1660–1800*, Princeton: Princeton University Press.

Beattie, J. (1977) 'Crime and the Courts in Surrey 1736–1753' in Cockburn, J.S. (ed.) *Crime in England, 1550–1800*, London: Methuen. pp. 159–161.

Benney, M. (1948) *Gaol Delivery*, London: Longmans, Green and Co.

Bochel, D. (1976) *Probation and After-Care, Its Development in England and Wales*, Edinburgh and London: Scottish Academic Press.

Bouffard, L.A. (2005) 'The Military as a Bridging Environment in Criminal Careers: Differential Outcomes of the Military Experience', *Armed Forces and Society*, 31(2): 273–295.

Bouffard, L., and Laub, J. (2004) 'Jail or the Army: Does Military Service Facilitate Desistance from Crime?' in Maruna S., and Immarigeon, R. (eds) *After Crime and Punishment*, London: Willan. pp. 129–151.

Craig, J. and Connell, N.M. (2013) 'The All- Volunteer Force and Crime: The Effects of Military Participation on Offending Behaviour', *Armed Forces and Society*, doi: 10.1177/0095327X13507258.

Devereux, S. and Griffiths, P. (2004) *Penal Practice and Culture, 1500–1900: Punishing the English*, London: Palgrave Macmillan.

Elder, G.H. (1986) 'Military Times and Turning Points in Men's Lives', *Developmental Psychology*, 22(2): 233–345.

Emsley, C. (2013) *Soldier, Sailor, Beggarman, Thief: Crime and the British Armed Services since 1914*, Oxford: Oxford University Press.

Farrall, S. (2002) *Rethinking What Works With Offenders*, London: Willan Publishing.

Foucault, M. (1977) *Discipline and Punish: The Birth of the Prison*, London: Penguin Books.

Galiani, S., Rossi, M. and Schargrodsky, E. (2010) 'Conscription and Crime: Evidence from the Argentine Draft Lottery', *Economics of Culture, Institutions and Crime*, Jan. 20–21, Milan.

Gard, R. (2007) 'The First Probation Officers in England and Wales 1906–1914', *British Journal of Criminology*, 47(6): 938–954.

Godfrey, B. (2011) 'Historical and Archival Research Methods' in Gadd, D. Karstedt, S. and Mesner, S. (eds) *The Handbook on Criminology Research Methods*, New York: SAGE.

Godfrey B. and Johnston, J. (2013) 'On License: The Financial and Personal Costs of the Convict License System', Social Science and History Association Conference, Chicago, November 22nd.

Godfrey, B., Cox, D. and Farrall, S. (2007) *Criminal Lives: Family, Employment and Offending*, Clarendon Series in Criminology, Oxford: Oxford University Press.

Godfrey, B., Cox, D. and Farrall, S., (2010) *Serious Offenders*, Clarendon Series in Criminology, Oxford: Oxford University Press.

Hay, D., (1982) 'War, Dearth and Theft in the Eighteenth Century: The Record of the English Courts', *Past and Present*, 95: 117–160.

Holmes, R. (1915) *My Police Court Friends With the Colours*, Edinburgh and London: William Blackwood and Sons.

Holmes, R. (1916) *Walter Greenway, Spy. And Others, Sometime Criminal*, Edinburgh and London: William Blackwood and Sons.

Irwin, J. (1970) *The Felon*, New Jersey: Prentice Hall.

Jamieson, J., McIvor, G., and Murray, C. (1999) *Understanding Offending Among Young People*, Edinburgh: The Stationery Office.

Jewkes, Y. and H. Johnston (2011) 'The English Prison during the First and Second World Wars: Hidden Lived Experiences of War', *Prison Service Journal*, 198: 47–51.

King, P. (2000) *Crime, Justice and Discretion in England, 1740–1820*, Oxford: Oxford University Press.

King, P. (2002) 'War as a Judicial Resource. Press Gangs and Prosecution Rates, 1740–1830' in Landau, N. (ed.) *Law, Crime and English Society, 1660–1830*, Cambridge: Cambridge University Press. pp. 97–116.

Landau, N. (2002) 'Introduction' in Landau, N. (ed.) *Law, Crime and English Society, 1660-1830*, Cambridge: Cambridge University Press.

Laub, J. H., and Sampson, R.J. (2003) *Shared Beginnings, Divergent Lives: Delinquent Boys to Age 70*, Cambridge, MA: Harvard University Press.

Laub, J., Nagin, D. and Sampson, R. (1998) 'Trajectories of Change in Criminal Offending: Good Marriages and the Desistance Process', *American Sociological Review*, 63: 225–238.

Meisenhelder, T. (1977) 'An Exploratory Study of Exiting from Criminal Careers', *Criminology*, 15(3): 319–334.

Mischkowitz, R. (1994) 'Desistance from a Delinquent Way of Life?' in Weitekamp, E.G.M. and Kerner, H.J. (ed.) *Cross-National Longitudinal Research on Human Development and Criminal Behaviour*, Boston: Kluwer-Nijhoff.

Munsche, P. (1981) *Gentlemen and Poachers: The English Game Laws, 1671–1831*, Cambridge: Cambridge University Press.

Page, M. (1992) *Crimefighters of London. A History of the Origins and Development of the London Probation Service 1876–1965*, London: Inner London Probation Service.

Palk, D. (2006) *Gender, Crime and Judicial Discretion, 1780–1830*, Suffolk: Boydell and Brewer.

Radzinowicz, L. (1968) *A History of English Criminal Law and Its Administration from 1750, Vol. IV: Grappling for Control*, London: Stevens.

Rodger, N.A.M. (1986) *The Wooden World: An Anatomy of the Georgian Navy*, London: William Collins.

Roodhouse, M. (2013) *Black Market Britain, 1939–1955*, Oxford: Oxford University Press.

Rose, A. (1954) *Five Hundred Borstal Boys*, Oxford: Basil Blackwell.

Ruggles-Brise, E. (1916) *The Times*, September 26th.

Sampson, R. J. and Laub, J. H. (1993) *Crime in the Making: Pathways and Turning Points Through Life*, London: Harvard University Press.

Sharpe, J. (1984) *Crime in Early Modern England 1550–1750*, London: Longman.

Shore H. (2012) 'Reformatory School Horrors: Investigating the Akbar Scandal in 1910', ESRC Modern Activism Conference, Liverpool, 27–30th June.

Shover, N. (1983) 'The Later Stages of Ordinary Property Offender Careers', *Social Problems*, 31(2): 208–218.

Thomas, D. (2003) *An Underworld at War: Spivs, Deserters, Racketeers and Civilians in the Second World War*, London: John Murray.

Vanstone, M. (2007) *Supervising Offenders in the Community: A History of Probation Theory and Practice*, Aldershot: Ashgate.

Warr, M. (1998) 'Life Course Transitions and Desistance from Crime', *Criminology*, 36 (2): 183–212.

Wetzell, R. (2000) *Inventing the Criminal. A History of German Criminology, 1880–1945*, Chapel Hill and London: University of North Carolina Press.

Wiggin, M. (1948) *My Court Casebook*, London: Sylvan Press.

Williams, R. (1985) *Crime and the Rural Community in Eighteenth-Century Berkshire, 1740–1789*, PhD thesis, University of Reading.

Wood, S. (1932) *Shades of the Prison House. A Personal Memoir*, London: Williams and Norgate.

Wright, J.P., Carter, D.E., and Cullen, F.T. (2005) 'A Life-course Analysis of Military Service in Vietnam', *Journal of Research in Crime and Delinquency*, 42(1): 55–83.

5 Through the lens of war

Political imprisonment in Northern Ireland[1]

Ruth Jamieson

Northern Ireland is not a war. You are joking. Right?

(British soldier, in Clarke, 1983, loc 2955)

Introduction

Operation BANNER (1969–2007) in Northern Ireland was the British Army's longest continuous deployment, and the conflict was the most serious security situation it had faced since the Second World War.[2] Despite the scale of the violence, warranting the involvement of the Army, the British government's position throughout 'the Troubles' was that they were dealing with a crime problem and *not* a war or insurgency. But, as the above quote illustrates, that was not a view shared by the soldiers on the ground. Some 3,600 people were killed and around 47,500 were injured over the course of the conflict. As Bloomfield (1998) argues, the level of death and injury may not seem 'too calamitous' when compared with other armed conflicts, but when considered against the small scale of Northern Ireland (slightly smaller than Yorkshire, with a population about the size of Birmingham) and the fact that the most deprived urban communities suffered disproportionately,[3] the intensity of the violence is easier to grasp in human terms: 'If the UK as a whole ... had experienced death pro rata, there would have been a total of over 130,000 violent deaths' (Bloomfield, 1998, para 2.5). The conflict also resulted in the imprisonment of over 30,000 people for conflict-related or terrorist-type offences. That represents an incarceration rate of one in 56. So, if a political conflict of equal intensity had occurred in Great Britain, then pro rata *over 1 million* people would have been imprisoned – a crime wave indeed.

The question of whether the political violence was absolutely defined as either 'war' or 'crime' was pivotal in determining both the legitimacy of particular actions and the legal liabilities and privileges accorded to different actors.[4] The struggle to define violent actions as either 'crimes' or 'acts of war' and the status of actors as either 'ordinary criminals' or 'political prisoners' escalated into a brutal and protracted 'jail war' (McEvoy, 2001; Mulcahy, 1995; English, 2003). The issue of political violence and imprisonment lies at the intersection of war, crime and politics. This chapter draws on political ex-prisoners' accounts to consider how and to what extent their self-understanding as soldiers or prisoners of war shaped their experiences of long-term imprisonment and served to mitigate or aggravate its destructive effects.

Historical context of the conflict and the state response to it[5]

The fundamental antagonism in Northern Ireland was and remains the constitutional question of whether the six counties that comprise it should be reunited with the south of Ireland or remain part of the United Kingdom. Northern Ireland has been an insecure and unsettled political entity since it was established in 1921. From the beginning, unionists have feared a republican uprising (either from within or from the south) and have never fully trusted the British government's commitment to its defence.[6] For that reason, the newly devolved Northern Ireland statelet was set up to ensure a Protestant ascendancy. The Special Powers Act of 1922 gave the Stormont government autonomy in law and order matters and extensive emergency powers to deal with any threat of insurrection or subversion.[7] However, because it had no authority to raise or control its own army, it had to rely for its security on a criminal justice system enhanced by special powers and an armed police force. The Royal Ulster Constabulary (RUC) and special constabulary were set up to ensure that 'every able-bodied Protestant male could be uniformed and armed to defend the state' (Ellison and Smyth, 2000: 20).[8] The IRA conducted military campaigns into Northern Ireland during the 1930s, 1940s, 1950s and 1960s, but the combination of armed police and special criminal justice measures were enough to quash these incursions without calling on Britain for assistance.

The immediate cause of 'the Troubles' in 1969 was not IRA violence, but a public order crisis arising out of civil rights marches and counter-demonstrations by loyalists and unionists. The policing of the marches and disorder in Londonderry/Derry and Belfast by the RUC and B-Specials was heavy-handed and partisan, and the violence escalated into arson, the forced displacement of people and armed skirmishes between paramilitary groups. Once it became clear that the RUC and B-Specials could not contain the situation, the Stormont government asked the British Government to send in troops. The British Army arrived on 14th August 1969 on 'Operation BANNER'. Initially the Army was deployed in an 'aid to the civil power' capacity and was tasked with supporting the local police in maintaining public order. Consequently it was bound by the same 'minimum force' rule as the local police. By March 1972 the violence had become so serious that direct rule was imposed.

The rationale for a criminal justice response

> In this as in so many other aspects of life here, I fear it is not being acknowledged that the army is engaged in fighting an enemy, in suppressing an insurrection, in effect conducting a war.
>
> (Lt. Gen. Sir Frank King, 3rd April 1974)

> A war no politician admitted is a war at all.
>
> (Clarke 1983, loc 3125)

The presence of the British Army in Northern Ireland opened out the possibility that the failing police-led criminal justice approach to dealing with worsening political violence might be jettisoned in favour of an *openly* military response. But that never happened.[9] One reason for this was that defining the political violence as domestic 'crime' had a number of practical and rhetorical advantages. For example, defining the situation as crime negated the legitimacy of the PIRA[10] campaign and limited the legal rights of paramilitary actors and any recourse they might have to external courts as 'combatants'. Cassese (1981: 417) observes:

> To acknowledge that rebels are entitled to invoke international rules implies that they are outside both the physical and legal control of the national authorities ... to suggest that insurgents cannot rely on international law means that the only body of law applicable to them is domestic criminal law.

However, the criminal justice approach involved operational disadvantages. Although treating the IRA as 'ordinary criminals' who should be dealt with by domestic criminal law removed their treatment from the constraints of humanitarian law, it also fettered the state's use of force against them. Treating political violence as a criminal conspiracy involved a civilianisation of the military and put soldiers on the same legal footing as their police counterparts, who could engage PIRA using only minimum force. The General Officer Commanding of the British Army in Northern Ireland was so concerned about the negative impact on operational efficiency and morale of the Army if soldiers who breached the minimum force rule by using unwarranted lethal force were 'convicted and sent to prison for actions arising out of operational incidents' that he wrote to the Attorney General arguing that the principle of equality before the law should be disregarded in Northern Ireland on the grounds that

> the law keepers are to be regarded as no different from the law breakers, that the forces of law and order and the forces of the enemy are to be on the same footing, is, to my view, playing directly into the enemy's hands.
>
> (Lt. Gen. Sir Frank King, 3rd April 1974)

He did not think that the civilian minimum force rule should apply to the Army because it implied a 'mentality of defence', which was 'anathema to military training, tactics and operating procedure' (King, 1974). He further suggested that prosecuting soldiers was not in the public interest and argued for *de facto* immunity from prosecution for law keepers who killed or injured civilians while on duty except where there was the 'clearest evidence of gross misbehaviour'. There is an important argument to be made about the selective nature of political justice in conflict situations (Kirchheimer, 1961) and it has been ably made by a number of commentators (Bennett, 2013; Cadwallader, 2013; Lundy, 2013; Ní Aoláin, 2000). The focus here, however, is on how the various antagonists made sense of the violence they were involved in and how that understanding shaped their actions.

As in other counter-insurgencies, the politics of intervening in Northern Ireland became a more vexing issue for the government than operations themselves (Galula, 1964), and so the skirmishes and explosions on the streets of Northern Ireland were mirrored by a bitterly fought political contest over whether the violence should be defined as crime or war.

The 'spin war'

> Counterinsurgency is an unusual form of warfare – one in which law and legitimacy figure prominently as a means to defeat a nation's enemies.
>
> (Nachbar, 2012: 37)

All the various antagonists (republican and loyalist paramilitaries, politicians, the Army, the RUC, the British government and its Northern Ireland Office) prosecuted their own 'spin wars' in tandem with their operations on the ground (Thomson, 2010). Each antagonist constructed its own 'discursive contention' from well-rehearsed narratives of causality to allocate moral responsibly between themselves and others (Haunss, 2007; Tilly, 2008). For example, government spokespersons cast the members of PIRA as 'thugs, gangsters, psychopaths' who had no community support and whose actions were fanatical, irrational, indiscriminate and motivated by personal pathology – just like 'ordinary' criminals. Any statements from PIRA were dismissed as 'propaganda' and the events of the conflict were rarely discussed in historical and political context. Conversely, the British government framed its own motivations as neutral and disinterested, its police as patient and impartial 'law keepers' and its troops' actions as professional, measured and rational (Curtis, 1998; Rolston and Miller, 1996; Rolston and Miller, 1996). Against this, PIRA framed its own violence as part of a national war of liberation against forces of colonial occupation. It considered its prisoners 'POWs' (prisoners of war) and insisted that their political motivation be recognised in the prison regime, a point they were prepared to fight for to the bitter end. As a consequence the jails became another battlefield (Clarke, 1987).

Through the lens of war

There was no automatic congruity between the official line that the political violence was a crime problem and the way in which the conflict was experienced on the ground. The government could insist that they were dealing with a criminal conspiracy, not a rebellion or insurgency, but many British soldiers felt they were fighting 'a war nobody will call a war' (Clarke, 1983, loc 2532). Given the intensity of the violence and the very concentrated deployment of troops in a few 'hard' areas, it is not surprising that those at the sharp end of the shootings, cordons, curfews, patrols and house searches experienced the situation as 'war'. In his review of Operation BANNER General Jackson admitted that the British Army's handling of the situation in Northern Ireland had been a harsh overreaction, especially in the early period (1969–1972/ 3) when there had been a 'desire to sort the Micks out' and 'to take out PIRA' (MOD, 2006, para 8–11). This tendency to see their mission through an interpretive frame of war that demanded maximum force against identifiable 'enemies' was especially marked among the lower ranks patrolling the streets of Belfast and Derry.[11] Soldiers' accounts of serving in Northern Ireland are entirely at odds with the idea that what they were fighting was a crime wave (for example in Asher, 1990; Clarke, 1983; Lindsay, 1998; Wharton, 2008, 2010). Their understandings of what they were experiencing and doing was mediated through the frame of war. The concepts of the enemy, allies, command structures and rules of engagement organised the meaning of action and simultaneously mobilised powerful moral emotions. For these British soldiers, PIRA was 'the enemy' or 'the enemy with a thousand faces' when hidden in the community; Catholic civilians were 'bog wogs', 'Micks' or 'Fenian bastards' and their rifles 'Paddy whackers' (Asher, 1990; Clarke, 1983; Wharton, 2008, 2010). Likewise, PIRA had its own hostile counterpoint to these epithets – soldiers were 'Brits', 'The Hun' and varieties of the standard expletives. Of course, the other principal protagonists (loyalists, government, police and prison officers) all had their own versions of the enemy, rules and so on. As Melucci (emphasis added, 1995: 45) observes, 'Passions and feelings, love and hate, faith and fear are all part of a body *acting collectively* …. There is no cognition without feeling and no meaning without emotion.' In spite of the government's definition of the conflict as a crime problem, members of the Army and paramilitary organisations thought and felt they were at war. So it is unsurprising that paramilitary prisoners would regard themselves as prisoners of war.

I want to turn now to the question of how and to what extent paramilitary prisoners' self-understanding as soldiers or prisoners of war shaped their experiences of long-term imprisonment and served to mitigate or aggravate its destructive effects.[12] My interest is in understanding the discursive construction of prisoner identity and resistance, not in offering a history of Northern Ireland prison policy or events in the 'jail war'.[13]

The 'jail war' as a moral contest

> What took place between 1976 and 1981 was a war. The British government tried to defeat the republican struggle through a policy of degradation, isolation, beatings and criminalisation. They did not succeed.
>
> (H-Blocks OC (commanding officer), Brendan Hughes, in English, 2003: 203)

However one classifies the conflict in Northern Ireland – criminal conspiracy or insurgency – 'taking out PIRA' through internment and the criminal justice system produced an exponential growth in the prison population and the prisons became another theatre of war. The prisons were the spatial and social setting of a moral contest between political offenders and the state (Kirchheimer, 1961; McConville, 2003). The stakes were high and extended beyond the prison. Historically the English response to political offending (for example, the Chartists, Fenians and Suffragettes) was to deal with it through criminal law and to reject the idea that 'political motive or objective as such and in itself, should secure for the offender a different mode of punishment or a different penal regime' (Radzinowicz and Hood, 1979: 421). The British government briefly departed from this policy in Northern Ireland when it granted 'special category status' (SCS) to paramilitary prisoners in 1972, though it later rescinded this recognition of political motivation in an attempt to delegitimise paramilitary organisations in the jail. The 'criminalisation' policy that replaced SCS resulted in a 'jail war' (1976–1981) that 'escalated nastily, stage by stage, through gradually intensifying attritional battles' (English, 2003: 191). Northern Irish jails (Long Kesh/The Maze, Armagh, Magilligan) became new battlefields for a bitter and protracted moral contest between political offenders and the state over the recognition of political motivation.

As noted earlier, the British state took the position that the political violence in Northern Ireland was part of a terrorist criminal conspiracy by PIRA. Ergo, the motivation of its members was criminal, not political. There was no such thing as political motivation:

> There is no such thing as political murder, political bombing or political violence. There is only criminal murder, criminal bombing and criminal violence. We will not compromise on this. There will be no political status.
>
> (Margaret Thatcher, 5th March, 1981a)

Against this, republican prisoners asserted a moral right to engage in a war of national liberation from British colonial occupation. Hence they saw themselves as prisoners of war:

> I am a political prisoner because I am a casualty of a perennial war that is being fought between the oppressed Irish people and an alien, oppressive, unwanted regime that refuses to withdraw from our land.
>
> (Bobby Sands, 1981: 7)

Their loyalist counterparts experienced imprisonment as contradictory and for that reason their resistance to criminalisation was more muted (McEvoy, 2001: 33). Although Loyalist prisoners recognised the legitimacy of the British government, they saw themselves as 'imprisoned patriots of Ulster' who were being punished unfairly, since 'their only crime was loyalty':

> I felt being inside was unfair – what I did was for my country.
>
> (UVF/RHC prisoner, in Crawford, 1999: 97)

Loyalist prisoners were more reluctant to protest against the British government's criminalisation policy than republicans were because doing so might be seen as siding with republicans (Crawford, 1999: 56). Nevertheless there was some accommodation and reciprocity between republican and loyalist prisoner groups when it was in their mutual interest, for example, when demanding better food or segregation.

Prison as a crucible of identity and resistance

> The meaning and entire experience of their imprisonment was mediated by their political beliefs, whether one agrees with them or not.
>
> (Hamber, 2005: 94)

The 'ideological docking' of PIRA 'was with the heritage of the 1916 Rising, the War of Independence and the United Irishmen' (Hughes, 2011: 18). This provided a reservoir of themes, vocabularies ('volunteer', IRA, 'risen people'), strategies (a 'long war' of attrition, hunger strikes, seeking public support) and expectations (the harshness and intransigence of the authorities) that could be drawn on to make sense of the present (McConville, 2003).[14] Their history of imprisonment was central to the political education of republicans and it imparted a kind of 'self-assumed obligation to keep faith with the past' (McConville, 2003: 10). The 1980 hunger strikers referenced that sense of obligation in their statement: 'not wishing to break faith with those from whom we have inherited our principles, we now commit ourselves to a hunger strike' (H-Block Blanketmen, 1980 in English, 2003: 192). One republican former prisoner who had been a hunger striker said,

> It's like an onus that you feel has been put on you to do things .... All of these things governed and determined your character, which may well have been out of kilter with your natural character. I was never inclined to kill anybody, or to go and shoot anybody, or to do robberies. I grew up in a family environment that was different. There was no politics in my family and here I was thrown into this massive sea change that was taking place around us ... and I suddenly found myself in positions

whereby I had to take decisions, actions ... to carry out actions which I didn't want to do. But I felt an obligation to do so.

(Blanketman and hunger striker, Jamieson and Grounds, 2002)

The presence of the Army on the streets reinforced the republican 'volunteer's' sense of being under occupation (Hamber, 2005) and part of a 'war of liberation' (like fighters in Algeria, Vietnam, South Africa).[15] By contrast, loyalists had no history of political imprisonment before 'the Troubles' so they drew on the larger theme of military service for Britain in construction of their collective identity, for example their loyal military service and sacrifice at the Somme, or their defence of the union against home rule (Graham and Shirlow, 2002, Rolston, 1995). It is significant that the contemporary influences on loyalists' self-understanding as being engaged in 'counter-terrorism' involved an identification with the British security forces.

Collective political identity was pivotal in the formation of prisoner resistance to the H-Blocks regime, and the prison served as a crucible for reshaping their collective political identity and galvanising ideological commitment. New elaborations of the republican prisoner identity, the 'blanket man', the 'squeaky booter' developed as the jail war proceeded.[16] This process worked through the interplay of cognitive, social and emotional elements (Melucci, 1989, 1995). Their goals, means and environment of action were interpreted through the cognitive framework of war and the military and shared through relationships and the development of 'emotional recognition' (trust, rapport, empathy) between individual prisoners (Melucci, 1995).

Resistance

Two imperatives guided republican resistance to criminalisation. The first was their self-understanding as soldiers in a war who had a duty to continue the fight in captivity, to respect the military command structure and discipline, and to try to escape (Walzer, 1969). The PIRA prisoners in Long Kesh/ The Maze signalled this by referring to themselves as the 'Fourth Battalion of Belfast Brigade of PIRA' while the women in Armagh prison called themselves 'A Brigade'. The second imperative was the rejection of criminal status. In her analysis of ANC prisoner resistance in Robben Island, Fran Buntman (2003: 127–8) identifies two distinct modalities of resistance, the categorical and the strategic. Categorical resistance involves open defiance of prison authorities as the articulation of political principle whereas strategic resistance, however, involves instrumental compliance with authority for the purpose of using the prison to further longer-term organisational goals. An example is the ANC's attempt to create a 'truce-like' situation with the authorities in order to create the space for ANC organisational development both inside and outside the prison Buntman (2003: 129).

For the protesting ('nonconforming') prisoners in the H-Blocks and republican wings of Armagh prison, the critical issue was the symbolic and practical recognition of their political status in the prison regime. They rejected criminal status absolutely and demanded segregation by political affiliation. The British government understood that republicans were determined to get control of the prison using a 'well-thought-out strategy of doing this by whittling away at the prison regime' (English, 2003: 204), and there was continuous interplay between the authorities' assertion of penal power and the prisoners' resistance to it, the one shaping the other. Their resistance strategies reflected the different phases of prison policy on the treatment of 'politicals'[17] and consequently the development of resistant agency was contingent and progressive (Corcoran, 2006: 140).

Resistance to reactive containment (1969–1975)

Prior to the granting of special category status to paramilitary prisoners in 1972, anyone who had been remanded or sentenced for political offences was held in Crumlin Road prison Belfast, Magilligan prison or Armagh prison under an 'ordinary' (criminal) regime in which there was no segregation or free association but inmates were not required to wear prison uniform. In August 1971, the Stormont government introduced internment without trial for suspected members of PIRA. At first the internees were detained under a special non-criminal regime in Crumlin Road prison and on the *Maidstone*, a prison ship moored in Belfast Lough, but they were later moved to special detention camps at Magilligan prison and Long Kesh Detention Centre. About six months after the introduction of internment, the PIRA OC, William McKee, led 40 prisoners on hunger strike in Crumlin Road, demanding the same treatment as the internees on the grounds they were both political prisoners. For a number of pressing pragmatic reasons the government granted 'special category status' (SCS) to prisoners held for political offences and they also were moved to Long Kesh to join internees. By 1975–1976 almost all paramilitary prisoners had special category status.

> SCS amounted to de facto political status and a POW regime. We didn't mind what they called it; we knew what it was.
> (William McKee, in Crawford, 1999: 25)

The Long Kesh compounds became the symbolic and physical locus of political status and regime. The physical environment of Long Kesh looked and felt like a prisoner-of-war camp. Both the internees and special category prisoners were housed in Nissan huts in separate compounds or 'cages' on the old World War II Long Kesh military base. The Army patrolled the compound perimeter and conducted searches of the grounds for the prison staff. Both internees and special category prisoners had a similar POW-type regime that involved no prison work and no prison uniform and allowed free association, weekly visits and parcels and unlimited mail.

During the special category/reactive containment period, the republican prisoners' resistance was primarily strategic, aimed at preserving group cohesion and discipline by controlling the compounds. The SCS compound system, organised within the framework of military command, asserted military authority through parading, drilling and discipline and reinforced the idea of POW captivity. Each group had its own commanding officer, a quartermaster and staff officers for intelligence, escape, welfare and education. The different republican and loyalist organisations had their own compounds and, whenever possible, interposed their command authority in prisoner interactions with staff. The POW cognitive frame was reinforced by the way the SCS regime was administered (Crawford, 1999: 28–32). Under the SCS system prisoners applied to particular paramilitary groups to have their political status 'ratified' so that they could be accepted onto the wings or compounds controlled by that particular group. The prison authorities recognised the Long Kesh 'camp council' which was made up of the OCs of the different paramilitary groups. At one stage the republican OC insisted on vetting ('for their own protection') which prison staff would be allowed to come into contact with individual republican prisoners. According to the Northern Ireland Office, the real aim of all this was

> to minimise prison staff control and to maximise paramilitary control over the inmates. Establishment staff invariably find a paramilitary officer interposed between them and the special category prisoners they want to contact, for whatever reason.
>
> (CJ4/1687, NIO 26th September, 1977, para 4)

> Having established their authority within the [SCS] compounds the prisoner commanders use it to debrief new commitals, organise indoctrination and weapons training classes, initiate escape attempts, hold disciplinary hearings and generally further the aims of their respective organisations.
>
> (CJ4/1687, NIO 26th September 1977, para 5)

When Lord Gardiner reviewed the system in 1975 he described the introduction of special category status as a 'serious mistake' and 'unfair to ordinary criminals, often guilty of far less serious crimes, who are subject to normal prison discipline':

> we can see no justification for granting privileges to a large number of criminals convicted of very serious crimes, in many cases murder, merely because they claim political motivation. It supports their own views which society must reject, that their political motivation in some ways justifies their crimes.
>
> (Gardiner Report, 1975, at 33–35)

On Gardiner's recommendation, both internment and special category status were ended. Anyone sentenced for a political offence committed after 1st March 1976 would be treated as an ordinary criminal and sent to cellular accommodation in the newly built H-Blocks. The Long Kesh site was renamed 'HMP Maze' to signal this change in policy. The cellular blocks were designed to enable more effective staff control over the inmates and the prison space, and with a view to curtailing the influence of military command structures. Ultimately the H-Block accommodation and criminalisation policy was aimed at undermining the legitimacy of the republican and loyalist paramiliary groups as military and political entities both inside and outside the prison.

Resistance to criminalisation (1976–1981)

The ending of special category status represented a symbolic and practical rejection of the idea that paramilitary prisoners were entitled to the privileges of POWs either in terms of the prison regime they were held under or any hopes they might nurture about an amnesty at the end of the conflict. However, the effectiveness of the criminalisation policy was undermined by the fact that special category status was never taken away from paramilitary prisoners who already had it. The result was that two completely different prison regimes holding people convicted of the same offences existed a few hundred yards apart on the same site. The special category compounds continued to operate a humane containment/prisoner of war type regime until the last SCS prisoner was released in 1992. These compounds were adjacent to the new highly punitive criminal regime in the H-Blocks where, from the start, there was a concerted effort to exert the disciplinary power over the inmates through unbending rule enforcement and the punishment of each and every rule infraction (McEvoy, 2001: 236). These policy changes produced a situation where the Northern Ireland prison population contained four types of prisoner. First there were SCS prisoners under their own relaxed POW regime. Then there were non-SCS paramilitary prisoners in the H-Block criminal regime who fell into two groups: protesting/non-conforming prisoners and conforming prisoners. Finally there were ordinary non-political prisoners ('ordinaries', 'ordinary decent criminals' or 'ODCs'). Conforming paramilitary prisoners and ordinary criminal prisoners were held on the same wings and there was no segregation by political affiliation.

The ending of special category status and introduction of the criminalisation policy in 1976 reflected the government's determination to claw back control over the paramilitary prisoners and to enforce normal prison discipline on them in order to neutralise their claims to be politically motivated. Although both republican and loyalist protesting prisoners were determined they would not submit to a criminal regime, loyalist protests tended to be intermittent and short-lived. The focus of the discussion which follows is on how the collective political identity of republican prisoners shaped their resistance to criminalisation.

For the whole of the criminalisation period (1976–1981), republican resistance to the ordinary regime was categorical, that is to say openly defiant of the prison authority and regime. Likewise, the prison authorities refused categorically to meet their demands, despite the escalating intensity of the protests from the 'blanket' to a 'no wash', then a 'dirty' protest and finally to hunger strikes. Although the protesting prisoners remained uncompromising in their rejection of criminal status, they did make strategic and tactical accommodations with the prison regime where it served their broader political aims or operational needs. For example, protesting prisoners would submit to wearing the prison uniform for visits in order to garner information, or exchange communications ('comms') and contraband items. After the 1981 hunger strike, protesting republicans changed tack and engaged in non-confrontational strategic resistance and outward compliance with the prison regime. They used this hiatus to regroup, gain education, and plan escape. The very brief outline of the development of the republican protests is included below to provide necessary context for the discussion of identity and coping which follows it. My interest here is in the 'jail war' as a moral contest and how collective identity mediated prisoner coping and resistance rather than in detailing a history of political imprisonment.

The blanket protest (1976 to 1st December 1980)

The first republican prisoner sentenced after the criminalisation policy came into effect on 1st March 1976 was Kieran Nugent. He refused to put on a prison uniform when he arrived in the H-Blocks and he was put into his cell naked with only a blanket to cover him and, because prison rules did not allow inmates to leave their cells without clothes, he was put on 24-hour lock up. Others soon joined him 'on the blanket' and by 1978 there were 300–400 blanketmen. These protesting prisoners lost all remission,[18] and were entitled to no exercise, no free association, no reading material other than a bible and no radio, television or recreation. They had one 30-minute visit per month and limited letters. The republican protesters made five concrete demands[19] which would give them back the equivalent of the special category regime (and implied political status) that SCS prisoners had in the compounds. The H-Block staff seemed intent on breaking the protesters through a campaign of petty harassment, beatings and humiliation (Crawford, 1999; Campbell *et al.*, 1994; Coogan, 1980; Hamber, 2005; McKeown, 2001; McEvoy, 2001; Miller, 2003; Jamieson *et al.*, 2010) and the frequent use of punishment cells or 'the boards'. It is not clear how much of this effort to break the prisoners was in response to top down Northern Ireland Office (NIO) policy and how much was staff-led practice on the wings.[20] But one of the ironic effects of this harsh treatment, apart from the infliction of suffering on the blanketmen, was that it strengthened their group cohesion and resolve. The protesters literally were held together by hate:

> The screws treated us like dirt. They hated us and did everything they could to break our morale and spirit. It was our hatred for the screws which kept our morale so good, in the circumstances.
>
> (Republican H-Block prisoner, in Crawford, 1999: 88)

The 'no wash' or 'dirty' protest (18th March 1978 to 1st December 1980)

After over a year and half on the blanket without gaining any concessions from the prison authorities and in the teeth of an increasingly vicious conflict with the staff over showering and humiliating body searches, the republicans escalated the blanket protest to a 'no wash' protest where prisoners refused to leave their cells. The no wash protest rapidly spiralled into a 'dirty' protest because of a conflict over slopping out and prisoners began smearing their excrement on the walls of their cells.[21] When the dirty protest reached the limits of the bearable, the protesting republican prisoners decided they had to hunger strike.

Hunger strikes (23rd October to 18th December 1980, 1st March to 3rd October 1981)

Out of desperation, exhaustion and a recognition that they had reached a stalemate, the prisoners decided to mount a hunger strike. And they knew from the moment they embarked on it that there would probably be a fast to the death because two IRA prisoners had recently died on hunger strike in England.[22] Seven men started their fast on 23rd October 1980 and were joined by three Armagh women on 1st December.[23] This first hunger strike lasted for 53 days and was ended when the men mistakenly thought the government had acceded to their five demands. Once it became clear to the prisoners that they had not won, they mounted their second hunger strike which resulted in the deaths of ten men. That hunger strike was a signal moment in the 'jail war', where the protesters exerted intense moral pressure on the state in an attempt to show their willingness to suffer, endure and die for their political beliefs.

Through these successive moments of attrition and resistance – nakedness, no wash, dirty protest and finally the hunger strike – the gendered body became an instrument of resistance (Aretxaga, 1995; Feldman, 1991; Foucault, 1977; McEvoy, 2001; Corcoran, 2006). Their bodies, which were the subjects of penal power, were reclaimed as sites where power was redirected back against authority (Feldman, 1991). Penal power was exerted on women's bodies though strip-searching, but when the women redirected it back at the authorities during the dirty protest by smearing excrement and menstrual blood on the walls of their cells, their actions gained tremendous emotional and moral force outside the prison where it provoked an almost visceral response (Corcoran, 2006; Murray, 1998; Weinstein, 2006). Margaret Thatcher's comments on the 1981 hunger strike highlights the problem that arousing these moral emotions caused for her government:

> Faced with the failure of their discredited cause, the men of violence have chosen in recent months to play what may well be their last card. They have turned their violence against themselves through the prison hunger strike to death. They seek to work on the most basic of human emotions – pity – as a means of creating tension and stoking the fires of bitterness and hatred.
>
> (Margaret Thatcher, 28th May 1981b)

Turning the prison inside out

The blanket, no wash and hunger strike protests had the effect of 'turning the prison inside out' (McConville, 2003: 5). The republican prisoners were able to reach out and draw the outside into the 'jail war' through law, politics and targeted violence. They mounted legal challenges and orchestrated local and international campaigning on their behalf (for example by the H-Block Armagh Committee).[24] They were also able to retaliate against their mal-treatment in the jail by declaring prison officers 'legitimate targets' for assassination on the outside. At the beginning of the criminalisation period PIRA had issued a statement saying:

> we are prepared to die for the right to retain political status. Those who try to take it away must be fully prepared to pay the same price.
>
> (IRA statement 27th March 1976, in Coogan, 1980: 65–66)

Both republican and loyalist groups issued threats against named prison staff who were alleged to have been the most brutal and abusive, but other prison staff were killed for no other reason than that they were prison officers. Even so the most significant instance of prisoners reaching out beyond the prison was the election of Bobby Sands to the Fermanagh-South Tyrone seat in April 1981, a few weeks before he died on hunger strike. His election changed everything. The unambiguous community support for the protesting prisoners established the political nature of the conflict and took the steam out of the criminalisation policy, but not before nine more men died.

Strategic resistance and managerialism (1981–1998)

What was begun in 1976 ended in 1981

(Tom Hartley, in English, 2003: 203)

The hunger strike was a Pyrrhic victory for the government because it eventually acceded to the same 'five demands' that it had so resolutely rejected throughout the 'jail war' period. After the end of the 1981 hunger strike, the focus of prison policy shifted from breaking the H-Block prisoners to managing them (1981–1998). Republican prisoners responded to this more managerialist approach with a shift in its resistance from categorical defiance to a more instrumental and strategic conformity. It took the form of outward compliance with the ordinary regime in order to create the space for regrouping and rebuilding the morale and discipline of republican prisoners. There was some concern among the republican officers in the H-Blocks that conforming PIRA prisoners had been 'individualised' on the ordinary wings and that their ties to the republican movement had been weakened. There was a perception that the conforming prisoners had become focussed on keeping their heads down, not losing remission, just doing their time and getting out (McKeown, 2001) so the republican leadership developed a strategy to retake the conforming wings and build up the PIRA command and communication structures within them (McKeown, 2001). This 'task force' strategy was inspired by the Viet Cong's hiding among the hordes of North Vietnamese refugees fleeing south. It involved ordering selected staunch republicans to leave the protests so that they would be sent to the mixed (loyalist and republican) conforming wings and, once they got there, they were to re-establish the PIRA command structures and lines of communication among the republican prisoners held there. Once that had been achieved the second phase of the strategy was to go for segregation, which would enhance and consolidate republican influence and discipline. One way they did this by exploiting the power of prison rumour to give loyalists the impression that republicans were arming themselves with makeshift knives to attack them with (McKeown, 2001). Less than two years after adopting the task force strategy they had achieved segregation and 38 PIRA prisoners effected a classic Colditz-like escape from the Maze which boosted morale and had significant propaganda value.[25]

The jail war as a political and psychological contest

I now turn to the question of how individual prisoners experienced their imprisonment during the miserable conditions of the H-Block protests and how and in what ways political commitment and collective identity mediated their cognitive and emotional understanding of jail war. Research on the effects of political imprisonment indicates that political commitment and group belonging can mitigate the negative effects of long-term imprisonment (Jamieson and Grounds, 2005, 2008; Kanninen *et al.*, 2002; Maercker and Schützwohl, 1997; Neria, 2000; Punamäkai *et al.*, 2008; Zalkin *et al.*, 2003). In their study of coping among Palestinian political ex-prisoners Punamäkai *et al.* (2008) found that no coping styles or strategies could protect prisoners

completely from the negative impacts of their captivity, but that strong ideological commitment, collective sharing and active problem-solving promoted
resilience and lessened negative psychological effects. Punamäkai *et al.* (2008)
make a distinction between emotion-focussed situational coping and problem-
solving coping strategies. They found that emotion-focussed, introspective
coping was associated with greater trauma-related mental health problems
while problem-solving coping, which is characterised by the assertion of
agency, trying to change hardships and engage constructive activities, and
information seeking and planning, enabled political prisoners to survive
better (Punamäkai *et al.*, 2008). In the H-Block context, resistance, even when
expressed through the abject bodies of the hunger strikers, constituted a form
of problem-solving coping. In this way both defiant categorical resistance and
instrumental strategic compliance can be seen as exercises of political agency.

Protesting republican prisoners resisted criminalisation through their collective political identity which was expressed through the group boundaries,
subculture and discipline, and sustained emotional connection between its
members (Melucci, 1995). And their collective identity was continuously
remade through the interplay of penal power and resistance:

> It was us or them, there were no shades grey. When you went in there you
> knew you were at war. They tried to turn you into a criminal but that
> only made you more conscious of what you were, a political prisoner. If it
> were any different they wouldn't have had to try so hard.
>
> (Republican H-Block prisoner, in Crawford, 1999: 99)

> there was them and us. They would keep us in and we were different from
> ordinary prisoners. We weren't criminals. We had that great political
> inner strength that kept us that way. We had our own structure, our own
> organisation; we had our own OC and our own structure and so forth. So
> the screws were not in control. We were in control.
>
> (Blanketman and hunger striker, in Jamieson and Grounds, 2002)

The experience of political imprisonment could harden individual resolve and
strengthen group ties:

> Before I went into prison I may have had some reservations about
> everything we do. I learnt better – prison educates you in that way.
> There's only one reality, them and us, and the armed struggle.
>
> (Republican H-Block prisoner, in Crawford, 1999: 89)

The blanketmen talked about how, in the harsh and isolated conditions of the
H-Blocks, the collective identity and the moral and cognitive frame of war
and revolution formed a kind of reality bubble around them:

we were enveloped in a shit-covered bubble of protest, an ugly world where nothing else existed ... as we fortified our spirits to face the immediate challenge of surviving each day, to win through somehow.

(O'Rawe, 2005: 41)

I was able to sustain things, or not sustain things but to endure things, which I would never in my life thought I would be able to endure and become involved in nasty things as well that I didn't think I was capable of. So it's an extraordinary situation made me do strange and extra-ordinary things and I mean, to spend three years scribing shit on a wall ... and think you're a revolutionary. You read about these jokes about people doing it in homes, in sanatoriums who think they're Napo-leon Bonaparte – there was me spreading the shite on the wall thinking I was Ché Guevara.

(Blanketman, in Jamieson and Grounds, 2008)

We lived in an unreal dimension in that we thought there was a revolution going on.

(Blanketman and hunger striker, in Jamieson and Grounds, 2002)

Political identity and group structure buttressed protesting prisoners against attempts to break their will:

it was a prisoner of war camp, it was run on those grounds, where the officer would come down, and go into the H-blocks where you were locked up seven days a week, 24 hours a day under protest ... I didn't want to be individualised. I didn't want to be treated as they would call it – an 'ordinary decent criminal.' I didn't want to be criminalised. I wanted to stress that I was in for a political offence and I wanted to be treated as such.

(Blanketman, in Jamieson and Grounds, 2002)

Protesting prisoners were sustained by their shared understanding of the situation and sense of belonging to a group where they found trust, empathy, loyalty, and emotional recognition. Ironically, joining the protest could get you through:

The thing about going on protest is this feeling of family. You're with your own, and as long as you're with your own, nothing can touch you.

(Republican woman prisoner, in Corcoran, 2006: 209)

And being in the protesting group offered protection as well as a daily reinforcement of one's political identity and belonging:

If you argued with one of them you argued with fifty. These guys were dedicated. They had done the blanket protests, dirty protests, and they had done the hunger strikes. They seemed to have an attitude that they were some sort of elite regiment, and when they came down they started getting into the Loyalists. The Loyalists went on protest to get away from them.

> (UDA prisoner, O'Rawe, 2005: 244)

The presence of a command structure made it a lot easier.
> (Republican who had been held in an English prison, in
> Jamieson and Grounds, 2002)

The protesting republican prisoners and their officers understood the importance of strong emotional bonds in sustaining group cohesion and political commitment:

> I think in the prison, especially during the blanket, dirty type protest, there was a genuine comradeship bordering on love which developed among the people there because of the hardship we had been through, because of the mental torture and the physical torture and the starvation. A great comradeship built up there to the point where ten people died for it.
> (Blanketman and hunger striker, in Jamieson and Grounds, 2002)

But negative emotions like hate also worked as a defining and unifying force:

> It's funny, but you hate them so much it keeps you going – even wee things to annoy them can keep your spirits up for days.
> (UDA/UFF, H-Block prisoner, in Crawford, 1999:113)

We hated them and they hated us, and that got worse and worse.
> (UVF/RHC, in Crawford, 1999: 88)

Relationships with prison staff really couldn't have been much worse. It was mutual hatred.
> (Republican H-Block prisoner, in Crawford, 1999: 114)

A striking aspect of these accounts is that the people engaged in the protests did not necessarily view their actions as remarkable. One republican who spent his imprisonment on the blanket and later went on hunger strike said that although he did not consider himself to be 'super staunch', he never doubted he would go on protest. He 'just thought it was the right thing to do' (McKeown, 2001: 52). PIRA was aware of the importance of the group in sustaining individual political commitment and bolstering personal coping and capacity to resist (McKeown, 2001: 92). The blanketmen had private personal selves as well as political selves, and imprisonment placed considerable stress on both. Of necessity, the H-Block prisoners had to adopt a certain stoicisim about their situation. The expression, 'do your whack', was a reminder that low moods were contagious and they all had to try to contain their negative feelings so that they did not make things harder for others. One blanketman and hunger striker said that he had consciously adopted a 'hard-edged political stance of mental austerity' and avoided any daydreaming or sentimentality while he was in prison (Jamieson and Grounds, 2002). His austere stoicism proved a more effective coping strategy than emotion-focussed, avoidant and distractive coping. The important determining factor in how effectively prisoners coped with the stress of incarceration was the ability to be flexible in their coping strategies and knowing what they could and could not control. Emotion-focussed coping is effective when the situation is uncontrollable (Punamäkai et al., 2008) and the prisoners seemed to understand that they needed to accept what they could not control:

> You had to accept it. You were living in a 9x6 cell. Nine feet by six with another person. The door was locked 24 hours a day. What could you do?
> (Blanketman and hunger striker, in Jamieson and Grounds, 2002)

> I focused on why I was in Jail – for the war.
> (Blanketman and hunger striker, in Jamieson and Grounds, 2002)

> I seen myself as a soldier, which I was, and what really got me through that period was concentrating on getting out, and trying to escape, and reading and doing political activism and so forth.
> (Blanketman, in Jamieson and Grounds, 2002)

> People who haven't got idealism have nothing to keep them going. They do time, big time, hard time.
> (Republican blanketman and hunger striker, in Jamieson and Grounds, 2002)

Republicans were able to withstand the squalid conditions of H-Block protests partly because they expected it. An important element of their political education had been learning about republican prison history. Most would have been familiar with the observation of Terence MacSwiney, who died on hunger strike in 1920, that 'It is not they who can inflict the most, but they who can suffer the most, who will prevail' (MacSwiney, 1920, cited in Costello, 1995: 115). Experiencing imprisonment through the lens of war was pivotal in republican prisoners' resistance to criminalisation and the penal power of the state. Punamäkai et al. (2008: 2) distil very clearly how such political commitment can mitigate the effects of incarceration:

> Ideological commitment serves as a contextual resource for active coping responses; it provides the possibility of interpreting and attributing causes

and consequences of trauma in meaningful, consoling and encouraging ways, sharing experiences and disclosing emotions with others, all contributing to empowerment and successful recovery.

The prisoners' ideological commitment and militarised structure of both republican and loyalist prisoners undoubtedly enabled their more active coping. In particular republican collective identity and high group solidarity buoyed individual prisoners up and provided a degree of protection from the more negative impacts of long-term imprisonment, especially the extreme stress and hardship of the blanket, dirty and hunger strike protests.

Conclusion

I think it is important to look at endings.

> It should be recognised that the Army did not 'win' in any recognisable way; rather it achieved its desired end state, which allowed a political process to be established without unacceptable levels of intimidation.
>
> (MOD, 2006, para 855)

In a spin war, who defines wins. Despite the fact that the Good Friday Agreement of 1998 recognised the political motivation of paramilitary prisoners in its provision for their early release, their conflict-related convictions have never been expunged (McEvoy, 1998). There has been no amnesty for political offences. Political ex-prisoners are still subject to 'residual criminalisation' in the form of legislative, attitudinal and practical barriers to full citizenship that stem from having a record for a conflict-related conviction (Shirlow and McEvoy, 2008: 94). This level of residual criminalisation involves significant and routine stigmatisation and restriction of politically motivated former prisoners without any foreseeable end point. Nevertheless, a vocal section of the Northern Ireland polity fervently holds the view that further punishment should be imposed on political ex-prisoners retrospectively in order to deliver justice for victims. Thus new legislation (Ann's Law) has been passed in the name of victims to disqualify ex-prisoners from being appointed as special advisors to members of the Legislative Assembly.[26] In tandem with this there are currently equally rancorous debates about the prosecution of historical crimes committed by members of the security forces and 'On the Runs'. However, notwithstanding all that heated contention, perhaps the most pressing item of unfinished business is the growing population now nearing 100 of dissident republicans imprisoned for their involvement in post-1998 political violence. Those 'dissident' prisoners also construct their identity through the lens of war and Irish political history and try to reprise the most recent republican prison history in their own dirty protests and hunger strikes to demand segregation and political status. They too are sustained by their collective identity and political commitment in the same way that the blanketmen were and are just as determined not to be broken. If the Long Kesh/Maze prison war has taught us anything, it is that the seeds of a political resolution were sown in jail only after attempts to break prisoners were abandoned (Shirlow and McEvoy, 2008).

Notes

1　Thanks to Expac and Seesyu Press for granting me permission to quote material from a report written for them in 2002. The full reference for this report is: Jamieson, R. and Grounds, A.T. (2002) *No Sense of an Ending: The effects of long-term imprisonment amongst Republican prisoners and their families*, Monaghan: Seesyu Press.

2　Before Operation BANNER there were only three resident infantry battalions in Northern Ireland, but by the worst year of the conflict (1972), there were 27,000 military personnel in Northern Ireland, i.e. more than the number of British soldiers deployed for the invasion of Iraq in 2003.

3　See INCORE (1999).

4　For example, in non-international armed conflicts, including 'wars of liberation', combatants may use lethal force and may be lawfully killed or captured. If captured, they are entitled to protection under the Additional Protocols to the Geneva Convention as prisoners of war (POWs) who should be released without prosecution at the end of hostilities as long they have not violated the laws of war. If, on the other hand, the violence is defined as crime, then state actors, whether the police or army, may only use *minimum force* in arresting those using political violence. The use of lethal force (shoot-to-kill) is prohibited. See Finlay 2010.

5　For clear and accessible accounts of the history of Northern Ireland, see Farrell (1976); O'Leary and McGarry (1996); Stewart (1977).

6　Enoch Powell, Ulster Unionist MP for South Down, described the British Foreign Office as a 'nest of vipers' and 'nursery of traitors' who were mounting a 'Fifth Column' operation in Ulster (Powell 1980).

7　The Civil Authorities (Special Powers) Act (Northern Ireland) 1922 gave the Stormont Government an array of special powers that were the envy of the apartheid regime in South Africa. These included wide powers for entry and search, imposing curfews, detention without charge or trial, banning of books, banning public assemblies and prohibiting inquests. The Special Powers Act was in effect for 50 years until it was replaced the end of 1972 under direct rule by the Northern Ireland (Emergency Provisions) Act of 1973. These and later amendments of emergency powers legislation (1978, 1987 and 1996) allowed for arrest without warrant, holding suspects for 7 days, juryless special courts for terrorism-related offences, the use of involuntary statements as evidence even when obtained through maltreatment of suspects, the use of evidence from non-testifying witnesses and delays in the notification of an accused's family and in access to legal counsel where it might interfere with information gathering. See Hogan and Walker (1989) and Walsh (1983) for overviews of the use of emergency powers in Northern Ireland.

8　The Ulster Special Constabulary (USC) was openly sectarian. It was comprised of 5,500 paid full-time A-Specials recruited from the loyalist paramilitary Ulster Volunteer Force, another 19,000 part-time unpaid B-Specials or 'B-Men' and a further 7,500 unpaid, uniformed C-Special reserves. Although the 'A' and 'C' specials were disbanded in 1922, the 'B'-Specials operated until 1970, when the locally recruited Ulster Defence Regiment (UDR) replaced them. Many 'B-Men' and members of the loyalist UVF were recruited into the UDR (O'Leary and McGarry 1996, 126). See also Ellison and Smyth 2000.

9 The fact that British forces conducted covert shoot-to-kill operations has been acknowledged only to the extent of Prime Minister Cameron issuing an apology in 2012 for 'shocking' levels of collusion between loyalist paramilitaries, the RUC and the Army in the killing of the solicitor Pat Finucane. See Cadwallader (2013); Dillon (1991); Kitson (1971); Murray (1990); Rolston (2000); and Urban (1993).

10 The Provisional IRA (PIRA) split from the IRA in 1969 and became the largest and most active republican group. Most Government and Army references are to 'PIRA'.

11 The Army was well aware that the behaviour of some troops, particularly that of the Parachute Regiment, was a problem. Some Army officers had even requested that '1Para' be kept out of their patrol areas. It had killed 10 civilians in Bally-murphy in August 1971 and six months later in Derry on Bloody Sunday shot 27 civilians, killing 13. To date no prosecutions have been brought for any of these killings. According to one journalist, the Paras were '"frankly disliked" by many officers here, who regard them as little better than thugs in uniform. I have seen them arrive on the scene, thump up a few people who might be doing nothing more than shouting and jeering, and roar off again. They seem to think they can get away with whatever they like.' Simon Hoggart, *Irish News*, 26 January 1972.

12 I draw on prisoner and staff accounts of the 'jail war' in Jamieson and Grounds (2002, 2008); Jamieson *et al.* (2010); Campbell *et al.* (1994); Corcoran (2006); Crawford (1999); Hamber (2005); McKeown (2001); Miller (2003); Ryder (2000).

13 See instead McEvoy (2001) and Corcoran (2006).

14 It must be said that Irish political history was a resource that could be mined by anyone. For example, when, in a *World in Action* interview, the Minister of State at the Northern Ireland Office was asked what would happen if a hunger striker died, he cited a precedent from Ireland: 'Well, he dies. He is carried out in a coffin as the fasting prisoners in the republic, in Dublin, were carried out in coffins in 1940.' (*World in Action*, 25 November 1980).

15 This identification with 'comrades' in other national liberation struggles was not new. Earlier generations of republicans had done the same, e.g. Frank Gallagher, Irish hunger striker of the 1920s reading books on the colonisation of Africa (Gallagher, 2008:14).

16 'Blanketmen' were republican prisoners who participated in the blanket protest against criminal status. 'Squeaky booters' were blanketmen who quit the protests wearing prison issue clothing including new boots that squeaked when they walked off the wings.

17 McEvoy (2001) identifies these policy phases as 'reactive containment' (1969–1975), 'criminalisation' (1976–1981) and 'manageralism' (1981–1998).

18 Protesting prisoners lost a day of remission for every day that they were on protest.

19 These included the restoration of lost remission and the right to wear their own clothes at all times, to free association in the blocks, not to do prison work and the right to access educational and recreational facilities.

20 Most accounts of the H-Blocks to date are from a prisoner perspective, but it is clear that during the criminalisation protests the situation was micro-managed from on high. See, for example, the NIO note, 'Protesters/Conformers Analysis as at 25 July 1977, Male Prisoners with PIRA Associations' (PRO, CJ4/ 1687, 1977).

21 Apparently inspired by Jimmy Boyle's successful 1968 dirty protest in HMP Inverness (O'Rawe 2005, p.32). See Coogan, 1980.

22 See Beresford, 1987; Coogan, 1980; O'Malley 1990.

23 The women were allowed their own clothes so did not go on the blanket, but they did refuse prison work and participated in the no wash protest. See Corcoran 2006.

24 See Ross (2011).

25 See the Hennessey Report (1984).

26 Civil Service (Special Advisers) Act (Northern Ireland) 2013.

References

Aretxaga, B. (1995) 'Dirty Protest: Symbolic Overdetermination and Gender in Northern Ireland Ethnic Violence', *Ethos*, 23(2): 123–148.

Asher, M. (1990) *Shoot to Kill: A Soldier's Journey Through Violence*, London: Viking.

Bennett, H. (2013) '"Smoke Without Fire"? Allegations Against the British Army in Northern Ireland, 1972–1975', *Twentieth Century British History*, 24(2): 275–304.

Beresford, D. (1987) *Ten Dead Men: The Story of the 1981 Irish Hunger Strike*, London: Harper Collins.

Bloomfield, K. (1998), 'We Will Remember Them: Report of the Northern Ireland Victims Commissioner', Belfast: Stationery Office. Available: http://cain.ulst.ac.uk/issues/victims/docs/bloomfield98.pdf.

Buntman, F.L. (2003) *Robben Island and Prisoner Resistance to Apartheid*, Cambridge: Cambridge University Press.

Cadwallader, A. (2013) *Lethal Allies: British Collusion in Ireland*, Cork: Mercier Press.

Campbell, J.B., McKeown, L. and O'Hagan, F. (1994) *Nor Meekly Serve My Time: The H-block Struggle, 1976–1981*, Belfast: Beyond the Pale.

Cassese, A. (1981) 'The Status of Rebels under the 1977 Geneva Protocol on Non-international Armed Conflicts', *International and Comparative Law Quarterly*, 30 (2): 418–439.

Clarke, A.F.N. (1983) *Contact*, London: Martin Secker &Warburg.

Clarke, L. (1987) *Broadening the Battlefield: the H-Blocks and the Rise of Sinn Fein*, Dublin: Gill and Macmillan.

Coogan, T.P. (1980) *On the Blanket: The H-Block Story*, Dublin: Ward River Press.

Corcoran, M. (2006) *Out of Order: The Political Imprisonment of Women in Northern Ireland 1972–1998*, Cullompton: Willan.

Costello, F.J. (1995) *Enduring the Most: The Life and Death of Terence MacSwiney*, Kerry: Brandon.

Crawford, C. (1999) *Defenders or Criminals? Loyalist Prisoners and Criminalisation*, Belfast: Blackstaff Press.

Curtis, L. (1998) *Ireland: The Propaganda War – The British Media and the Battle for Hearts and Minds*, London: Pluto Press.

Dillon, M. (1991) *The Dirty War*, London: Arrow Books.

Ellison, G. and Smyth, J. (2000) *The Crowned Harp: Policing in Northern Ireland*, London: Pluto Press.

English, R. (2003) *Armed Struggle: A History of the IRA*, Basingstoke: Macmillan.

Farrell, M. (1976) *The Orange State*, London: Pluto.

Feldman, A. (1991) *Formations of Violence: The Narrative of the Body and Political Terror in Northern Ireland*, Chicago: University of Chicago Press.

Finlay, C. J. (2010) 'Terrorism, Resistance and the Idea of the "Unlawful Combatantcy"', *Ethics & International Affairs*, 24(1): 91–104.

Foucault, M. (1977) *Discipline and Punish: The Birth of the Prison*, New York: Pantheon.

Gallagher, F. (2008) *Days of Fear: Diary of a 1920s Hunger Striker*, Dublin: Mercier.

Galula, D. (1964) *Counterinsurgency Warfare: Theory and Practice*, London: Greenwood Publishing Group.

Gardiner, Lord. (1975) 'Report of a Committee to Consider, in the Context of Civil Liberties and Human Rights, Measures to Deal with Terrorism in Northern Ireland. CMND. 5847', London: HMSO.

Graham, B. and Shirlow, P. (2002), 'The battle of the Somme in Ulster memory and identity', *Political Geography*, 21(7): 881–904.

Hamber, B. (2005) *Blocks to the Future: An Independent Report into the Psychological Impact of the 'No Wash/Blanket' Prison Protest*, Derry: Cúnamh.

Haunss, S. (2007) 'Challenging Legitimacy: Repertoires of Contention, Political Claims-Making, and Collective Action Frames' in Hurrelmann, A., Schneider, S. and Steffek, J. (ed.) *Legitimacy in an Age of Global Politics*, London: Palgrave Macmillan. pp. 156–172.

Hennessey, Sir James. (1984) 'Report of an Inquiry by HM Chief Inspector of Prisons into the Security Arrangements at HM Prison, Maze Relative to the Escape on Sunday 25th September 1983, Including Relevant Recommendations for the Improvement of Security at HM Prison, Maze. (H.C. 203 of 1983–1984)', London: HMSO.

Hogan, G. and Walker, C. (1989) *Political Violence and the Law in Ireland*, Manchester: Manchester University Press.

Hoggart, S. (1972) 'Army Call To Bar Paratroops', *The Guardian* 26 January, p. 1. (Accessed 21 November 2014.) The Guardian The Observer Digital Archive, available at http://pqasb.pqarchiver.com/guardian/doc/185586400.html?

Hughes, J. (2011) 'State Violence in the Origins of Nationalism: The British Reinvention of Irish Nationalism 1969–1972, Paper for the Nationalism and War Workshop', Montreal: McGill University (24–26 March). Available at http://personal.lse.ac.uk/HUGHESJ/images/StateViolenceintheOriginsofNationalism.pdf.

INCORE. (1999) 'Final Report, The Cost of the Troubles Study (COTT)'. Available at www.incore.ulst.ac.uk/publications/pdf/cottreport.pdf.

Jamieson, R. and Grounds, A.T. (2002) *No Sense of an Ending: The Effects of Long-term Imprisonment amongst Republican Prisoners and their Families*, Monaghan: Seesyu Press.

Jamieson, R. and Grounds, A.T. (2005) 'Release and Readjustment: Perspectives from Studies of Wrongfully Convicted and Politically Motivated Prisoners' in Liebling, A. and Maruna, S. (eds) *The Effects of Imprisonment*, Cullompton, Devon: Willan.

Jamieson, R. and Grounds, A.T. (2008) *Facing the Future: Ageing and Politically-Motivated Former Prisoners in Northern Ireland and the Border Regions*, Monaghan: EXPAC.

Jamieson, R., Shirlow, P. and Grounds, A.T. (2010) *Ageing and Social Exclusion among Politically-motivated Former Prisoners in Northern Ireland*, Belfast: Changing Ageing Partnership.

Kanninen, K., Punamäki, R. L., and Qouta, S. (2002) 'The Relation of Appraisal, Coping Efforts, and Acuteness of Trauma to PTS Symptoms among Former Political Prisoners', *Journal of Traumatic Stress*, 15(3): 245–253.

King, Lt. Gen. Sir F. (1974) WO 296/144, Letter to the Attorney General, 3 April 1974

Kirchheimer, O. (1961) *Political Justice: The Use of Legal Procedure for Political Ends*, Princeton, NJ: Greenwood Press.

Kitson, F. (1971) *Low Intensity Operations: Subversion, Insurgency and Peacekeeping*, London: Faber and Faber.

Lindsay, J. (1998) *Brits Speak Out: British Soldier's Impressions of the Northern Ireland Conflict*, Derry: Guildhall Press.

Lundy, P. (2013) 'Submission to the Multi-party Group Chaired by Richard Haass'. Available: http://eprints.ulster.ac.uk/28252.

McConville, S. (2003) *Irish Political Prisoners, 1848–1922: Theatres of War*, London: Routledge.

McEvoy, K. (1998) 'Prisoners, the Agreement, and the Political Character of the Northern Ireland Conflict', *Fordham International Law Journal*, 22(4): 1539–1576.

McEvoy, K. (2001) *Paramilitary Imprisonment in Northern Ireland: Resistance, Management, and Release*, Oxford: Oxford University Press.

McKeown, L. (2001) *Out of Time: Irish Republican Prisoners, Long Kesh, 1972–2000*, Belfast: Beyond The Pale.

Maercker, A. and Schützwohl, M. (1997) 'Long-term Effects of Political Imprisonment: A Group Comparison Study', *Social Psychiatry and Psychiatric Epidemiology*, 32: 435–442.

Melucci, A. (1989) *Nomad of the Present*, Philadelphia: Temple University Press.

Melucci, A. (1995) 'The Process of Collective Identity', in Johnston, H. (ed.). *Social Movements and Culture*, London: Routledge. pp. 41–63.

Miller, S. (2003) *On the Brinks*, Galway: Wykin de Worde.

Ministry of Defence (MOD). (2006) 'Operation Banner: An Analysis of Military Operations in Northern Ireland, Army Code 71842. Prepared under the Direction of the Chief of General Staff'. Available: www.vilaweb.cat/media/attach/vwedts/docs/op_banner_analysis_released.pdf.

Mulcahy, A. (1995) 'Claims-making and the Construction of Legitimacy: Press Coverage of the 1981 Northern Irish Hunger Strike', *Social Problems*, 42(4): 449–467.

Murray, R. (1990) *The SAS in Ireland*, Dublin: Mercier Press.

Murray, R. (1998) *Hard Time: Armagh Goal, 1971–1986*, Dublin: Mercier Press.

Nachbar, T. (2012) 'Counterinsurgency, legitimacy, and the rule of law', *Parameters*, 42(1): 27–38.

Neria, Y. (2000) 'Posttraumatic Residues of Captivity: A Follow-Up of Israeli Ex Prisoners of War', *Journal of Clinical Psychiatry*, 61(1): 39–46.

Ní Aoláin, F. D. (2000) *The Politics of Force: Conflict Management and State Violence in Northern Ireland*, Belfast: Blackstaff Press.

Northern Ireland Office (NIO) (1977) [CJ4/1687] (26 September). 'E.N. Barry Briefing on "Special Category Compounds", Annex I'.

O'Leary, B. and McGarry, J. (1996) *The Politics of Antagonism: Understanding Northern Ireland*, (2nd edition), London: Athlone Press.

O'Malley, P. (1990) *Biting at the Grave: The Irish Hunger Strikes and the Politics of Despair*, Belfast: Blackstaff Books.

O'Rawe, R. (2005) *Blanketmen: An Untold Story of the H-Block Hunger Strike*, Dublin: New Island.

Powell, E. (3 January 1980) Speech to the Annual Institution Supper of the Dundonald Orange Lodge, Northern Ireland, Thatcher Archive, PREM19/279 f123. (Accessed 18 November 2014.) Available at: http://fc95d419f4478b3b6e5f-3f71d0fe2b653c4f00f32175760e96e7.r87.cf1.rackcdn.com/A8EFA9DAF0D64E3AA2313AF76EE7463E.pdf.

Punamäki, R. L., Salo, J., Komproe, I., Qouta, S., El-Masri, M. and De Jong, J. T. (2008) 'Dispositional and Situational Coping and Mental Health among Palestinian Political Ex-prisoners', *Anxiety, Stress, & Coping*, 21(4): 337–358.

Radzinowicz, L. and Hood, R. (1979) 'The Status of Political Prisoner in England: The Struggle for Recognition', *Virginia Law Review*, 1421–1481.

Rolston, B. (1995) *Drawing Support 2: Murals of War and Peace*, Belfast: Beyond the Pale.

Rolston, B. and Miller, D. (ed.) (1996) *War and Words: The Northern Ireland Media Reader*, Dublin: Beyond the Pale.

Rolston, B. (2000) *Unfinished Business: State Killings and the Quest for Truth*, Belfast: Beyond the Pale.

Ross, F.S. (2011) *Smashing H-Block*, Liverpool: Liverpool University Press.

Ryder, C. (2000) *Inside the Maze*, London: Methuen.

Sands, B. (1981) *The Diary of Bobby Sands*, Dublin: Sinn Fein.

Shirlow, P. and McEvoy, K. (2008) *Beyond the Wire*, London: Pluto Press.

Stewart, A.T.Q. (1977) *The Narrow Ground: Aspects of Ulster 1609–1969*, London: Faber.

Taylor, P. (1996) 'Reporting Northern Ireland' in Rolston, B. and Miller, D. (ed.) *War and Words: The Northern Ireland Media Reader*, Dublin: Beyond the Pale. pp. 67–79.

Thatcher, M. (1981a) 'Speech at Parliament Buildings, Stormont', 5th March. Available at: www.margaretthatcher.org/document/104589.

Thatcher, M. (1981b) 'Speech at Stormont Castle Lunch', 28th May. Available at: www.margaretthatcher.org/document/104657.

Thomson, M. (2010) 'Britain's Propaganda War during the Troubles/The Spin War in Northern Ireland', 22nd March. Available at: http://news.bbc.co.uk/1/hi/uk/8577087.stm.

Tilly, C. (2008) *Credit and Blame*, Princeton, NJ: Princeton University Press.

Urban, M. (1993) *Big Boys' Rules: The SAS and the Secret Struggle against the IRA*, London: Faber and Faber.

Walsh, D.P.J. (1983) *The Use and Abuse of Emergency Legislation in Northern Ireland*, London: The Cobden Trust.

Walzer, M. (1969) 'Prisoners of War: Does the Fight Continue After the Battle?', *American Political Science Review*, 63(3): 777–786.

Wharton, K. (2008) *A Long Long War: Voices from the British Army in Northern Ireland 1969–1998*, Solihull: Helion and Co.

Wharton, K. (2010) *Bloody Belfast: An Oral History of the British Army's War Against the IRA*, Stroud Spellmount: The History Press.

Weinstein, L. (2006) 'The Significance of the Armagh Dirty Protest', *Éire-Ireland*, 41 (3): 11–41.

Zalkin, G., Solomon, Z. and Neria, Y. (2003) 'Hardness, Attachment Style and Long Term Psychological Distress among Israeli POWs and Combat Veterans', *Personality and Individual Differences*, 34: 819–829.

6 Veteran coming-home obstacles

Short- and long-term consequences of the Iraq and Afghanistan wars

William Brown

Introduction

> I looked down at the girl. She was maybe 12 years old. She could have been 15. Who knows? Who cares? Delbert and Ryan were right. She didn't have a fucking face anymore. The brains were exposed from the front of her skull and already turning gray. Brains did that after a while. I assumed it had something to do with the air hitting them. Plus, these brains had to contend with the heat of the burned-out *hootch*. Her right arm had been ripped from its shoulder socket. The socket was blackened, but there was a shiny red gooey substance that seemed to coat the cuplike socket where her arm once had been attached to her body. I don't ever recall seeing the arm. Her right leg was twisted into some grotesque position, sort of like a twisted piece of licorice. I wondered how that leg got so twisted. What difference did it make? She was dead.
>
> (Brown, 2005: 251)

The young girl, noted above, died in June 1968—somewhere in the Central Highlands of South Vietnam. This event occurred after a bullet hit a U.S. soldier on the left side of his head. He was dead. An older Vietnamese male lay near the young girl. He was also dead. There was an AK47 on the floor of the burned-out *hootch*. We carried the soldier, wrapped in a poncho, to an LZ (Landing Zone) for transport back to the rear area. It took nearly three hours to reach the LZ. The body was loaded onto a helicopter. The helicopter lifted off and left the area. The soldier was gone. *It don't mean nothing* was uttered by many soldiers standing on the edge of the LZ. This phrase was often used by *grunts* (Infantrymen) to avoid any emotional thoughts or feelings while serving in a war zone. Emotion can interrupt concentration. Concentration helps protect the soldier from being wrapped in a poncho and carried to an LZ. Besides, if you survived, there was plenty of time for emotion when you got back home.

Many veterans reflect on their war experiences. People often wonder why veterans continue to revisit those experiences. Civilians often ask—*Why don't they just get over it?* A veteran may learn to *live with it*, but it is doubtful that he or she will ever *get over it*. These experiences *are for life*. Some veterans are successful in suppressing the after-effects of war, while other veterans are less fortunate. Some veterans reflect on those experiences regularly, while others obscure those experiences until confronted with a situation that triggers their thoughts of war.

It is pointless to engage in a discussion about veterans returning from war while ignoring the topic of *war*. War experiences have lasting effects on many veterans' post-military behavior. Professionals often sanitize the concept of war verbally and in their writings. For example, Hardt and Negri (2004: 3) describe war as an, "armed conflict between sovereign political entities, that is, during the modern period, between nation-states". Most combat veterans would agree that war is a combination of death, killing, sacrifice, and survival.

The Iraq war produced 4,804 coalition military deaths, which include 4,486 Americans, 179 British, and 139 military service member deaths from other nations. The war in Afghanistan, as of February 27 2014, has produced 3,424 coalition military deaths. Those deaths include 2,313 American, 447 British, and 664 military personnel from other countries (Iraq Coalition Casualty Count, 2014). There appears to be a tendency to ignore the number of civilian casualties produced during war. A recent study reveals that the Iraq war produced more than 500,000 civilian deaths. U.S.-led coalition forces were responsible for the majority of violent civilian deaths, which include men and women. Most of those deaths resulted from gunshots rather than *media-popularized* car bombs and Improvised Explosive Devices (Hagopian *et al.*, 2013). The war in Afghanistan has undoubtedly produced many civilian deaths. While it is true that coalition forces did not cause all of these deaths *directly*, they are at least *indirectly* responsible for many civilian deaths by their mere presence in that country. The *actual* number of civilian deaths resulting from wars in Iraq and Afghanistan is unknown. After 39 years since the fall of Saigon, in 1975, inconsistency prevails regarding the number of Vietnamese civilians killed in that war. Numbers range from just under 1 million civilian deaths (Hirschman *et al.*, 1995) to perhaps as many as 3.8 million, which includes both Vietnamese combatant and civilian deaths (Obermeyer *et al.*, 2008). Direct or indirect participation in activities that produced civilian casualties often plague many veterans after they return from war.

This chapter centers on the after-effects of war and the impact those effects have on many veterans returning to civilian culture. Veterans returning home from war often search for their identities. Many veterans feel that they do not *fit* in the civilian community. They often leave the military and enter the civilian culture only to discover that their military identity conflicts with civilian culture, standard expectations. This is particularly true for veterans who deployed to combat areas and is further aggravated with multiple deployments. Exposure to horrific war experiences often exacerbates the difficulties in veteran efforts to find his or her place in civilian culture. Those experiences may include handling/uncovering bodies or human remains, witnessing children twist in agony after a hostile confrontation where civilians became casualties, or being in close proximity to wounded or killed members of the veteran's unit. The more combat exposure that veterans encounter in a war zone the more likely they will experience individual identity and/or cultural adaptation problems, which include relationship disintegration, difficulties securing and/or maintaining employment, problems advancing their education goals, substance abuse, or self-isolation, for example. These problems can enhance the probability of veteran criminal justice entanglements or veteran suicides.

The after-effects of war were problematic for veterans of previous wars. World War II combat veterans brought memories of their war experiences home with them (Wood, 2006), as did many Vietnam veterans (Emerson, 1976; Caputo, 1977; Turse, 2013), as do Iraq and Afghanistan veterans today (Hoge, 2010; Goodell and Hearn, 2011).

Much of the data presented in this chapter is from interviews conducted with nearly 250 Iraq/Afghanistan veterans since 2008. The veterans in this study are from two independent groups. Group 1 includes over 160 Iraq and Afghanistan veterans from 16 states across America. The second group includes over 80 Iraq/Afghanistan veteran defendants in criminal cases, where I conducted sociological evaluations used by defense attorneys in state and federal courts. These evaluations were for pre-trial negotiations, trial, and sentencing mitigation purposes. Official military documents, which include discharge documents (DD 214), verified that veterans in both groups had deployed to Iraq and/or Afghanistan.

Military total institution/military culture

While a veteran's war experiences often obstruct attempts to be successful in civilian culture, the indoctrination and training they received as recruits also contribute to problems confronting them after leaving the military. Their indoctrination and training occurred within the military total institution (MTI). Total institutions share similar characteristics. First, all aspects of an individual's life occur in the same location and apart from the larger society. Second, most people are treated the same. Third, all phases of the individual's day and night are programmed and closely monitored. Finally, everyone must accept, adapt, and comply with the total institution's rules, values, expectations, and standards (Goffman, 1961). The military meets the criteria of a total institution. These social and cultural constructs exist in all military total institutions throughout the world.

Previous research related to the MTI has focused on the roles of military instructors (Bamberger and Hasgall, 1995), assimilation into the MTI through military training (Zurcher, 2007), and the MTI's influence on veterans returning to the civilian culture and the probability of entanglement in the criminal justice system (Brown, 2008, 2010, 2011, 2014; Brown *et al.*, 2013). All of these studies rely on the basic foundation of total institutions set forth by Goffman.

Obedience, discipline, survival, and *sacrifice* are principle components of the MTI foundation. *Obedience* mandates submission to superiors and the directives and orders that they initiate—to obey all orders without hesitation or question. *Discipline,* in military settings, is a requirement that military personnel develop a mental and moral character consistent with the expectations of military culture—to look and behave as a soldier, sailor, airman, or Marine. *Survival* is another component in the MTI foundation. Military personnel who are unable to survive reduce the chances of other personnel surviving—thus, reducing the prospect of the military completing its mission. *Sacrifice,* relative to military personnel, is a component that includes relinquishing one's individuality to the ultimate sacrifice—sacrificing one's life (Brown, 2008).

The MTI begins with recruitment. The primary objective of military recruitment is to identify and induct individuals who will most likely adopt and adapt to the values, rules, beliefs, and expectations of the military—*young adults.* As one former Marine recruiter stated,

> My job was to go into high schools and convince those kids that joining the Marines would be in their best interest. Many times, I had to meet their parents and convince them their child was not going to be in danger. I often downplayed the possibility of deployment. Sometimes, when parents asked about the possibility of deployment I would change the subject .... Four of the kids I recruited got killed in Iraq—those are just the ones I know about. I did what I had to do to make my quota—that is how I justify what I did. Now that I am out, I have problems with that justification.[1]

One of the principle MTI goals of early military training is to remove the sense of individualism from the recruit. Civilian culture promotes individualism, while the military encourages the importance of the group. This is one of many culture shock confrontations experienced by recruits (Brown, 2014). Often, modern civilian cultures classify or rate people by their individual accomplishments. For example, civilian societies tend to recognize wealthy individuals as successful, often attributing that success to the individual, while failure is a term applied to someone who lives in poverty. In the military, the importance of individual accomplishments is not nearly as significant as group achievements. The group is responsible for completing the military's mission. The military recognizes individual accomplishments, but that recognition generally occurs within the context of an individual's performance within the group.

At the onset of military training, leadership values of the military are introduced to recruits. In combat situations, veterans with lower rank may be required to assume leadership roles if the original unit leader becomes disabled or is eliminated. Leadership values include loyalty, duty, respect, selfless service, honor, integrity, and personal courage (LDRSHIP). *Loyalty* requires military personnel to always be there for members of their unit—

regardless of the conditions or situation. *Duty* mandates that military personnel follow and comply with the rules and guidelines of the military, and fulfill their responsibilities. *Respect* requires military personnel to obey those with higher rank and respect those of lower rank. *Selfless service* requires military personnel to forever place the mission and the needs of others before one's own needs. *Honor* is respecting and complying with military tradition, and dedication to reaching the goals of the military. *Integrity* requires military personnel to be honest and truthful to others and to themselves, regardless of the consequences. *Personal courage* requires military personnel to always accept responsibility for their actions, regardless of the outcome (Headquarters, Department of the Army, 2006).

Regimentation and *esprit de corps* are two crucial elements of the MTI. Regimentation fosters strict organization and control, while *esprit de corps* produces enthusiasm, devotion, and strong regard for the honor of the group, which are essential elements within all branches of the military. These elements encourage rigorous competition that promotes the goals of all military systems—to defeat the enemy—to win.

Military training is an intensive and concentrated process. MTI indoctrination begins in Basic Training or Boot Camp. Following successful completion of Basic Training or Boot Camp, recruits are required to complete AIT (Advanced Individual Training). There are two primary training classifications germane to the military—tactical and technical training. The focus of tactical training meets the needs of Military Occupational Specialties (MOS) in the area of combat arms (i.e. Infantry, Armor, Artillery, Combat Engineers, etc.). Military personnel trained in the combat arms receive technical training, which often focuses on weaponry or other devices related to combat operations. Computer operators, mechanics, communication experts, medical providers, and other occupations related to military support units receive extensive technical training relative to their MOS.

Instantaneous reaction to critical confrontations or situations and forestalling of all emotional influences are two crucial elements addressed during recruit training. Recruits must demonstrate compliance with these elements during their initial training. Training cadres convey to recruits, early in their military training, that hesitation in their response to orders or when confronted with a critical situation can result in their death or the death of their *buddies*. Individual and group punishments are tactics used by training cadres when recruits hesitate or fail to perform adequately during the training process. Degradation and humiliation are tactical tools used by Drill Sergeants and Drill Instructors to increase the recruit's level of stress, improve the recruit's physical capabilities, and instill the importance of instantaneous reaction—to act or react without hesitation—in a combat situation (Brown, 2014).

A U.S. Army veteran talked about his perceptions of, and experiences in, Basic Training.

The first couple of weeks of Basic Training sucked. I thought I was in good physical condition when I went but I wasn't. The constant harassment by the Drill Sergeants nearly drove me crazy. They called us worthless and lazy. If someone in the platoon screwed up we were all punished. They were on our asses constantly. After a while, the harassment and punishment lightened up. I eventually started to think and act like a soldier. I started to develop pride in myself. Instead of feeling sorry for myself, I began to realize that I was a team member. I was responsible for the guys in my squad and they were responsible for me. After my deployment to Afghanistan, I learned the value of what all that training was about.[2]

Another veteran, reflecting on her own experiences in Basic Training and the impact that training had on her and her performance during deployment to Iraq, said,

One of the biggest changes I recall was that I could accomplish things in the military that I would never even attempted to do if I hadn't joined the Army. I also realized that I was a part of something much larger, and other people relied on me to perform at my best. I thought I was a responsible person before I joined, but after I completed medic training I realized that other people's lives depended on my job performance. Serving in Iraq changed me. The training prepared me for experiences that I faced during deployment. I was a good soldier.[3]

Military training continuously reinforces military cultural expectations, while simultaneously expunging the recruit's civilian cultural remnants. This process involves the constant degradation of civilian values, rules, and expectations, while repeatedly promoting winning and/or the glorification of killing the enemy. Cadence lyrics, used during drills, marching, or running, often devalue and/or degrade civilians. Cadence also installs the idea that killing is not only acceptable but also encouraged. Killing human beings is not a natural act that one engages in. Most people require programing and training to willingly take the life of another human being (Grossman, 1995).

Most of the veteran participants and veteran defendants that I interviewed said they joined the military to serve their country, while others said they had a desire to do something with their lives. Nearly 69 percent of these veterans said their parents had not served in the military. Over one-half of the veterans said their family strongly supported their decision to join the military. Most veterans said that the primary thing they learned during their initial military training was to defeat or kill the enemy, followed by improvement in weapons proficiency, and the importance of relying on and protecting their *buddies*. About 35 percent of the veterans said they received the most training in physical conditioning, followed by nearly 28 percent who said weapons training, and 23 percent who said discipline training. Most veterans said the thing they liked most about their initial military training was the level of self-confidence they developed. When asked to describe the one part of their training that they disliked most, the vast majority said group punishment. When asked to identify the most scathing cadence content used during their initial military training, over 40 percent said references to killing the enemy, followed by nearly 24 percent who said the glorification of killing, 20 percent who said dehumanizing the enemy, and about 14 percent who said the degradation of civilians and civilian culture values. When asked to describe their primary function in the military after they completed their initial training nearly 35 percent said to kill the enemy, while over 27 percent said to protect their "buddies," and 23 percent said to serve their country.

War: lasting consequences

Many Iraq and/or Afghanistan veterans returning home from war are reluctant to discuss their participation in war. Some veterans try avoiding discussions or even thinking about their own war-related experiences. Typically, the more gruesome the experiences the less willing veterans are to share those experiences with non-veterans. Their unwillingness to share their experiences with *outsiders* (non-veterans) is understandable. After returning from Vietnam in 1969, it took me over 36 years to write about my own *ghosts of war* (Brown, 2005). One problem confronting many veterans is the distinctions between acceptable and unacceptable behavior that exist amongst military and civilian cultures. Behavior that is encouraged, required, and expected in a war zone often conflicts with many of the rules, values, and expectations of civilian culture. As one Afghanistan veteran stated,

> We would force our way into a home and make everyone get against a wall or get down on the floor. Sometimes they were dressed. Other times they weren't. We ransacked their homes looking for weapons or something. I had no problem doing those things when I was in Afghanistan. I mean they could have been the fucking enemy ... the problem is now when I think about it. It is like I participated in a bunch of burglaries and put all those people through all that shit.[4]

Behavior that complies with the ROE (rules of engagement) is acceptable within the military culture. For example, the ROE allows military personnel to detain civilians if they interfere with the completion of the assignment or mission, or if required for self-defense. These rules also specify that it is permissible to fire into a civilian populated area or building if the enemy is using them for military purposes or if military personnel find themselves confronted with a self-defense situation. In a war zone, these rules make sense; they particularly make sense to those who find themselves confronted in combat situations. In a war zone, the completion of the military mission is more essential than the safety and protection of civilians.

The content of many veteran war experiences can be quite graphic, and many veterans are hesitant to disclose the details of those experiences to a society that embraces individualism, and does not understand the influence and requirement of the group-oriented culture promoted in a war zone. One veteran said,

> I wanted to talk about some of the experiences I had in Iraq and Afghanistan, but I don't talk about them. I guess it is because I was a little confused. I mean some of the things I did over there were completely legitimate, but back here people would think those things are bad. I don't want people at home to think I am bad.[5]

While many veterans believe that those who have never been in war lack the capacity to understand their war experiences, another reason why many veterans do not discuss their war experiences with non-veterans is that their previous attempts to share their experiences resulted in negative responses. A female veteran talks about her attempt to discuss a deployment experience she encountered with a long-time friend.

> My friend and I went to school together. I joined the Army, while she remained at home and went to a junior college. When I got back, we hung around each other for a while. She kept asking me question about Iraq. I tried avoiding her questions. Finally, one day I just started talking to her about an incident that I was involved in on convoy duty. I talked about the I.E.D. (Improvised Explosive Device) explosion that killed three soldiers. The more I talked about the incident the more she became disturbed. Finally, I guess I realized that she really didn't want to hear my story.[6]

One veteran describes an incident he encountered while serving in Iraq.

> We came up to a vehicle destroyed by an I.E.D. We all ran over to the vehicle. Everyone inside was dead. I remember grabbing a soldier in the back of the vehicle by his legs. Blood was everywhere. He had a big hole on the right side of his head. When I pulled on his legs I saw shit coming out of the hole in his head. We got all the bodies out. My hands had blood all over them.[7]

In previous wars, veterans who served in the infantry or other combat arms occupations were more likely to experience traumatic events during war. Today, in the modern era of warfare, those who served in supportive roles in war zones also experience traumatic events. A female veteran who deployed to Iraq and performed duties in a medical unit said,

We were going down the road and I saw these bodies lying alongside the pavement. They were civilian bodies. One of them was a child. He might have been 6 or 7 years old. I don't know. I mean, I think about it still, and it makes me ask the question—why? I still don't know why. I try to explain it to myself, but I have no real answer.[8]

Throughout the interviews, veteran participants and veteran defendants provided many accountings of war experiences that were similar to those noted above. Some of their experiences were much more scathing than those noted above, while others were less scathing. Some veterans displayed emotion as they talked about their war experiences, while other veterans demonstrated emotional numbness.

Welcome home

Welcome home has become a celebratory ritual for many families and friends of veterans returning home from war. Reuniting with family members, former friends, and associates, for many veterans, is an anticipated festive activity. However, many veterans find that re-joining family and friends can also have an unfavorable outcome. As one Afghanistan veteran noted,

My girlfriend and other friends had a welcome home party for me a couple days after I got home from Afghanistan. I thought it would be a cool event. However, shortly after I arrived it seemed like everyone asked questions about what I did in Afghanistan. Eventually, some of those assholes started asking me questions related to combat. I was asked many times, if I had killed anyone or if I saw bodies. I got really pissed off. I got really drunk and passed out. The good thing about the party was that I realized if I drank a lot, and passed out, I didn't think about the war. I broke up with my girlfriend and haven't seen any of the others since the party. I still can't believe they asked me those questions.[9]

The most inflammatory question that family members and/or former friends ask veterans today is, "Did you kill anyone over there?" Over 90 percent of the veterans I interviewed said family members and/or former friends had confronted them with this question when they returned home from deployment. Most veterans said this question, more than any other inquiry, was most upsetting and often resulted in the veteran "shutting down" and/or distancing her/himself from the individual(s) who presented the question.

Turning to an earlier war—Vietnam—previous research found that 55 percent of Vietnam veterans had experienced high to very high combat exposure (Barrett et al., 1996). Vietnam veteran readjustment research identified four primary stressors/exposure dimensions among male Vietnam veterans, which include exposure to combat, exposure to abusive violence and related conflicts, deprivation, and loss of meaning and control. This study concluded that, while many Vietnam veterans were able to adjust to civilian life, many continued to experience mental problems more than a decade after leaving military service. This study also concluded that veterans with PTSD (Post-traumatic Stress Disorder) were at risk for relationship problems, substance abuse, unemployment, depression, and violent behavior (Kulka *et al.*, 1990). Among nearly 104,000 OEF/OIF (Operation Enduring Freedom/Operation Iraqi Freedom) veterans initially seen at U.S. Department of Veterans Affairs (DVA) health care facilities, 25 percent received mental health diagnoses, and nearly one-half of those veterans were dually or multiply diagnosed. PTSD was the most common service-related mental health diagnosis (Seal *et al.*, 2007). Another study found that 20 percent (about 300,000) of all OIF/OEF veterans were exhibiting symptoms of PTSD or major depression. The rates of PTSD and major depression occurred most frequently among members of the U.S. Army and U.S. Marines who were no longer on active duty. Exposure to combat was the primary predictor. Nearly one-half of the veterans seeking treatment from the DVA received minimally adequate treatment. These researchers argued that, if PTSD and serious depression are not treated, or if they are under-treated, there will be significant increases in suicide, drug and alcohol abuse, marital problems, and unemployment, for example. The estimated cost of treating PTSD and serious depression among OIF/OEF veterans for two years ranged from U.S. $4 billion to $6.2 billion (Tanielian and Jaycox, 2008). As many as 665,000 veterans may be submitting PTSD claims to the DVA, which takes into account the large percentage of military personnel serving multiple deployments (Atkinson *et al.*, 2009). The DVA's Fifth Annual Report (2007) suggests that at least 30 to 40 percent of Iraq veterans will face serious psychological problems associated with PTSD. Military personnel were more likely to report substance abuse, family problems, and symptoms of PTSD six months following their return from war (Waters, 2007). According to data revealed in the Mental Health Advisory Team (MHAT) IV Final report (2006) over one-half of the soldiers and Marines in Iraq who tested positive for a psychological injury expressed concern that their fellow service members would perceive them as weak. Nearly one-third were concerned that a mental health diagnosis would result in negative consequences to their career.

Richards *et al.* (1989) identified higher than expected rates of reported alcohol abuse among military personnel returning from past conflicts. Kulka *et al.* (1990) found that about 75 percent of male Vietnam combat veterans with PTSD had high levels of alcohol consumption, and that alcohol was the most common comorbid disorder among men with PTSD. Some studies compared individuals exposed to trauma but who did not meet the criteria for PTSD, individuals without traumatic experiences, and individuals with PTSD. Those individuals with PTSD were at a higher risk for developing alcohol-related problems (Stewart, 1996). Meisler (1996) found that between 60 and 80 percent of combat veterans with PTSD met the criteria for alcohol and substance abuse. Research supports the argument that PTSD is associated with changes in alcohol consumption (McFarlane, 1998).

While extensive investigations of alcohol misuse after veterans return from the current wars in Iraq and Afghanistan are wanting, service members who deploy and experience combat exposures are at higher risk of new-onset heavy weekly drinking, binge drinking, and alcohol-related problems. This study identified a strong association between combat deployment in Iraq and Afghanistan and alcohol-related problems (Jacobson *et al.*, 2008). The causes of alcohol use among OEF/OIF soldiers were dissimilar and quite possibly linked to reunification with family and friends, stress associated with reintegration, and self-medicating PTSD and other depressive symptoms (Meis, 2010).

Many variables related to Iraq and Afghanistan veterans' experiences returning home from war were contained in the interview schedule used throughout my study. One specific area of inquiry addressed relationships. The inability to develop or maintain relationships increases the likelihood of self-isolation. Before entering the military over 60 percent of the veterans whom I interviewed described their ability to develop relationships as either good or very good, while about 26 percent said average. After their military service, fewer than 15 percent said their ability to develop relationships was either good or very good, and about 28 percent said average. When asked to describe their ability to maintain relationships, 65 percent said either good or very good, while 26 percent answered average. After leaving the military, only 10 percent described their ability to maintain relationships as either good or very good, while just over 20 percent answered average. Most veterans said that many of their previous relationships disintegrated shortly after they returned home. The primary reason veterans provided for their disintegrating relationships was that they no longer had anything in common with their former friends, family, and spouse. Self-isolation often begins when the ability to develop and maintain relationships dissolves. For many veterans, alcohol became the replacement for their disintegrated relationships. Alcohol use or misuse accommodates self-isolation.

Over 80 percent of the veterans I interviewed said they used alcohol before they entered the military. That percentage increased to over 96 percent when asked about their alcohol use after leaving the military. Among those veterans who used alcohol before joining the military, over 50 percent said they used alcohol either weekly or monthly. Over 60 percent of those veterans who used alcohol after leaving the military said they used alcohol at least once per week or more. When asked to provide the reasons they chose to use alcohol, before entering the military, nearly 90 percent said peer pressure or enjoyment (e.g. parties). Fewer than 6 percent said they used alcohol for either depression or anxiety problems. After leaving the military, over 70 percent said they used alcohol for depression and anxiety issues, and most of these veterans said they preferred drinking alone—in isolation.

Veterans and crime

Austin Hamon, a French sociologist, once noted that war enables the reversal of the typical moral value of men's actions, and that living through war educates people for war, not peace (Hamon, 1918). Edith Abbott's (1927) research noted that during the U.S. Civil War males in the prison population across America decreased significantly. After the Civil War, there was a massive increase in the number of male prisoners. Abbott (1927) also noted significant increases of veteran prisoners in both England and the United States following World War I. Robert Casey (1923) discussed the mental health problems associated with returning veterans from World War I and the relationship of those problems to increased criminal involvement. In 1985, there were an estimated 100,200 veteran prisoners in state and federal prisons throughout the U.S. By 1998, the estimated number of veteran prisoners increased to 156,400 (Mumola, 2000). The BJS (Bureau of Justice Statistics) noted that the number of veteran prisoners in state and federal prisons declined to an estimated 140,000 in 2004, and Iraq-Afghanistan veterans made up 4 percent of veterans in both state and federal prison (Noonan and Mumola, 2007). In 2007, a study of the Marion County Jail in Salem, Oregon revealed that over 5 percent of their prisoners were veterans. In a 2011 study, approximately 10 percent of the prisoners in that jail were veterans (Brown *et al.*, 2013). In 2013, a national survey of veteran incarceration in state prisons was conducted. This study revealed astounding differences in veteran incarceration rates among the 18 randomly selected states. The states with the lowest percentage of incarcerated veterans were Connecticut (2.3 percent) and California (2.7 percent). Jurisdictions with the highest percentage of incarcerated veterans were Oregon (19.1 percent) and Nevada (11.3 percent). The average percentage of incarcerated veterans in state prisons among the 18 randomly selected states was 7.1 percent. Thus, many veterans return home for a brief period only to experience *redeployment* to jail and prison.

Throughout the vast majority of veteran defendant cases I have worked with, the veterans had no juvenile or criminal histories before entering the military. Nearly all of these veterans graduated from high school. A significant number of these veterans had some type of employment history before entering the military. Most of the veteran defendants had no disciplinary or legal problems during their military service. Over 75 percent of the veteran defendants had problems with alcohol misuse leading up to the instant offense that resulted in their arrest. Nearly 65 percent of these veteran defendants had been engaging in some form of self-isolation at the time of their arrest. One purpose for conducting this study was to identify differences between the veteran participants and the veteran defendants. The only significant distinction found was that the veteran defendants *got caught*. Nearly 41 percent of the veteran participants had engaged in illegal behavior after leaving the military but that behavior did not result in an arrest.

Military suicides

Another remnant of war is *veteran suicide*. The BBC News (2013) reported that in 2012 more British soldiers and veterans committed suicide than British military-related deaths in Afghanistan. Unlike the U.S., the British government does not record suicide rates among ex-soldiers. A military spokesperson for the Ministry of Defence stated that active-duty military suicides were extremely rare and much lower than the civilian rate of suicide in England (Telegraph, 2013). Recent data, provided by the U.S. Department of Veterans Affairs (DVA), indicate that 22 veterans commit suicide each day in the United States. Veterans 50 years old and over make up 69 percent of veteran suicides (Kemp and Bossarte, 2013). The U.S. Department of Veteran Affairs reported that male veteran suicides, under the age of 30, increased by 44 percent. Female suicides increased by 11 percent. Among the 22 veteran suicides per day, five are patients in the DVA health system (Kemp, 2014). A study of veteran suicides in California found that World War II veterans were nearly four times more likely to commit suicide than their non-veteran age counterparts, while younger veterans are more than two times more likely to commit suicide than their non-veteran age counterparts (Glantz, 2010).

Conclusion

Thank you for your service. In America, this is the most frequently used statement people—including officials—use to greet veterans returning home. This greeting makes many veterans uncomfortable. This is particularly true for those veterans who served in combat zones. Most combat veterans served to help and protect their buddies—not to serve their country. Veterans are more likely to appreciate greetings such as *welcome back* or *welcome home.*

Nearly all of the veteran participants and defendants I interviewed talked about problems they experienced in their attempts to receive adequate treatment and services. Most of these veterans who sought treatment through the DVA for medical issues indicated that the treatment was adequate. However, when asked about their experiences with DVA mental health services, most veterans who applied or received mental health treatment described their experiences as hideous. The most significant problem related to providing mental health services for veterans is the insufficient number of available mental health professionals. Mental health case managers and counselors are overwhelmed with the number of veterans needing and seeking treatment. Long waiting lists for veterans attempting to seek treatment and long periods between treatment sessions are frustrating and discouraging for many veterans (Institute of Medicine, 2010). A rarely mentioned issue is that most of the mental health providers are not veterans. Veterans with PTSD and other anxiety and/or depression issues often have problems trusting non-veterans— regardless of the academic credential or professional labels of mental health providers. Providers must acquire and practice cultural competency. They must become aware of distinctions between the military and civilian cultures. The development of a multidisciplinary approach, which could include Anthropologists, Psychologists, and Sociologists—to name but a few—to explain veteran behavior, would be a giant step forward.

Cultural *incompetence* aggravates the problem of veterans entangled in criminal justice. The legal system must consider changes in the model they currently use. Prosecutors typically challenge the relevance of information related to the veteran defendants' military culture. Many judges concur with those prosecutors by disallowing that information to juries. Prosecutors often present arguments, in their motions to disallow testimony regarding military culture, that information about a veteran's military history is simply a collection of excuses. There is a substantial difference between an *excuse* and an *explanation*. Finally, it would be most beneficial in veteran criminal cases if defense attorneys would learn and present the importance of cultural competency, as it applies to veterans and the military, to the trier of fact—judges and/or juries.

How might society prepare for the after-effects of war? Regardless of geographic locations, many options are available to alleviate some of the problems confronting veterans returning from war. If a country insists on *playing war*, they have an ethical obligation to inform the citizens they recruit about the *realities of war*. One of those realities is that veterans returning home from war often return a completely different person. Second, there should always be adequate medical and mental health services available for veterans coming home from war. If a country cannot afford those services, that country should not play war. Finally, family members and friends of veterans must stop asking veterans stupid questions, such as "Did you kill anyone over there?" These issues pertain to all countries involved in war. After all, war is war.

Notes

1 A statement from an anonymous male veteran who served in the U.S. Marine Corps with two deployments to Iraq.
2 A statement from an anonymous male veteran who served in the U.S. Army in Iraq and Afghanistan.
3 A statement from an anonymous female veteran who served in the U.S. Army in Iraq.
4 A statement from an anonymous male veteran who served in the U.S. Marine Corps with one deployment in Iraq and two deployments in Afghanistan.
5 A statement from an anonymous male veteran participant who served in the U.S. Army and who deployed twice to Iraq.
6 A statement from an anonymous female veteran participant who served in the U.S. Army in Iraq.
7 A statement from an anonymous male veteran defendant who served in the U.S. Marines in Iraq.
8 A statement from an anonymous female veteran who served in the U.S. Army in Iraq.
9 A statement from an anonymous male veteran who served in the U.S. Marines in Iraq and Afghanistan.

References

Abbott, E. (1927) "The Civil War and the Crime Wave of 1865–70." *Social Service Review*, 1(2): 212–234.

Atkinson, M.P., Guetz, L., and Wein, L.M. (2009) "A Dynamic Model for Posttraumatic Stress Disorder Among U.S. Troops in Operation Iraqi Freedom," *Management Science*, 55(9): 1454–1468.

Australian Government Department of Veteran Affairs (2007) *Annual Report 2006-7*, Canberra, Australia. Available: www.ag.gov.au/cca.

Barrett, D.H., Resnick, H.S., Foy, D.W., Dansky, B.S., Flanders, W.D., and Stroup, N. E. (1996) "Combat Exposure and Adult Psychosocial Adjustment among US Army Veterans Serving in Vietnam, 1965–1971," *Journal of Abnormal Psychology*, 105(4): 575–581.

Bamberger, P. and Hasgall, A. (1995) "Instructor Role in Educational Organizations Having the Characteristics of Total Institutions," *Journal of Educational Administration*, 33(3): 68–85.

BBC News. (2013) "UK Soldier and Veteran Suicides 'Outstrip Afghan Deaths'." Available: www.bbc.co.uk/news/uk-23259865.

Brown, W.B. (2005) "It Means Something: The Ghosts of War" in Berger, R.J. and Quinney, R. (eds) *Storytelling Sociology: Narrative as Social Inquiry*, Boulder, CO: Lynne Rienner.

Brown, W.B. (2008) "Another Emerging Storm: Iraq and Afghanistan Veterans with PTSD in the Criminal Justice System," *Justice Policy Journal*, 5(2). Available: http://www.cjcj.org/news/5574.

Brown, W.B. (2010) "War, Veterans, and Crime" in Herzog-Evans, M. (ed.) *Transnational Criminology*, Netherlands: Wolf Legal Publishers.

Brown, W.B. (2011) "From War Zones to Jail: Veteran Reintegration Problems," *Justice Policy Journal*, 8(1). Available: www.cjcj.org/news/5579.

Brown, W.B. (2014) "Spinning the Bottle: A Comparative Analysis of Veteran Defendants and Veterans Not Entangled in Criminal Justice" in Hunter, B. (ed.) *The Attorney's Guide to Defending Veterans in Criminal Court*, DC Press.

Brown, W. B., Stanulis, R. Theis, B., Farnsworth, J., and Daniels, D. (2013) "The Perfect Storm: Veterans, Culture and the Criminal Justice System," *Justice Policy Journal*, 10(2). Available: www.cjcj.org/news/6871.

Caputo, P. (1977) *A Rumor of War*, New York: Holt, Rinehart and Winston.

Casey, R.J. (1923) "The Lost Legion: 20,000 Veterans are in Prison—How Many of Them Ought to be in the Hospital," *The American Legion Weekly*, 7: 24–27.

Emerson, G. (1976) *Winners and Losers: Battles, Retreats, Gains, Losses and Ruins from the Vietnam War*, New York: Harcourt Brace Jovanovich.

Glantz, A. (2010) "Suicide Rates Soar among WWII Vets, Records Show," *The Bay Citizen*. Available: www.baycitizen.org/news/veterans/suicide-rates-soar-among-wwii-vets.

Goffman, E. (1961) *Asylums: Essays on the Social Situation of Mental Patients and Other Inmates*, New York: Doubleday.

Goodell, J. and Hearn, J. (2011) *Shade it Black: Death and After in Iraq*, Philadelphia: Casemate.

Grossman, D. (1995) *On Killing: The Psychological Cost of Learning to Kill in War and Society*, New York: Little, Brown and Company.

Hagopian, A., Flaxman, A.D., Takaro, T.K., Esa, S.A., Shatari, A., Rajaratnam, J., Becker, S., Levin-Rector, A., Galway, L., Hadi Al-Yasseri, B.J., Weiss, W.M. Murray, M.J. and Burnham, G. (2013) "Mortality in Iraq Associated with the 2003–2011 War and Occupation: Findings from a National Cluster Sample Survey by the University Collaborative Iraq Mortality Study," *PLOS Medicine*, DOI: 10.1371/journal.pmed.1001533.http://www.plosmedicine.org/article/info%3Ad oi%2F10.1371%2Fjournal.pmed.1001533.

Hamon, A. (1918) *Lessons of the World War*, London: T Fisher Unwin.

Hardt, M., and Negri. A. (2004) *Multitude: War and Democracy in the Age of Empire*, New York: Penguin Books.

Headquarters, Department of the Army (2006) "Army Leadership: Competent, Confident, and Agile," (FM 6–22) Washington, DC: Headquarters, Department of the Army.

Hirschman, C., Preston, S., and Loi, V.M. (1995) "Vietnamese Casualties During the American War: A New Estimate," *Population and Development Review*, 21(4) 783–812.

Hoge, C.W. (2010) *Once a Warrior Always a Warrior: Navigating the Transition from Combat to Home, Including Combat Stress, PTSD, and TBI*, Guilford, CT: Globe Pequot Press.

Institute of Medicine. (2010) *Returning Home from Iraq and Afghanistan: Preliminary Assessment of Readjustment Needs of Veterans, Service Members, and Their Families*, Washington, DC: The National Academies Press.

Iraq Coalition Casualty Count. (2014) Retrieved from: http://icasualties.org.

Jacobson, I.G., Ryan, M., Smith, T.C., Amoroso, P.J., Boyko, E.J., Gackstetter, G.D., Wells, N.S., and Bell, T.S. (2008) "Alcohol Use and Alcohol-Related Problems Before and After Military Combat Deployment," *JAMA*, 300(6): 663–675.

Kemp, J. (2014) "Suicide Rates in VHA Patients through 2011 with Comparisons with Other Americans and other Veterans through 2010," Washington, DC: Veterans Health Administration.

Kemp, J. and Bossarte (2013) *Suicide Data Report, 2012*, Washington, DC: Mental Health Service—Suicide Prevention Program, Department of Veterans Affairs.

Kulka, R., Schlenger, W., Fairbank, J., Hough, R., Jordon, B., Marmar, C., and Weiss, D. (1990), *Trauma and the Vietnam Generation: Report of Findings from the National Vietnam Veterans Readjustment Study*, New York: Burner-Mazel.

McFarlane, A.C. (1998) "Epidemiological Evidence about the Relationship between PTSD and Alcohol Abuse: The Nature of the Association," *Addictive Behavior*, 23 (6): 813–825.

Meis, L.A. (2010) "Intimate Relationships Among Returning Soldiers: The Mediating and Moderating Roles of Negative Emotionality, PTSD Symptoms, and Alcohol Problems," *Journal of Traumatic Stress*, 23(5): 564–572.

Meisler, AW. (1996) "Trauma, PTSD and Substance Abuse," *PTSD Research Quarterly*, 7 (4): 1–8.

Mental Heath Advisory Team (MHAT) IV. (2006) "Operation Iraqi Freedom: Final Report," Office of the Surgeon Multinational Force-Iraq and Office of the Surgeon General, U.S. Army Medical Command.

Mumola, C.J. (2000) "Veterans in Prison or Jail," Bureau of Justice Statistics: Special Report, Washington DC: U.S. Department of Justice.

Noonan, M.E. and Mumola, C.J. (2007) "Veterans in State and Federal Prisons, 2004," Bureau of Justice Statistics: Special Report, Washington DC: U.S. Department of Justice.

Obermeyer, Z., Murray, C.J.L., and Gakidou, E. (2008) "Fifty Years of Violent War Deaths from Vietnam to Bosnia: Analysis of Data from the World Health Survey Program," *BMJ*, 336(7659): 1482–1486.

Richards, M.S., Goldberg, J., Rodin, M.B., and Anderson, R.J. (1989) "Alcohol Consumption and Problem Drinking in White Male Veterans and Nonveterans," *American Journal of Public Health*, 7(8): 1011–1015.

Rouche, J.D. (2007) *The Veteran"s PTSD Handbook*, Washington, DC: Potomac Books, Inc.

Seal, K.H., Bertenthal, D., Miner, C.R., Sen, S., Marmar, C. (2007) "Bringing the War Back Home: Mental Health Disorders among 103,788 US Veterans Returning from Iraq and Afghanistan Seen at Department of Veteran Affairs Facilities," *Archives of Internal Medicine*, 167(5): 476–482.

Stewart, S.H. (1996) "Alcohol Abuse in Individuals Exposed to Trauma: A Critical Review," *Psychological Bulletin*, 120(1): 83–112.

Tanielian, T. and Jaycox, L.H. (ed.) (2008) *The Invisible Wounds of War: Psychological and Cognitive Injuries, Their Consequences, and Services to Assist Recovery*, Santa Monica, CA: Rand Corporation.

Telegraph (2013) "More British Soldiers Commit Suicide than Die in Battle, Figures Suggest," Available: www.telegraph.co.uk/news/uknews/defence/10178403/More-British-soldiers-commit-suicide-than-die-in-battle-figures-suggest.html.

Turse, N. (2013) *Kill Anything That Moves: The Real American War in Vietnam*, New York: Metropolitan Books.

U.S. Department of Veterans Affairs (2007), *Fifth Annual Report of the Department of Veterans Affairs Undersecretary for Health Special Committee on Post-Traumatic Stress Disorder*, Washington, DC: Department of Veteran Affairs.

Waters, R. (2007) "Iraq War's Mental Impact Grows Months After Return," Bloomberg News, 14th November. Available: www.bloomberg.com/apps/news?pid=newsarchive&sid=anALPscp4c.Y.

Wood, E.W. (2006) *Worshipping the Myths of World War II: Reflections on America's Dedication to War*, Washington, DC: Potomac Books.

Zurcher, L.A. (2007) "The Naval Recruit Training Center: A Study of Role Assimilation in a Total Institution," *Sociological Inquiry*, 37(1): 85–98.

Part 3

War, sexual violence and visual trauma

7 Sexual and sexualized violence in armed conflict

*Christopher W. Mullins and
Nishanth Visagaratnam*

Introduction

Sexual assault, and a host of other sexualized violences, routinely occur during armed conflicts. It is typically assumed that this takes the form of soldiers raping civilian women. While these events do occur, the nature and variety of sexual assault and other sexualized violences is more complex. Both men and women are targets for rape and gendered violence of a highly sexualized nature. We use the term 'conflict sexual assault' to refer to coerced sexual contacts that occur in the course of an armed conflict occurring in either an active combat zone or an occupied territory. In addition, conflicts produce highly sexualized violences, that is, those actions which do not involve sexual contact but are clearly sexualized and highly gendered. Torture involving the victim's genitals, mutilation of the same, and being stripped naked in front of others for the purposes of humiliation are all examples seen in both historical and recent conflicts. Such acts are sometimes referred to as 'gender-based violence', as they are motivated by and given symbolic meaning from gender norms and expectations. We will use the terms 'sexualized' and 'gender-based' interchangeably here.

From antiquity through the early modern era, rape's association with warfare was a result of the chattel status women that held. Where women are seen as property, they are seen as plunder. The rules of war in these historical periods gave the victors the right to appropriate the property of their enemies; this extended to legitimating temporary sexual access to women or abducting them and taking them as wives, either for the short term of a campaign or permanently. Even in contemporary contexts, war rapes may be more prevalent in societies where women have few social or legal rights (i.e. certain sub-Saharan African conflicts). While the norms about plunder began to shift in the nineteenth century (see Sandholtz, 2007), rules about sexual violence were slower to be modified. Changes in behaviour lagged further behind. As we will explore in this chapter, the raping of the enemy's women was first officially prohibited in the later nineteenth century. By the early twenty-first century, domestic and international law universally criminalize such behaviour. Yet, widespread sexual violence persists in many conflicts. Though, as

Wood (2006, 2009) has pointed out, the amount of sexual violence does vary within and between conflicts and, as we will explore here, it can take a variety of functional types. This chapter will examine the types and contexts of sexual violence in armed conflicts, focusing on those towards the end of the twentieth century and the start of the twenty-first. It begins with a brief overview of extant legal prohibitions, then two cases are examined in depth: Sierra Leone and Sri Lanka.

Law

Sexual violence in armed conflict is criminalized in both international and domestic law. This has been the case since the mid-nineteenth century. The first formal code of conduct applied to the behaviour of soldiers in combat, US Army General Order 100, was issued in April of 1863 during the United States civil war. The so-called Lieber code was the first extensive set of codified rules for the operation of armies in the field (Witt, 2012). Section II, Article 44 explicitly criminalizes 'All wonton violence committed against persons in the invaded country', it specifically mentions rape and establishes that a superior can order the offender to 'be lawfully killed on the spot'. Anecdotal discussions of its applications appear in histories of the war, but there has not been a systematic analysis of military commission records to determine the extent or contexts of its use. The Lieber code is important not only due to its lasting influence on the U.S. Uniform Code of Military Conduct, but due to its influence on later treaties and other nations' codes regulating their own armed forces. It becomes a model that other states quickly adopt for their own use.

General Order 100 also served as the foundation of later international treaties on the conduct of warfare, including the 1864 Geneva Convention, the 1874 International Declaration Concerning the Laws and Customs of War and the Hague Conventions of 1889 and 1907. While the 1864 convention focuses on the treatment of soldiers by an opposing army (it only mentions civilians in the context of those helping to retrieve injured combatants), the other agreements are more broadly focused. They do not directly mention sexual assault, but contain provisions for the protection of civilian populations that would clearly include rape. For example Article 38 of the 1874 convention protects 'Family honour and rights, and the lives and property of persons, as well as their religious convictions and their practice'. Western culture at the time would definitely see rape as a violation of family honour and rights, even if it did not accord women equal social and legal rights. Herein lies one of the motivating factors for the more systematic use of sexual violence in armed conflicts that will be explored below. The rape of a woman is seen literally and symbolically as a failure of the men obligated to protect her. It is both a physical and social attack.

Currently, the Four Geneva Conventions and their attendant protocols stand as the most widely adopted standards of the conduct of armed forces in the field. A total of 194 of the 195 currently recognized independent states have adopted the 1949 conventions (the new state of South Sudan being the exception), with 166 also adopting the two additional protocols of 1977. Thus, the 1949 Conventions have effectively universal jurisdiction and the 1977 protocols nearly so. While the 1949 agreements do not mention sexual assault by name, as with earlier treaties, it seems to be clearly covered by existing language. Article 3 of the Fourth Geneva Convention prohibits military actors from abusing civilians, specifically referencing violence, hostage taking, and 'outrages upon personal dignity' (Article 3 (c)). These provisions would seem to cover sexual and sexualized violences. The 1977 protocols use much more specific language. Additional Protocol I provides specific protection for women against 'rape, forced prostitution and any other form of indecent assault' (Article 76 (1)). Article 77, Section 1 extends the same protection to children. Protocol I only applies to international conflicts, but Protocol II, covering non-international conflicts, protects all people from 'outrages upon personal dignity, in particular humiliating and degrading treatment, rape, enforced prostitution and any form of indecent assault' (Article 4 (e)). Thus, by the later twentieth century, there is strong international agreement prohibiting war rapes.

The most recent international law focused on military matters is the Rome Statute of the International Criminal Court, currently ratified by 122 states. The statute created the first permanent International Criminal Court (ICC), designed to try individuals responsible for mass atrocity. Language in the statute concerning sexual and sexualized violence is much more specific and encompassing. Under the Rome Statute, sexual violence against men and women by combatants or other representatives of the state can be charged as a war crime, a crime against humanity or a form of genocide, depending on the actual actions and the nature of the conflict in which they occur. In the context of genocide, systematic rape would violate Article 6, Section (b), 'causing serious bodily or mental harm'. As we will examine below, systematic sexual assault is a frequent characteristic of genocide events; it is one mechanism of population elimination.

As part of Crime Against Humanity, Article 7, 1 (g) prohibits 'Rape, sexual slavery, enforced prostitution, forced pregnancy, enforced sterilization, or any other form of sexual violence of comparable gravity'. Such provisions would apply to the behaviour of a repressive state using violence against its own citizens or those of another state, whether or not there is an ongoing conflict event. Concerning war crimes, Article 8, 2 (b) (xxii) prohibits 'Committing rape, sexual slavery, enforced prostitution, forced pregnancy, as defined in Article 7, Paragraph 2 (f), enforced sterilization, or any other form of sexual violence also constituting a grave breach of the Geneva Conventions'. Article 8 applies to actions committed during either an international or internal armed struggle.

Not only does the Rome Statute contain the clearest and most specific language about sexual assault and other sexualized violences, the

International Criminal Court's Office of the Prosecutor has shown a high degree of interest in prosecuting leaders on such charges. To date, the ICC has issued arrest warrants for 26 people; 16 of those warrants list sexual violence charged as both war crimes and crimes against humanity. From 2008 until 2012, US law professor Catharine MacKinnon served as Special Gender Adviser to the Prosecutor. The ICC's jurisdiction is not universal; it was designed as a complementary court to step in when states were unwilling or unable to adjudicate violations. For the ICC to have jurisdiction the conflict must occur in the territory of a state's party, be voluntarily submitted to the court by a state or be granted by the United Nations Security Council. This does not grant impunity to most belligerents, as prohibitions against sexual violence versus civilians (and prisoners) are contained within the Four Geneva Conventions and their attendant Protocols.

National military codes of conduct tend to prohibit this behaviour as well. For example, soldiers serving in the United States Army have faced legal sanctions for rape of civilians since the issuing of the above-mentioned Lieber code. Currently, the US Uniform Code of Military Justice, for example, specifically prohibits rape (Chapter 47, subchapter X, article 120), stalking (ar120b), rape of a child (ar120c) and other sexual misconduct (ar120d). While it is likely that not every solider who has committed sexual violence during the conflicts in Iraq and Afghanistan has faced a Court Martial, there have been trials and convictions of especially egregious cases committed by troops in the field as well on bases at home. The UK's Armed Forces Act 2006 prohibits Disgraceful Conduct of a cruel or indecent kind (sec 23) and all actions that are criminalized in England and Wales (sec 42 Criminal Conduct). These provisions clearly prohibit sexual assault. The UK has convicted soldiers of sexual assaults and sexualized violence in the recent Iraq and Afghanistan conflicts as well, though again, we do not know the true frequency of these acts, nor do we know the likelihood of prosecution and conviction. In sum, extant law thoroughly criminalizes sexual assault and other forms of sexualized violence that occur during an armed conflict. Yet the actual application of these laws appears to be infrequent.

In addition, whilst sexualized forms of violence appear to be ubiquitous Wood (2006, 2009) points to their variability. They vary in frequency, in motivation and in kind. We can generally characterize these acts into one of three types by looking at both motivation of the offender and contextual elements of the offence: opportunistic assault, forced confinements for the purpose of sexual availability and violences that are used as express military tactics. These categories are based on the first author of this chapter's work on rape during the Rwandan genocide (see Mullins 2009a, 2009b) but are applicable to non-genocidal conflicts as well, with some additional tactical uses seen. However, whilst some are developing large N data sets for statistical analysis, rich case studies are an excellent way to develop a more grounded theory of war rape. So, in this chapter we shall analyse two cases: Sierra Leone and Sri Lanka. Both cases are civil wars with long durations that have recently been concluded. Both show variation in use of sexual violence by belligerent parties and provide different contexts for exploration.

Sierra Leone

Sierra Leone, a former UK colony on the West African Atlantic coast, is home to 16 ethnic groups and is religiously diverse. It is just under 73,000 square miles in size. Its primary economic revenues come from agriculture, but it is better known for its diamond mines in the eastern portion of the country. It was these very minerals that enticed Charles Taylor, president of neighbouring Liberia, to support the rebel forces. Six years after Sierra Leone gained independence in 1961, the All People's Congress (APC) took control of the state. Like in many other one-party states in the region, the APC's government was widely seen as corrupt, nepotistic and inefficient. The primary insurgent group, the Revolutionary United Front (RUF) was composed of numerous factions, but primarily organized in Liberia by Foday Saukoh with the financial and military assistance of Taylor's regime. Supported heavily by Liberian militias, the RUF launched their invasion from the neighbouring nation on 23rd March 1991, starting a ten-year war that is well known for its brutality, massive kidnapping of children as a recruitment strategy, epidemic looting and wide-spread sexual violence.

Initially the Sierra Leonian Army (SLA) opposed the RUF as well as the Nigerian-led Economic Community of West African States Monitoring Group (ECOMOG) which had been initially deployed in Sierra Leone to control Taylor's Liberia. Groups of traditional hunters and warriors, the Kamajor, self-organized to oppose the RUF and later in the conflict they would also clash with government and ECOMOG forces as well. Starting in 1993, pro-government militias – termed Civil Defence Forces (CDF) – were organized and in 1995 the government hired Executive Outcomes, a South African 'security' service, to provide additional military assistance. In May of 1997, a coup led by Major Koroma ousted then President Kabbah and produced a new government that called itself the Armed Forces Revolutionary Council (AFRC), with an army composed primarily of disaffected SLA troops. The AFRC abolished political parties and declared a ruling council composed of military officers. The next month the AFRC reached out to and united with the RUF. Then, breaking with their early negotiation with ECOMOG, they announced elections and returned to civilian rule in four years.

Kabbah's exiled government received support from ECOMOG forces and the CDFs to retake control of the country by mid-1998. July of that year saw the establishment and deployment of The United Nations Observer Mission in Sierra Leone (UNOMSIL). As a response to rebel success, in October the mission was increased in size and became the United Nations Mission in Sierra Leone with much more peacekeeping responsibilities. By the end of the year the rebel groups had retaken control of about half the country, including the diamond fields. In January of 1999, the RUF/AFRC attacked and took control of the capital, Freetown, in an atrocity-filled campaign that they called 'Operation No Living Thing'. The three-week occupation was infamous for crimes against civilians. July of 1999 saw the government and rebel groups agree to the terms of the Lomé accords, but fighting within rebel groups and between the rebel forces and government forces continued. It was not until May of 2002 that the RUF officially disarmed and transformed itself into a political, rather than military, organization.

Forces from all sides committed sexual violence against civilians, including ECOMOG and UN forces. It is generally agreed that the RUF committed more, and more severe atrocities, in general, and sexual violence crimes specifically. Within the RUF, Liberian contingents are often pointed to as the worst offenders. In his testimony before the Truth and Reconciliation Commission (TRC), retired Captain Kosia, an RUF officer, directly blamed Liberian troops for all atrocities, including sexual violence, directly admitting he and his officers could not control them. He did acknowledge though, 'when the boys were at the front lines, it was difficult for the high command to know what they were doing' (The Truth and Reconciliation Commission, 2003: 62). He also acknowledged the taking of 'bush wives' as a common practice. Among native forces, the CDF were believed to be the best-behaved group; this is often explained by the fact that they were protecting their communities and were not deployed in other regions. However, it is difficult to ascertain responsibility for many of the war crimes, including sexual violence, which occurred. Individuals would float from one force to the next; so-called 'sobels', (soldiers by day, rebel by night), would maintain their SLA affiliations and duties during the day, but at night participate in RUF activities.

The brutality of the conflict, especially after the Freetown campaign, has become notorious. In addition to systematic sexual violence by the RUF, and frequent sexual violence by other participants, many other crimes occurred. Rebels would use machetes to amputate civilian's limbs and cut out tongues to dissuade civilians from giving information to the government. Amputations increased in advance of elections to reduce turnout. They also abducted thousands of children to be pressed into service as child soldiers. Whilst many women became armed combatants, more became 'bush wives'. SLA and ECOMOG forces executed prisoners and suspected collaborators extra-judicially.

Through examining testimonies given to the TRC, we can see how sexual violence was a central experience of many Sierra Leonean women during the civil war. This resource, of course, is not a complete account of all crimes experienced: only certain people chose to come forward and may not have disclosed some victimization experiences. The stigma of being sexually assaulted in Sierra Leone is quite strong, providing victims with a strong incentive not to disclose their experiences (see MacKenzie, 2010). Out of 40,242 incidents reported to the TRC 3.3 per cent were for sexual violence: Rape (n=626, 1.6 per cent), Sexual Abuse (n=486, 1.2 per cent) or Sexual Slavery (n=191, 0.5 per cent). No males reported a rape or sexual slavery incident but 299 of the sexual abuse cases were male. It should also be noted that of the 5,968 people who reported having been abducted, 2,058 were female. While not universal, many sources claim that abducted females were raped by one perpetrator, or a gang of militia, as soon as they got back to camp. It seems likely that even amongst those who were willing to give testimony to the commission, they were not willing to disclose everything they experienced. The Truth Commission report provides narratives of assaults by all combatant groups. As prior work has pointed out (Cohen, 2013; MacKenzie, 2012), the RUF committed the greatest number of atrocities; the CDF had the fewest incidents attributed to them.[1]

Typically, opportunistic assaults occurred during raids on civilian villages. The RUF were particularly dependent on raiding for supplies, and other raids were also directed toward the abduction of children. While looting and kidnapping was taking place, sexual assaults would occur by lone assailants or in groups. In some villages, the RUF would gather captives in a central location and rape the women and girls in front of their husbands, fathers and brothers. On other occasions, the rebels would order civilians to commit atrocities on each other. For example, a former RUF abductee described such an event in his testimony before the TRC. He had just been abducted by a group, commanded directly by Foday Saukoh, the head of the RUF. They forced him to carry ammunition boxes as they travelled. Soon the troops entered a village,

> where many people had been captured, and there was fire on many of the houses. When we dropped the boxes, I saw my mother and father; they were naked. There were also other people there. They ordered all the women to haves sex with their fathers; and all the men were ordered to have sex with their mothers. I shouted out that I had never done that. They asked me to identify my mother. When we got to the top of the bush, they put them all in a house, sprinkled petrol on the house and set the house on fire.
>
> (The Truth and Reconciliation Commission, 2003: 124)

This was not a unique occurrence (see MacKenzie, 2012). Once back in camp, abducted females were again raped, with a larger portion of these assaults being group assaults. Afterwards, most were given to a male as a 'bush wife'. She would then be responsible for cooking, to maintain a living area and be sexually available. Most seem to have had one 'bush husband', but others mentioned having a series of them. However, as many of the women who gave testimony to the TRC pointed out, being a 'bush wife' was no protection against future assaults. Not only were they required to be available at their husband's every whim, but also when he left the camp on a mission, multiple men in the camp would assault the woman.

Seen in the context of Sierra Leonean traditional culture, this form of marriage is not totally aberrant, though a less desirable situation. Traditional culture does not place a high value on women and sees them firmly as the property of their fathers or husbands. Rape is often viewed as a property crime, as it leaves the victim a less desirous marriage partner and thus reduces her bride price or presents the potential that her father will have to continue to support her long past an age where she should have left his household. A legally acceptable remedy in the wake of a rape was for the perpetrator to marry his victim. In part, this explains why some 'bush wives' stayed with their 'bush husbands' after the conflict. Such behaviour is further explained by the diminished marriage prospects they faced after having been a 'bush wife'. Despite this, many women who gave testimony to the TRC did indicate that they had established new romantic relationships in the post-conflict environment. While some rape victims described being shunned by husbands and family members, others claimed their husbands and/or families were supportive of them (which may be why they were willing to give public testimony to the TRC). Not all of the abducted girls became bush wives. A portion became active combatants, and this led Cohen (2013) to hypothesize that those units might rape less frequently. She found that not only was this not the case, but also women soldiers often participated in rapes of newly abducted girls. They would hold the victim down while males assaulted her and would themselves use objects to perpetrate sexual assaults.

Whilst women experienced the vast majority of sexual and sexualized violence, men were victimized as well. The testimonies given to the TRC contain one case of a male rape, though it is probable that most victimized men would not bring their experiences into a public forum such as the TRC. Men also experienced much sexualized violence other than rape. We have previously mentioned the cases where men were made to watch as their mothers, wives and daughters were raped, as well as instances where men were made to rape relatives. Men taken captive were routinely stripped naked in front of the village for the purposes of humiliation. For example: a prominent chief's son testifying before the TRC, who had an antagonistic relationship with the RUF, described numerous interrogations and sexualized humiliations. During one instance, the RUF came to his house, stripped him naked and made him walk across the village to the interrogation centre so that everyone saw him disrobed. During that interrogation he was kicked repeatedly in the groin, becoming impotent afterwards. Other men were castrated either before or after they were killed. In one particularly barbaric incident the RUF killed a Kamajor commander and the son of a local paramount chief, castrated him and wore the organ on a string around his neck.

The rebels were clearly systematically using rape to terrorize, humiliate and control the civilian population. It is unknown whether or not the rebel high command explicitly adopted the strategy; on-the-ground commanders clearly approved of the rapes and on occasion issued orders demanding assaults. For example, Staff Alhaji, second in command of his unit, ordered a group of young women gang-raped as punishment for an escape attempt. However, it is clear that some rebels were punished for sexual assaults. Numerous testimonies indicate that at some point in the conflict, the RUF high command issued orders that rape was punishable by death. Former members of the RUF told commissioners during their testimony that they knew of soldiers being executed for such incidents. However, such punishments appear to have been rare and occurred later in the conflict. As discussed above, some Sierra Leonean commanders blamed the Liberian contingents of the RUF; it is clear they were not the only troops responsible for sexual violence. This turn at the end of the conflict, as well as the testimonies presented to the TRC, are likely an attempt by the RUF to appear legitimate and regain social support of the people as it began its shift from a rebel fighting force into a political governing force. As Wood (2006, 2009) has suggested, once forces expect to govern and if they seek the support of the people, they will be disinclined toward especially systematic use of sexual assault; rather, stronger attempts will be made to control troops' actions to engender popular support.

The long civil war in Sierra Leone devastated the country and its citizens. War crimes, including sexual violence, were committed by both sides, though to varying degrees. RUF troops were the most frequent perpetrators, though some effort appeared to be made toward the end of the conflict to reign in some of the violence. A number of factors contributed to high levels of assaults by the rebels. Command was clearly diffuse and weak in the RUF. The initial force was composed of poor, disaffected young men with little in the way of economic opportunities. With few, if any, social connections in the field of operations, there was little in the way of consequences for sexual violence. As the conflict wore on, such behaviour clearly became normalized in the RUF; newly abducted recruits learned that this was allowable, if not expected, behaviour. As Cohen (2013) points out, it no doubt assisted in group bonding and cohesion. The use of sexual enslavement, enshrined in the practice of taking 'bush wives', was undergirded by traditional Sierra Leonean culture and gender norms. The CDFs' infrequent commission of sexual assault is likely due to the nature of these units: they were local men organized to specifically defend their own communities. The militia had strong ties to the community and community members, which no doubt exerted a fair amount of social control on their actions. They had little to gain and much to lose from such behaviour. Similarly, the Kamajours were more locally focused forces, with stronger local ties, who perpetuated less sexual violence than rebel or state troops. However, it must be noted that the Kamajours did not fight a clean war. They engaged in extra-judicial executions and waged a campaign of terror against villages that they felt did not sufficiently resist the RUF. Existing evidence suggests that they did not rely on sexual violence in enacting their 'punishments' of 'collaborators'.

The sexual violence during this civil war was extensive, but exhibited quite a bit of variation across type, context and belligerent party. State and ECOMOG units did not deploy rape as a tactic in the conflict but are otherwise only distinguished from the rebels by committing fewer opportunistic assaults and taking fewer 'bush wives'. Of course, with the 'sobel' practices of state troops, the sexual violence they committed could easily be attributed to rebel groups. In the wake of the war, an ad hoc tribunal was established to prosecute those most responsible for the war-time atrocities. The Special Court for Sierra Leone brought indictments against AFRC, RUF and Kamajors leaders, as well as the Liberian President, Charles Taylor. Every indictment except the Kamajors case included charges of sexual violence.

Sri Lanka

Sri Lanka, formerly Ceylon, received its independence from the UK on 4th February 1948. In 1956, S.W.R.D. Banadaranike was elected Prime Minister and introduced the Sinhala Only Act of 1956, which recognized the Sinhalese language as the official language of the government. For the minorities, The Sinhala Only Act was a symbol of oppression; it ignited the beginning of a revolution for a separate state and equal rights. In 1958 parts of the act were reversed to the Tamil Language Special Provisions Act (De Silva, 1981). The total population of Sri Lanka is roughly 21,481,334 constituting 73.8 per cent Sinhalese, 7.2 per cent Sri Lankan Moors, 4.6 per cent Indian Tamils, 3.9 per cent Sri Lankan Tamils, 0.5 per cent others, and 10 per cent unspecified (Central Intelligence Agency (CIA), 2013). A total of 69.1 per cent percent of the population is Buddhists (mostly practised by Sinhalese), 7.6 per cent Muslim, 7.1 per cent Hindu (mostly practised by Tamils), 6.2 per cent Christian, and approximately 10 per cent who are unspecified (CIA, 2013). A figure of 24.9 per cent are 0–14 years of age (male 2,705,953; female 2,599,717); 67.2 per cent are 15–64 years of age (male 6,993,668; female 7,313,440); and 7.9 per cent are 65 years of age and over (male 720,219; female 950,916) (CIA, 2013).

There have been close to three decades of ethnic conflict in Sri Lanka between the minority Liberation Tigers of Tamil Eelam (LTTE) rebels and the Sri Lankan government. In March 2004, LTTE commander, Colonel Karuna (Vinayagamoothi Muralitharan) stepped away from the LTTE to start his own group called the Tamil Makkal Viduthalai Pulikal (TMVP), because he did not judge Prabhakaran, the founder of the LTTE, to have treated eastern Tamils equally to northern Tamils. After President Mahinda Rajapaska was elected President in 2005, the military captured the LTTE-controlled Eastern Province during July 2007 and, in May 2009, the state took control over the northern province and defeated the LTTE, bringing the long, bloody war to an end (UTHR(J), 2009).

The almost three-decade long war in Sri Lanka resulted in at least 100,000 people killed and millions of Tamils and Sinhalese living as diaspora (Deedadayalan, 2011: xxiii). The state presented its perspective of the events unequivocally by controlling major institutions and resources (e.g. media, medical aid, educational funding) throughout the land to the cost of thousands of citizens (Weiss, 2012). According to the Sri Lankan government, they were freeing more than 300,000 Tamils from the LTTE, the 'bloodless' terrorists, and conducting the 'world's largest hostage rescue' (Weiss, 2012: xvii). During September 2008, the Sri Lankan government ordered many of the humanitarian agencies out of the Vanni area (one of the most war-stricken areas) and this worsened the conditions for civilians.

In Sri Lanka much of the sexual violence committed was targeted by the state soldiers, police officers and security forces against women and men associated with the minorities (Tamils) (Wood, 2006: 328). There have been reports of Tamil females experiencing various forms of sexual violence, such as gang rape after an arrest or detention at a checkpoint due to the suspicion that either they or a member of their family is in the LTTE (Wood, 2006). Wood (2006) notes that, whilst sexual violence does not appear to be widespread, sexual violence against Tamil women by the state has been, and this drove Tamil females to join the LTTE (Wood, 2006). Gender-based violence is ever present and existed in Sri Lanka during and after the war. It was committed for a number of reasons: for power, to control the population, for torture, to situate fear within the population, to shame, for potential ethnic cleansing and to acquire information. Such atrocities are made possible through sexual slavery, forced prostitution and rape.

There are two kinds of sexual violence utilized by the state towards the minority Tamils: one is custodial rape and the other is sexual torture of males and females (Wood, 2009). Sexual torture took place in detention camps, police stations and army bases in various forms, such as raping victims with plantain flowers soaked in chilies and other objects, applying electric shocks or chilies to the genitals, forced sexual relations with other prisoners and piercing genitals or slamming genitalia into a drawer (Wood, 2009). Violations experienced by victims at the internally displaced people (IDP) camps included, but are not limited to, sexual favours in exchange for food and the singling out of persons in camps with links to the Tamil insurgency (Human Rights Watch, 2009). Females with no other means of supporting themselves or their families were forced to sell sex for money and supplies, some females were raped outside of detention camps when the police removed them or military personnel and others, such as those involved with the LTTE, were raped in the detention centres.

Channel 4 surreptitiously videotaped the conditions of internment camps and found that female prisoners were forced to stand before male soldiers naked 'and made allegations of rape and chronic food shortages in the camp' (European Center for Constitutional and Human Rights, 2010: 15). Several cases of alleged rapes of 14-, 15- and 16-year-old girls at the internment camps appeared before the Vavuniyaa District Judge in October 2009; there was also a case of state soldiers raping a mentally disabled female Tamil youth at the Vavuniyaa hospital, a highly militarized area (European Center for Constitutional and Human Rights, 2010). Wood (2006) found a lack of sexual violence practised by the LTTE, although there are other forms of violence forced upon the civilians by the rebels, such as forcibly recruiting child soldiers and coercing its members to be suicide bombers. However, fear, stigma and the need for resources for survival are driving forces for the lack of reporting sexual violence by victims.

Tamil women were not the only targets of sexual violence at the hands of security forces. During the second uprising of the Janatha Vimukthi Peramuna from 1987 to 1990, Sinhalese women were targets of sexual violence at the hands of security forces (Human Rights Watch, 2013). Human rights organizations formally recognized over 1,000 cases of torture of Sinhalese men and women during police custody; over a two-year period many involved rape and sexual violence (Human Rights Watch, 2013). An example of the extent of this violence includes a Tamil woman being gang-raped in Amparai and later killed in a police station where they placed a grenade in her vagina (Wood, 2009); another includes the raping of females (children) at checkpoints and at military quarters (Wood, 2009).

Research presented by Fulu *et al.* (2013) from the United Nations multi-country study on men and violence in Asia and the Pacific questioned why it is that some men rape and what can be done to prevent it. However, there is perhaps an increased recognition that sexual violence is no longer a gender-based violence only experienced by women as victims and perpetrated by men; gender-based violence needs to be redefined to be inclusive of the experience of sexual violence by both men and women. Their study indicates that more women are treated as victims compared to men, but men are less likely to report victimization experienced, especially if it is sexual violence.

Sexual violence and rape experienced by Tamils took place in tandem with torture and degrading, inhuman treatment by state-sanctioned officers, such as the army, Criminal Investigation Department (CID), or other officers of the state (Human Rights Watch, 2013). The researchers from Human Rights Watch found that their participants seldom had access to resources that helped them with representation, medical or psychological aid, such as defence lawyers or doctors who could represent them without fear of retaliation. The perpetrators came from security forces, such as the Sri Lankan army, police officers and CID, as well as Tamils who worked in tandem with government efforts (Human Rights Watch, 2013). Not all detainees are released after they sign a confession or after they are prosecuted; instead, the report found that detainees were allowed to escape instead of being released after the perpetrators received a bribe (Human Rights Watch, 2013). 'KP', a 31-year-old male, explained that, in August 2011, he was picked up by security personnel north of Vavuniya and detained for nearly ten days in a small, dirty room (Human Rights Watch, 2013: 10). He described his abuse as including being burned with cigarettes, and beaten and sexually abused for a confession that he was a supporter and contributor to the LTTE whilst living outside Sri Lanka. During 'KP's' detainment, an officer

> forced himself on [the victim] and raped [him]. During questioning, the officials would squeeze [the victim's] penis. They would force [the victim] to masturbate them. One of them masturbated [the victim].
>
> (Human Rights Watch, 2013: 10)

There is a ritual in the process of such sexual violence during wartime in Sri Lanka, where groping, mocking, degradation and foreplay with words, psychology and physical touching are used to ignite the process. For instance, both female and male victims of sexual violence experienced the following before the perpetrators raped them: the victims were forced to strip, the officers groped the victims' breasts or genitals, and the perpetrators verbally abused and mocked them. Numerous medical reports corroborate evidence of sexual abuse, such as bites on the buttocks and breasts, cigarette burns found in the inner thighs and breasts and other sensitive areas, and sharp needles stuck in men's penises, and other cases found small metal balls inserted into the urethra by army personnel (Human Rights Watch, 2013: 11).

Evidence indicates that sexual violence was an occurrence in detention camps and detention spots by soldiers, police, members of the CID and the Terrorist Investigation Department (TID); cases not only occurred in battlegrounds but also at the Boosa and Kaluthara prisons, and at the Trincomalee police station (in the East) (Human Rights Watch, 2013). In one case, 'SV', a male asylum seeker deported from France, was detained by the CID at Colombo International Airport in December 2010. He recounts his experiences:

> I was kept in detention for more than a month. ... They asked me about my activities with the LTTE in France. They brought pictures of my participating in antiwar protests in France and accused me of betraying the government. ... I was locked in a dark room and my hands were tied in the position of a crucifix. I then was burned all over my arms in this position. ... I was raped many times. Two men would come to my room and one would hold me down. They would take turns raping me.
>
> (Human Rights Watch, 2013: 12)

In a 2013 ethnographic study of 28 refugees from Sri Lanka conducted by the second author of this chapter, 13 males and 1 female were either raped or sexually assaulted by the Sri Lankan security forces during or post-civil war. One 28-year-old male participant, 'Sutty', describes,

> They kept asking me to identify LTTE members in the camp, but I didn't know of any. We kept to ourselves most of the time. They didn't believe me, they held me down and put current to my genitals because they said I was not telling the truth.

An interview with another participant, 26-year-old 'Rich', goes as follows:

> Rich: He said I was LTTE, said I had to confess and sign the letter. I refused because I knew that if I signed the confession I would never see my family again. They hit me with whisky bottles, pvc pipes that had sand in it, and then the worst thing happened
>
> Interviewer: Can you talk a little about what happened?
>
> Rich: They made me give oral sex to the officers, they had sex with me, they took pictures while all of this was happening ... it's never been the same with my family since, I have not been able to be intimate with my wife because I relive that moment every day in my mind. I still have nightmares. At least I am alive with my wife and children.

A 24-year-old female, 'Amy', described her experience as unforgettable. Amy explained that her friends were taken away at the camp and, when they returned, they would cry because they were raped and some lost their virginity; some talked of not eating or committing suicide. She described her experience as unforgivable:

> Amy: I refused to sign the confession that I was LTTE. Yes, I am LTTE member but they would kill me if I signed it! They hit me with their hands and pinched me on my breast. I still refused to sign it. The big guy [of authority] ripped my clothes off and raped me while the other two [officers] watched. I begged him to stop. I was virgin before. I was bleeding [participant crying now]. He smelled of alcohol. I kicked and screamed but no one helped me. [Stopped crying and taking deep breaths]. What man will accept me now [for marriage]? I saw and experienced things no woman should go through.

There is shaming for Sri Lankan women associated with certain issues, specifically those related to sexual violence or sexual assault. When a woman exposes herself as a rape victim, there is the risk of ostracism from not just her family, but also her community and Sri Lankan society (Swiss and Jennings, 2006). Acts of victim blaming stem from the cultural expectations of gender roles within particular societies and subcultures within the island. Some of the consequences of exposing oneself as a victim of sexual violence is not being able to marry, rejection or abandonment by the spouse and relatives (e.g. in-laws and parents), unknown or indefinite detention in protective custody by the state, commitment of suicide either by the victim or by someone she knows (e.g. honour killing) and retribution from the predator that can range from the use of acid burns to murder.

Another major factor that Swiss and Jennings (2006) allude to is Sri Lanka's current state of mayhem within the criminal justice system, law enforcement and the state, where women who complain of sexual victimization or abuse are not appropriately protected or experience inappropriate redress and may become revictimized. They also point out that women who face such obstacles do not receive adequate treatment during the process (e.g. in making a complaint with the corrupt criminal justice system, receiving appropriate representation and services from lawyers, prosecutors, judges and the criminal justice system, and completing a case within the criminal justice system in less than 6 to 10 years, or at times longer). Although Swiss and Jennings (2006) focus on vulnerable women living in displaced areas, the conditions and experiences can also be extended, but not generalized to, all men due to fluidity in gender roles and gender expectations within Sri Lankan subculture. We suggest that the issues raised in this section are used as a prompt for further research into the sexual victimization experiences of both sexes.

Finally, The People's Tribunal on Sri Lanka Report conducted by the Permanent People's Tribunal on Sri Lanka (2010: 15), found that the government's unorthodox and forceful removal of the rebel group, LTTE, resulted in the government controlling the Tamil civilian population, whereby,

> The Government of Sri Lanka pursued military actions in violation of international law, including the Geneva Conventions and the Declaration of Human Rights. The resulting atrocities of rape ... brutalized and threatened the survival of the Tamil community. ... War crimes and crimes against humanity clearly appear to have been committed.

The Permanent People's Tribunal on Sri Lanka (2010) also found evidence of sexual abuse and rape used as a weapon of war throughout the war by government troops in dilapidated and war-affected villages and in welfare villages. The consequence of this atrocity led to many victims committing abortions and suicides due to shame brought on by cultural values and beliefs, family shame and mental trauma (Permanent People's Tribunal on Sri Lanka, 2010). However, the Committee of the Convention on the Elimination of Discrimination against Women (cited in European Center for Constitutional and Human Rights, 2011: 4) explains that 'reporting Non-Government Organizations (NGOs) rarely had access to relevant information' and Sri Lanka's State Report (see the Lessons Learnt and Reconciliation Commission's 2011 final report: Ministry of Defence and Urban Development, Sri Lanka, 2011) does not provide a thorough and unbiased analysis of gender-based violence and access to justice in the conflict zones. The Rehabilitation and Research Centre for Torture Victims (RCTV) in Denmark found sexual violence was used by the state against women as a method of torture to acquire information about the paramilitary rebels. The study noted that 'cases of sexual abuses were often not "discovered" and reported, even by organizations or persons working at the local level, due to issues of fear, stigma, shame, etc.' (RCTV, cited in European Center for Constitutional and Human Rights, 2011: 5).

Conclusion

Sexualized violence permeates armed conflicts. Rape, other forms of assault and humiliation are part and parcel of warfare. Yet, as seen in the two cases examined here, it varies. It varies in quantity and quality. Even well-disciplined troops, or troops with strong ties to the local population, will contain individuals who use the anarchy of an armed conflict to opportunistically commit an assault. Such attacks appear to increase as the relational and cultural distance between troops and civilians increases, especially when those civilians are associated with an enemy belligerent. When it occurs, sexual enslavement is strongly shaped by the immediate socio-cultural context. In Sierra Leone, the taking of 'bush wives' was influenced by traditional cultural norms for legitimated abduction marriages as well as a rapist being able to legitimate the relationship by marring his victim. Systematic use of sexualized violence can arise out of several contexts. As seen in Sri Lanka, Peru and Abu Ghraib prison (see Rothe *et al.*, 2009), it can be deployed as one of many forms of torture utilized during interrogations and as a more general exercise of power and control. Here, especially, is where we find much male victimization. When deployed in the field, systematic rape is typically associated with a 'total war' strategy where the belligerent force does everything it can to reduce the enemy's ability and will to maintain the conflict. Such approaches are more common in protected conflicts that are not brought to an end by more legitimate military means. Such was the case in Sierra Leone and the on-going conflict in the eastern Democratic Republic of the Congo (DRC). In this context, rape is used to reduce civilian morale and humiliate both the civilians raped and the fighting forces unable to protect non-combatants, and it serves as an attack on the group's very identity. In genocidal conflicts, systematic sexual assault serves as yet another tool to eliminate a population, as seen in Rwanda, Darfur and the former Yugoslavia (Hagan *et al.*, 2009; Hagan and Rynmond-Richmond, 2009; Mukamana and Brysiewicz 2008; Mullins 2009a, 2009b; Prunier 2008). Sexual assault and other forms of sexualized violence seem to be rarer when a belligerent seeks legitimacy in the eyes of civilians in the post-conflict landscape. In the two conflicts examined here, both the LTTE and the CDFs did not frequently victimize civilians in this way. The LTTE hoped to become a political power post-conflict with citizen support. The CDFs in Sierra Leone needed to maintain local support in the communities they planned to live in post-conflict. Similarly, states seeking to gain or maintain approval from other states will put more emphasis on good conduct from their soldiers. This was a factor in the low number of crimes committed by the Georgian Army in 2008, as Georgia was seeking closer ties with the European Union community (Mullins, 2011). Modern professional armies rarely use systematic sexual violence in the field or condone sexual slavery. Unfortunately, we have seen such forces use sexualized forms of torture in recent conflicts. It has been suggested that professionalized forces commit fewer opportunistic rapes than undisciplined, poorly trained militia in recent conflicts (i.e. DRC, Central African Republic, Sierra Leone). But without systematic evidence, the veracity of that claim is unknown.

While there is a lot we do know now about conflict rapes, there is still a lot we do not know. Conflict sexual assault and other forms of sexualized violence during wartime are increasingly getting the media and legal attention they deserve. It is also beginning to get academic attention from social scientists. As a field, criminology is theoretically and methodologically well suited to add to our knowledge base. There is still plenty of exploratory work to be done in publicly available archival materials, such as court records and TRC testimonials. These materials allow rich case studies to be done to better identify situations and contexts that increase or decrease sexual violence by armed forces. Qualitative interviews with victims about their wartime experiences are also very fruitful projects. These sorts of projects can help descriptively, typologically and in inductive theory building. Yet, we need to see systematic quantitative data collection for traditional theory testing. Some medical NGOs have conducted epidemiological surveys to measure the frequency and long-term health consequence of war rapes but often important social and incident data are not part of these survey instruments. Social scientists should seek out partnership in the medical community to collect such important data on victims. Also, criminologists interested in war crimes in general need to make connections with the UN, crisis relief NGOs and other such organizations that collect various forms of data during and after conflicts to take advantage of other ongoing information gathering. Such data will help shed light on the true prevalence of this behaviour and assist in developing better theoretical models of war rapes.

Note

1 Three in total and only cases of sexual abuse, not rape or slavery, and these are attributed to the Kajamors.

References

The Truth and Reconciliation Commission. (2003) 'Transcripts of TRC public hearings Sierra Leone Truth and Reconciliation Commission: Appendix three'. Available: www. sierraleonetrc.org/index.php/view-the-final-report/download-table-of-contents/appendices.
Central Intelligence Agency (CIA). (2013) *The World Factbook 2013–2014*, Washington, DC: Central Intelligence Agency. Available: https://www.cia.gov/library/publica tions/the-world-factbook/index.html.
Cohen, D. K. (2013) 'Female combatants and the perpetration of violence: Wartime rape in the Sierra Leone civil war', *World Politics*, 65(3): 383–415.
Deedadayalan, P. (2011) *Post War Sri Lanka*, Bangalore: Other Media Communications.
De Silva, K. (1981) *A History of Sri Lanka*, Berkeley: University of California Press.
European Center for Constitutional and Human Rights. (2010) *Study on Criminal Accountability in Sri Lanka as of January 2009*, Berlin.

European Center for Constitutional and Human Rights. (2011) 'Alternative report on the implementation of the UN convention on the elimination of discrimination against women (CEDAW) – Sri Lanka "Woman and Armed Conflict"', Berlin.

Fulu, E., Warner, X., Miedema, S., Jewkes, R., Roselli, T. and Lang, J. (2013) 'Why do some men use violence against women and how can we prevent it? Quantitative findings from the United Nations multi-country study on men and violence in Asia and the Pacific, Bangkok: UNDP, UNFPA, UN Women and UNV'. Available from: http://asia-pacific.undp.org/content/dam/rbap/docs/Research%20&%20Publica tions/womens_empowerment/RBAP-Gender-2013-P4P-VAW-Report.pdf.

Hagan, J., Rynmond-Richmand, W. and Palloni, A. (2009) 'Racial targeting of sexual violence in Darfur', *American Journal of Public Health*, 99(8): 1386–1392.

Hagan, J. and Rynmond-Richmond, W. (2009) *Darfur and the Crime of Genocide*, New York: Cambridge University Press.

Human Rights Watch. (2009) 'War on the displaced: Sri Lankan Army and LTTE abuses against civilians in Vanni', New York: Human Rights Watch. Available: www.hrw.org/reports/2009/02/19/war-displaced.

Human Rights Watch. (2013) '"We will teach you a lesson": Sexual violence against Tamils by Sri Lankan security forces', New York: Human Rights Watch. Available: www.hrw.org/reports/2013/02/26/we-will-teach-you-lesson.

MacKenzie, M. (2010) 'Securitizing sex? Towards a theory of the utility of wartime sexual violence', *International Feminist Journal of Politics*, 12(2); 202–221.

MacKenzie, M. H. (2012) *Female Soldiers in Sierra Leone: Sex, Security, and Post-Conflict Development*, New York: New York University Press.

Ministry of Defence and Urban Development, Sri Lanka. (2011) *Report of the Commission of Inquiry and Lessons Learnt and Reconciliation: Final Report*. Available: www.defence.lk.

Mukamana, D. and P. Brysiewicz. (2008) 'The lived experience of genocide rape survivors in Rwanda', *Journal of Nursing Scholarship*, 40(4): 379–384.

Mullins, C.W. (2009a) '"We are going to rape you and taste Tutsi women": Rape during the 1994 Rwandan genocide', *The British Journal of Criminology*, 49(6): 719–735.

Mullins, C.W. (2009b) '"He would kill me with his penis": Rape during the Rwandan genocide as a state crime', *Critical Criminology: An International Journal*, 17(1): 15–33.

Mullins, C.W. (2011) 'War crimes in the 2008 Georgia-Russia conflict', *British Journal of Criminology*, 51(6): 918–936.

Permanent People's Tribunal on Sri Lanka. (2010) 'People's Tribunal on Sri Lanka Report', Dublin: Trinity College.

Prunier, G. (2008) *Darfur: A 21st Century Genocide* (3rd edition), Ithaca, NY: Cornell University Press.

Rothe, D., Kramer, R.C., and Mullins, C.W. (2009) 'Torture, impunity, and open legal spaces: Abu Ghraib and international controls', *Contemporary Justice Review*, 12 (1): 27–43.

Sandholtz, W. (2007) *Prohibiting Plunder: How Norms Change*, New York: Oxford University Press.

Swiss, S., and Jennings, P. J. (2006) 'Documenting the impact of conflict on women living in internally displaced persons camps in Sri Lanka: Some ethical considerations', Albuquerque: Women's Rights International. Available: www.womens-rights. org/Documenting/EthicsIDP.html.

University Teachers for Human Rights (Jaffna) (UTHR(J)) (2009) 'Let them speak: The truth about Sri Lanka's violence of war.' Available: www.new-just.eu.

Weiss, G. (2012) *The Cage: The Fight for Sri Lanka and the Last Days of the Tamil Tigers*, New York: Bellevue Literary Press.

Witt, J.F. (2012) *The Laws of War in American History: Lincoln's Code*. New York: Free Press.

Wood, E.J. (2009) 'Armed groups and sexual violence: When is wartime rape rare?', *Politics and Society*, 37(1): 131–161.

Wood, E.J. (2006) 'Variation in sexual violence during war', *Politics and Society*, 34(3): 307–341.

8 Normative visibility and artistic resistance to war

Wayne Morrison

> We command you, that you must bring to our Court the body of A.B. whom you have detained in prison under your custody, as it is claimed to us, together with the day and cause of your taking and detaining him, by whatever name the said A.B. may be known therein ... you are to undertake and receive that interrogation which our Court shall then and there consider and follow any order the Court may make in that regard. Hereof in no way fail, at your peril. For you have here this writ.

This is a modern translation of the medieval writ of Habeas Corpus, the so called 'great writ' or most famous of the 'extraordinary', 'common law', or 'prerogative writs', which were historically issued by the English courts in the name of the monarch to control inferior courts and public authorities within the kingdom (for continuing significance see May, 2011).

> The accused took a number of photographs of the executions and allowed X to take further photographs, although he knew that the photographing of such incidents was not permitted. These were for the most part pictures which showed the most deplorable excesses, many are shameless and utterly revolting. The photographs were developed in photographic shops in southern Germany and the accused showed them to his wife and friends.
> [Verdict] the accused shall not be punished because of the actions against the Jews as such. Jews have to be exterminated and none of the Jews that were killed is any great loss .... He should be excused .... Real hatred of the Jews was a driving motivation for the accused. But in the process he let himself be drawn into committing cruel actions ... which are unworthy of the German man and an SS officer .... It is not the German way to apply Bolshevik methods during the necessary extermination of the worst enemy of our people .... The accused jeopardised the discipline of his men. It is hard to conceive of anything worse than this.
> [B]y having these developed in photographic shops and showing them to his wife and friends, the accused is guilty of disobedience. Such pictures could pose the greatest risks to the security of the Reich if they fell into the wrong hands. It would be extremely easy for them to be leaked out of southern Germany to Switzerland and used for enemy propaganda

.... However [on the charge that this undermined the fighting spirit of Germany] the Court is convinced that the accused never even entertained the thought that the showing of such pictures to people of weak disposition could undermine the fighting spirit of the German people.

(Extracts from verdict against SS-Untersturmfuhrer Max Taubre, 24th May 1943, of the SS and Police Supreme Court in Munich, Klee *et al.*, 1991: 196)

Prologue – studying criminology: committing the perfect crime

I came to England in the early 1980s possessed of a law degree and Legal Professional qualifications from New Zealand, but for two-and-a-half years I made my living in sport, food and wine. Then, as my working holiday visa was to expire (and thus I would have to return to New Zealand), the leading female squash player at the squash centre where I was manager and co-licensee, Carol Willis, who was at that time a 'criminologist' at the Home Office (and Civil Service female squash champion) suggested I undertake post-graduate studies in criminology at the LSE. I knew neither what criminology was (although I had, like Jock Young, shared a flat for some time with a drug dealer), nor what and where the LSE was. To her credit, Carol got the forms, photocopied some articles by Paul Rock and David Downs and convinced me. I ended up doing the LLM, undertaking Theoretical Criminology, Applied Criminology, Sentencing and Penal Policy and Juvenile Justice. There my academic supervisor and lecturer for two courses was John Eryl Hall Williams. Eryl was a deeply humane man who ran, paradoxically, a most tediously boring course. I say paradoxically, because Eryl had crossed boundaries. While at the time of World War II (WWII) my father had volunteered and joined the Navy (and later at university I had joined the New Zealand Territorial Army), Eryl was a conscientious objector. He refused to join and from 1943 he was assigned to be part of a Quaker relief/medical team which in time followed the advance into Nazi-occupied Europe. Then, at war's end, he entered hell; he entered Belsen.[1] Eryl not only read about, but encountered, the piles of corpses, smelt the stench and drove an ambulance ferrying survivors around the extended camp. He who had objected to war experienced the existential outcome of the worst war – the 'War to Exterminate the Jews' – and not a word of this, not an inkling, ever entered into the courses he taught as a criminologist. Instead, when we read his *Criminology and Criminal Justice* (Hall Williams, 1982) war, the holocaust and genocide were not part of our criminological reality. It was as if they never existed, or, in Baudrillard's (2008) terms, they were 'the perfect crime'.

Contesting the perfect crime: normative visibility

Were it not for appearances, the world would be a perfect crime, that is, without a criminal, without a victim, and without a motive. And the truth would forever have withdrawn from it and its secret would never be revealed, for want of any clues [traces] being left behind. But the fact is that the crime is never perfect, for the world betrays itself by appearances, which are the clues to its non-existence, the traces of the continuity of the nothing. For nothingness itself – the continuity of the nothing – leaves traces. It is by this that the world betrays its secret. That is the way it allows itself to be sensed, while at the same time hiding away behind appearances.

(Baudrillard, 2008: 1)

Jean Baudrillard (like Jean-Luc Nancy, 2007) encourages us to understand globalisation in part as the disappearance of the traditional referential universe. In conditions of globalisation the 'world' is reconstituting; ideas of the centre and the periphery, of time and space, of locality and transcendence, of the nation-state and its vision, its borders, its organisation of violence, in particular its distinction between policing (internal state-applied violence) and waging war (external applied violence), need to be rethought and reinscribed.

This is an existential issue for criminology. Criminology – the 'logos' of crime – has been developed in the legacy of Thomas Hobbes (1991 [1651]), where he turned the question of life, of being here in this world, from being one of preparation of the other world, the world of the final judgment and our sentence by God into heaven or hell, into an issue of prolonging life herein. The fear of hell was replaced by fear of social anarchy (the 'natural condition of man', the 'warre' of all on all), and religious and artistic rhetoric was replaced by an obligation to talk of social organisation in terms of a language structured by ideas of a probabilistic science and geometrical precision. To the Sovereign was given the ability to define and to state through law, to order the 'just' and the 'unjust'; to his advisors, the task of reasonable discourse. Criminology grew as the use of reasoned discourse internal to the nation-state (with war as the prerogative of the Sovereign waged with external enemies); methodological nationalism ruled, even when criminological theory was presented as 'social theory of deviance' or 'general theory of crime'.

For all its sophisticated and thoughtful probing, *What is Criminology?* (Bosworth and Hoyle, 2011) demonstrates how we are still largely within that realm and how difficult it will be to break its contours. Designed to take stock of the discipline, it has an extensive range of contributors, but, while Katja Aas (2011: 417) seeks a criminology that will address 'the global geo-political imbalances of power', Chris Cunneen (2010: 115–37) points to a post-colonial potentiality for 'art and performance' and utilising more fluid representations of 'identity' for healing, Ben Bowling (2011) hints at the need for a global criminology and Stephan Parmentier (2011: 385) asks for 'transitional justice and international crimes' to have greater attention, the overall feel is that mainstream criminology is 'in a state of denial' to quote Parmentier (2011: 383). Kathleen Daly reminds us that 'the end product of doing criminology is written and spoken texts' (2011: 115) (although in a footnote considers that visual references will increase in importance); yet of war and genocide criminology hardly has spoken; they were not part of its referential universe:[2] so criminology murders the reality of the world. Let me make one comparison: in the Holocaust (1940–45) *c.* 6 million Jews (defenceless civilians) were killed by persons in face-to-face massacres or using tactics of 'industrial genocide' following the orders of the lawful Head of the Nazi State. In the twentieth century the total people killed by homicide according to the official criminal statistics in the US is less than 1 million. Thus it takes 6 centuries of the US homicide rate for the twentieth century to equal the Holocaust. Reflect, then, upon the circumstances under which a leading contributor to *What is Criminology?* feels able to state: 'it is necessary to overcome ... the false image... that depicts crime as planned, as crafty, as requiring 'tough' offenders' (Gottfredson, 2011: 39). *Contra* Gottfredson, let us recover Himmler's words:

> It is one of those things that is easily said. 'The Jewish people is being exterminated', every Party member will tell you, 'perfectly clear, it's part of our plans, we're eliminating the Jews, exterminating them, ha!, a small matter'. And then along they all come, all the 80 million upright Germans, and each one has his decent Jew. They say: all the others are swine, but here is a first-class Jew.
>
> And none of them has seen it, has endured it. Most of you will know what it means when 100 bodies lie together, when there are 500, or when there are 1000. And to have seen this through, and – with the exception of human weaknesses – to have remained decent, has made us hard and is a page of glory never mentioned and never to be mentioned.
>
> We have taken away the riches that they had, and I have given a strict order ... we have delivered these riches completely to the Reich, to the State. We have taken nothing from them for ourselves. A few, who have offended against this, will be [judged] in accordance with an order that I gave at the beginning: He who takes even one Mark of this is a dead man.
>
> We have the moral right, we had the duty to our people to do it, to kill this people who wanted to kill us. But we do not have the right to enrich ourselves with even one fur, with one Mark, with one cigarette, with one watch, with anything. That we do not have. Because at the end of this, we don't want, because we exterminated the bacillus, to become sick and die from the same bacillus.
>
> (Himmler, Speech to SS at Poznan, 4th October 1943; see Friedländer, 2007: 543–44)

The SS – a criminal organisation according to the IMT Nuremberg – characterised by discipline, 'decency', self-control, hardness: what kind of 'presence' do scholars involved in criminology portray as requiring explanation? It seems (with one or two exceptions, e.g. Alvarez, 2001, Morrison, 1995, 2006; Friedrichs, 2011) as if the Holocaust had not happened, as if Adolf

Eichmann – he who performed, with devotion and absolute self-control, the bureaucratic function that facilitated the murder of 6 million Jews – never existed. Thus, in *A General Theory of Crime* (Gottfredson and Hirschi, 1990) we are told that 'the idea of organised crime' is 'incompatible' with '[their] ideas of crime and self- control'; genocide is essentially just murder. Observing the trial of Eichmann, Hannah Arendt was of another opinion:

> Nothing is more pernicious to an understanding of these new crimes ... than the common illusion that the crime of murder and the crime of genocide are essentially the same, and that the latter therefore is 'no new crime properly speaking'. The point of the latter is that an altogether different order is broken and an altogether different community is violated.
>
> (Arendt, 1994: 272)

It is important to note what Arendt (1994: 269) visualised: 'the supreme crime ... the physical extermination of the Jewish people, was a crime against humanity, perpetrated upon the body of the Jewish people ...'. We have a new referential: humanity; and we retain locality: bodies, experiencing pain, and torment, both physical and psychological.

In a book-length piece (Morrison, 2006), I have outlined how I conceive that criminology has been constituted through a particular gaze of the local, as the defender of 'civilised space' and thus repressed all that is done in the name of the state or with the state's blessing in the 'other' world, most notably, the worlds of colonialism, genocide and war. A regime of the 'sensible' and normal practice was established. Thus we were told by a foremost criminologist who actually wrote on crime and war that 'criminology is not a normative, but a factual discipline' (Mannheim, 1965: 13), and both Mannheim and Eryl's (Hall Williams) opinion was that criminology was an applied science, engaged in '"piece-meal social engineering" which regards the "ends" as beyond its province' (Mannheim, 1965: 13). But what, then, differentiates the criminologist from Eichmann, if not contingency? For both Mannheim and Hall Williams there was little or nothing in criminology 'per se' that allowed one to make normative comments; if one did so, one did that as a voter, as an individual. What was the transcendent? For Mannheim and Hall Williams it was 'law'; thus criminology, as Mannheim accepted, must always follow the organisation of punishment and work within it (and thus he accepted, uncritically, the judgment of Nuremberg; Mannheim, 1965: 565). My response here is to claim that there is an inherent if basic normativity to the criminological enterprise – put shortly, a commitment not to social engineering but to 'justice'. But what is justice? The answers are long and tenuous and I share grounds with those who say that it may be too difficult to know the just, but at least we can know the unjust,[3] and the process of being just is to engage in the process of 'exposing' the unjust (I am simplifying Nancy, 2007). Hence I suggest a principle that I believe can be helpful in the endeavour of facing up to globalisation – a principle of normative visibility – and my examples will come from only two wars: the war on the Jews and the war on terror.[4] If they seem at first instance unrelated, they share at least one similarity: they are 'wars' not of state against state, but of the state (or allied states) against a vaguely specified enemy which does not enjoy any specific state's allegiance. What marks off these 'wars' from infantry assaults or the massive tank or air force encounters is precisely the lack of encounter: the other does not fight on the terms that are equitable to the heroics of a warrior ethos (and so the Nazi actions were called police actions or hygienic actions, and conversely a world war against a [mythical] Jewish-Bolshevik conspiracy; the war on terror faces terroristic attacks, insurgencies, actions of 'illegal non-combatants' or global civil war).

If criminology has been words, to what can it turn to 'present' presences repressed? Baudrillard (2008: 2) (and Chris Cunneen, 2010, in the art of the indigenous people of Australia) finds the artist an opponent to this 'absence of things from themselves':

> The artist, too, is always close to committing the perfect crime: saying nothing. But he turns away from it, and his work is the trace of the criminal imperfection. The artist is ... the one who, with all his might, resists the fundamental drive not to leave traces.

Again this may seem strange, for as David Freedberg (1989: 422) reminds us:

> The beautiful work of art does not – or should not – give cause for disturbance; and so we conveniently repress as many of the ways in which it is troublesome as we possibly can. If it is too troublesome, it is not worthy of enshrinement in a museum or it is not a work of art.

So the Nazi banned 'degenerate Art' (including the startling work of Otto Dix, deemed to be conducting 'a bolshevistic anti-war campaign', see Willett, 1998: 74); this is the tradition originating with Plato who banned poets (artists) from his ideal republic; only, of course, he did not. He banned those who would upset the vision of reality that the Philosopher Kings laid out.

I began by presenting two extracts. The first relates to the writ of Habeas Corpus (a writ is a command, an order to do something), known as the writ of freedom by which a person who has been detained secretly must be brought into the public gaze in an official court of the realm. This writ has been the most successful weapon of those who have sought to bring to light the fate of those detainees of the war on terror. Larry May discusses both the history of this writ and proposes it as the basis of a global due process emerging through an international criminal justice realm. I take the phrase 'normative visibility' from his loose formulations in which he sees three functions for the writ, which revolve around a 'principle of visibleness': first a minimal value in that the detained must be brought out from detention into a public hearing to hear the charges and to check the process leading up to incarceration and on the conditions of incarceration itself; second is the idea of status: hidden, the subject loses the status of participant in the human arena; and third, a protection against torture and those humiliations that work on the body: bringing the subject into our light allows us to see the marks and hear the account of being the object of power.

The second extract is from the verdict of the SS and Police Court in the case of an SS Officer who had been charged with disobedience and harming the war effort by instigating his labour unit into killing thousands of Jews and allowing photos to be taken of their actions. The SS Police Court commend his hatred of Jews, after all 'none of the Jews that were killed is any great loss' (and found innocent subordinates who beat Jews to death with shovels or who held up Jewish children in one hand shooting them with the other, as they were following orders), but found that he had been overzealous in engaging in killing operations that were not authorised and that a lack of organisation and proper oversight infected the discipline of his men; moreover he had allowed photos to be taken that could in the wrong hands reveal the nature of the operation to a wider world.

At first sight the very existence of this trial seems amazing: it is recognisable as 'law', as legal judgment laying out boundaries of the legal and non-legal, the punishable and the acceptable; but we have, after all, been given a narrative from the Nuremberg trials onwards of Nazi Germany as a state run by a group of criminals (trace the tactics of Justice Jackson and his language of a gang of international brigands who had seized power; for the visual presentation of this in Nuremberg trials, see Hartouni 2012), or where there was no real law: Nazi German law being the destruction of law. How, then, to explain the experience of SS Investigating Judge Konrad Morgen? During the war Morgen actively investigated rumours of theft and corruption at a number of camps, including Buchenwald, Lublin, Sachsenhausen, Oranienberg, Dachau and Auschwitz, and had prosecuted several SS Officers, including five concentration camp commanders, two of whom were executed.[5] Morgen – given the name the Bloodhound Judge – followed up the discovery by Police of smuggled gold and it became clear that this was dental gold from Auschwitz (Gross, 2010: 503). Calculating that dental gold was equivalent to between 25,000 and 100,000 corpses, he understood that mass killing was taking place and in his investigations found that this was just a fraction of the real killings. But what was the law? He soon realized that the killings were taking place under a *Führer* order, the commands of the supreme ruler and source of law in Nazi Germany.

Given that, it followed that the only basis on which he could proceed against Auschwitz officials, or against any of the concentration camp personnel, was if he could show that some killings were carried out by unauthorized individuals or for reasons not covered by legal normativity. As Fraser (2005 and an unpublished 2012 paper on the Nazi state) brings out, this attitude about the 'legality' of killing Jews was not limited to Morgen, but was one

Figure 8.1 Extermination of Polish Jews: album of pictures

This action, for which I have no hesitation using the term, 'crime', is located in an environment saturated with law. From the time that the Nuremberg laws were passed in 1935 and when the Jews obeyed the first order, the path to this action was laid out. But what does this photo reveal? The Album states that its existence is an act of resistance in that most of the images were taken by the Germans as momentos, but copies were secretly made by those entrusted in developing the negatives, and specifies that it relates to the Lomza ghetto and Einsatzgruppe action of August or September 1941. However, Janina Struk (2004: ch. 1) identifies a master copy which has a full profile of a German Officer on the right of the photo (only his arm protrudes in the image here) and the negative is in the archives with the caption, 'Sniaty – tormenting Jews before their execution 11.V.1943'. Many read such images in terms of an appeal for human rights and calls for action, but Hannah Arendt (1973: 299, 300, 301) is more cutting: 'The world found nothing sacred in the abstract nakedness of being human .... A man who is nothing but a man has lost the very qualities which make it possible for other people to treat him as a fellow-man .... We are not born equal; we become equal as members of a group on the strength of our decision to guarantee ourselves mutually equal rights. Our political life rests on the assumption that we can produce equality through organisation.' Does this image need a caption? The caption that Janina Struk found does not seem apt; I do not see the active tormenting (although this must have been a living torment for the victims); instead I see cold efficiency. I can sense the common humanity and I feel ashamed at the acts of covering the genitals as if they knew they would be looked at again, many years later. But I am removed. Daniel Goldhagen famously tried to convey the lived experience of these executions (Goldhagen, 1996), at least as he interpreted the perpetrators, but was overly emotive and subjective. The normativity of the event lies in the observing of the power of the 'inhumane' to destroy or to render invisible the human victim. For words of a poet that convey the lived experience of the victims see *Postcard 4* by Miklos Radnoti (1972), Hungarian poet murdered in the Holocaust. This is, of course, an 'impossible memory' in Derrida's terms. We are grasping for reality

Source: Taffet, G., ed. (1945) *Extermination of Polish Jews: Album of Pictures* (ZagLada Zydostwa Poliskiego: Album Zdjec) Centralna Zydowska Komisja Historyczna Polsce, Lodz (Central Jewish Historical Committee in Poland), p.80. Photographer unknown. Reproduced with kind permission from Emanuel Ringelblum Jewish Historical Institute.

which was deeply embedded in the normative legal universe in which the question was not the killing of Jews, but instead was posed in relation to the issue of who had the jurisdiction and power to kill Jews.[6] Therefore, for Morgen, the problem was not the killing of Jews, since this was at one and the same time consistent with the Nazi worldview and with understandings of positive legality under the *Füherprinzip*. The problem was limited to illegal killings of Jews, in pursuance of an equally, or perhaps more, illegal campaign of corruption and personal enrichment.[7]

But, you may say, that was merely the workings of a distorted system; surely after WWII everyone realized that there was no cover of any form of 'law' to this system? Yet this comes up against the reality that the de-Nazification proceedings before the *Spruchkammergericht* found that Morgen had 'maintained to the utmost the ethics of a truth-seeking judge and carried out the duty of a conscientious representative of the law. The court concluded that he could not, as an (ethical) SS judge, be called to account.' The result is that 'law' dealt with Nazism only by denying 'law's' existence, by putting it as a place beyond law, by repressing it in the name of civilization and claiming that our law is the real law.

I now turn to a contemporary image.

Daniel Heyman, a Jewish American artist, sought to 're-cover' the humanity of former detainees of Abu Ghraib Prison.[8] Between 2006 and 2008, Heyman joined the legal team around American lawyer Susan Burke, visiting Jordan and Turkey and taking the testimony of former prisoners held at Abu Ghraib (all of whom had been released without charge). Burke was seeking damages against private contractors, who provided interrogation and translation services, and were involved in the torture of detainees at Abu Ghraib and other military prisons. Over the course of five trips between 2006 and 2008, Heyman observed interviews with 40 former detainees of Abu Ghraib and later witnesses to the Blackwater/Nisour Square shooting that left 17 Iraqi civilians dead and 20 injured.

The detainees' testimony was taken in hotel rooms; as the detainees spoke, Heyman sketched. Heyman encounters language and physical presence – culturally mediated. The ex-detainees are slow to talk, but then talk with an increasing methodical power; narratives are broken, time becomes non-linear. Heyman transcribes parts of their testimonies directly onto his images. What dominates: image or language? Actually they intermix. But he presents words as accompanying (I hesitate to say 'belonging' to) human subjects with narratives to tell. The anonymous figures – hooded and caped, or naked in piles – in the infamous Abu Ghraib photographs (what Butler, 1990, calls 'the absent') become individuals. Farmers, doctors, shopkeepers, teachers, taxi drivers, husbands and fathers speaking of their fears for their families; they pose naturally, dressed as they were at the time of the interviews, most in Western-style clothing, some in a fe keffiyeh and thwab (the traditional Middle Eastern headdress and robe). The words denote trauma, overwhelming fear and humiliation. Heyman interprets; he selects particular

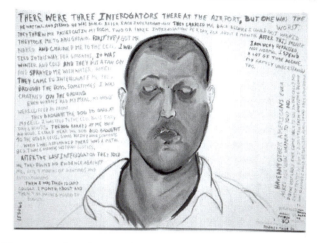

Figure 8.2 There were three interrogators there
This is a water colour of the head and shoulders of a man, surrounded by writing that
is somewhat difficult to read; one has to twist and turn to follow the lines. 'THEY
TOOK ME TO ABU GHRAIB', one section reads. 'FIRST THEY GOT ME
NAKED AND CHAINED ME TO THE CELL. I WAS TIED IN THIS WAY, FOR
6 MONTHS. IT WAS WINTER AND COLD AND THEY PUT A FAN ON AND
SPRAYED ME WITH WATER. WHEN THEY CAME TO INTERROGATE ME
THEY BROUGHT THE DOGS. SOMETIMES I WAS CHAINED ON THE
GROUND. EVEN WHEN I HAD MY MEAL, MY HANDS WERE CUFFED IN
FRONT'. 'AFTER EACH INTERROGATION', the narrative continues later,
'THEY CARRIED ME BACK BECAUSE I COULD NOT WALKED [sic]. THEY
THREW ME PASSED OUT IN MY ROOM'. On the bottom corner of the page:
'RELEASED MAY 2006. 30 MONTHS. THEY GAVE ME 20 DOLLARS'
Source: Daniel Heyman, *There Were Three Interrogators There*, watercolor on paper.
Watercolor in the David Winton Bell Gallery, gift of Mr. Richard Rubin by exchange.
Permission to use courtesy of the Artist and Cade Tompkins Projects

aspects of appearance and words to emphasise their common humanity and
reduce their 'distance' from us, to illustrate their normalcy.

Practices at Guantánamo Bay, Abu Ghraib, extraordinary rendition,
migration camps or extraordinary surveillance have been defined in terms of
states of exception, as 'black holes'. In these sites executive power (prerogative) trumps 'normal' judicial power in ways that were most commonly
reserved for colonial situations; however, as scholars who take Hobbes seriously, such as Carl Schmitt, Derrida and Agamben, note, beneath the normalcy of the law is always a relationship with the exceptional other. The state
of exception is thus – to paraphrase Schmitt – part of the conceptual voca-
bulary of theorising the state. If, in founding philosophical modernity, Hobbes
postulated that the pre-Sovereign normal state was that of a 'warre' of all
against all, then Law and Social Order is premised in an act of coming out of
that state; continual social order depends on the constant threat of the return
to a state of war (in particular, for Hobbes, civil war). Hobbes gave us the

idea of the founding act as a social contract; realists point to more violent foundations: 'order must be established for juridical order to make sense. A regular situation must be created, and sovereign is he who definitely decides if this situation is actually effective' (Schmitt, 1985: 13). Agamben (1998: 21) takes this further: to demonstrate an anterior, and exterior, sovereignty, he offers the exception, the exception to what the law is 'for the time being': 'only the sovereign decision on the state of exception opens the space in which it is possible to trace borders between inside and outside and in which determinate rules can be assigned to determinate territories'. Mainstream criminology is always the anterior, but it cannot even realize that boundaries exist, for these boundaries only become apparent when one attempts to encounter the question of who is the criminal, who is the victim, what is the transgression, in the space of the exception.

Those who are the objects of power in these black holes are beyond sight, or, more aptly put, they are in a particular sight; common to their accounts is that they perceive themselves as living dead:

> Even though I was alone, I never had any privacy because of the constant monitoring by video cameras, including the video camera in my cell that followed every little movement I made, and because my cell was regularly searched. In both cells, the ceiling and floor were all painted the same drab grey colour and I was not once allowed to see the sun or the sky for the more than twelve months I was in this facility.
>
> 32. The sealed in nature of this facility and the claustrophobia that I experienced contributed to my feeling that this detention facility and the facility in Afghanistan were essentially coffins. It especially felt that way to me because I was innocent. You die a little every day you are in prison because you are in a coffin for the living where you don't see, you don't hear, and there is nothing.
>
> In RE MOHAMED FARAG AHMAD BASHMILAH DECLARATION OF
> MOHAMED FARAG AHMAD BASHMILAI-1 pp. 64–65

There are, of course, more ways to disappear than to be kept in a (legal and physical) black hole: the US constantly claims that drone strikes are precision-targeted killing.

The development of the 'Drone War' post 9/11 was first characterised as the CIA's secret war on terror. The enemy was unseen, underground, often not in uniform: 'the hard thing is to know where and who your enemy is'. Identifying many on the CIA list of 'evil masterminds' – individuals at the intersection of Al Qaeda, Taliban and Pakistan militant groups – as being in the 'very dangerous', 'Wild West-like', perilous, 'lawless', remote tribal lands of North West Pakistan, the drones – named reapers, avengers, predators –

Figure 8.3 Image by an artist collective from Pakistan and the USA
Using social media sites, in particular Facebook and Twitter, #notabugsplat – a group
of Pakistani and American artists – make a dual statement: the actual installation
replaces the 'bug-like' images of humans with a large portrait of a child on a massive
banner, situated in a suburban field in the heavily bombed khyber pukhtoonkhwa
region (thus asking drone operators to consider child casualties), while the larger aim
is to make a statement against the increasing use of drone strikes by raising awareness
of the numerous civilian casualties. They claim 380+ drone strikes and 3,500+ dead,
including more than 200 children. In military slang, predator drone operators often
refer to kills as 'bug splats', since viewing the body through a grainy video image gives
the sense of an insect being crushed.
Source: By an artist collective from Pakistan and the USA, reproduced with
permission

enabled attacks to reach across borders and make 'serious enemies disappear
in a puff of smoke'. The balance of killing the target and collateral damage
(civilian deaths) was best 'played out by the "anger limit" of the Pakistan
populace'. Critics fear that the 'human' has disappeared from sight, the
images that the Drone commanders see are all too similar to that of the video
games that soldiers play for relaxation; conversely, supporters argue that
human soldiers are subjects of irrational rage but not a drone pilot/gun commander and that a lawyer is always present in the command station (phrases
taken from *CIA Confidential: Inside the Drone War*, a National Geographic
Programme, 2011).

The principle of normative visibility: an illusion, an interpretation or a contribution to rebuilding criminology as a collaborative enterprise?

Rosalind Hursthouse (1992: 63), an art theorist, puts forward a dramatic
account of the normative power that viewing certain works of art had on her
own concept of war:

> The words 'war is terrible' have some power; they evoke connections
> with suffering, blood, pain and loss. But the words 'military glory',
> 'honour', 'courage', have a similar power; they evoke connections with
> suffering, blood, pain and loss nobly borne, and reiterating 'but war is
> terrible', against those words ('Honour!' 'Courage!'), may start to seem
> feeble and stale. The familiar words invite, 'Well, war is terrible in some
> ways, but glorious in others; there are two sides to every question; you
> can see war in this way or in that way.' And that is what I used to think –

reluctantly, but perforce – that there were at least these two ways of thinking about or 'seeing' war. But then I was lucky enough to get to Madrid and see both Goya's paintings on war and Picasso's Guernica. Because I saw them all in the same week I do not know what effect they would have had if I had seen only Guernica or only the Goyas, or indeed, only one or the other of the Goyas, but I certainly know what the effect was of seeing all the paintings I did see. It created in me an image of 'war is terrible' which is dominatingly vivid. Now, when I look at pictures which represent war as glorious, or read poems, novels or plays about military glory, or honour and courage displayed in war, or see films about them, or hear music supposed to invoke a passionate willingness to fight for one's country or one's cause, Goya's and Picasso's paintings always come into my thoughts. 'No, no,' they always say, 'don't be fooled. This is the way it is – terrible, terrible'.

These are beautiful words, contemporary words. Throughout history war has been known to be hell at times, but equally portrayed as glorious, liberating, as the greatest endeavour that men can be involved in. But, from the time that Callot dared to set out in etchings a narrative of war's visibility (entitled *The Miseries of War, 1633–35*), war came to take on the character of atrocity. Reflecting on the horrors of the French suppression of the Spanish in 1808–14, Goya gave two masterful paintings (The Second and the Third of May, 1808, that can denote heroic resistance) but plumbed the depths of a new anarchy in his The Disasters of War set of etchings that he left unpublished (published in 1863, 35 years after his death). Here war is stripped of all glory, all pretence, and with and without reason. The distortions of war, that men sell their souls and engage in activities that 'domestically' would be regarded as crimes and severe sin, was the theme of a bitter *Westminster Review* article in 1844. The article by William R. Greg is structured by the belief that the initiative and good sense of the people when their 'vision' of war was freed from the shackles of power would usher in a new era of progress and stability. Yet the masses met World War I with joy and rushed to join in what promised to be heroic struggles. The art of the First World War struggled to cope; it was as if all the promises of the Enlightenment were laid waste on the pitted and mud-ridden fields of France and the devastation of industrial warfare. The sheer scale of death, and the ability of commanders to order tens of thousands of men to charge machine gun- and barbed wire-covered areas, to go to their certain death meant that it was difficult to see any individuality, to portray what for centuries had been seen as the divine spark in the human. It was said of the German drawer and etcher Otto Dix (who was a soldier) that his muse was 'nausea' and that the subject of his art was not the real world but the destruction of the real world; but what were the borders between the real and this 'other'? Or had the 'other' become the real?

Classically art was meant to reproduce the linkage between beauty and truth, to suppress the ugly as the evil; but now the all too visible destruction of a new war made the ugly true. However anti-war art became vulgar, that is to say democratic, the base of its emotional power that it appeals to everyone. Thus I struggle to find in the abstract art of Guernica an act of resistance to war. I rely on John Berger (1965: 118–19) to explain:

> Picasso did not try to imagine the actual event. There is no town, no aeroplanes, no explosion, no reference to the time of day .... Where is the protest then? It is in what has happened to the bodies – to the hands, the soles of the feet, the horse's tongue, the mother's breasts, the eyes in the head. What has happened to them in being painted is the imaginative equivalent of what happened to them in sensation in the flesh. We are made to feel their pain with our eyes. And pain is the protest of the body.

Guernica does little for me. Even though I accept that it is a work of passion and I appreciate it and admire its craftsmanship, I do not feel the humanity; Goya's etchings, on the other hand, strike hard. No wonder that many have hoped that the photograph would cut through any interpretative issues, would reveal an indisputable truth. Certainly the increasing existence of technologies of visual reproduction – such as the spread of the mobile phone with camera – grant a minimal form of Habeas Corpus by extending their capturing gaze into innumerable corners. We are consequently awash with images: thus I can appreciate the seemingly internal debate that Susan Sontag had (with herself) between writing *On Photography* and *Regarding the Pain of Others*. Many have misquoted her, as an oft repeated line is 'our failure is one of imagination, of empathy: we have failed to hold this reality [of atrocity] in mind' (Sontag, 2003: 7), which would appear an apt criticism of my lack of reaction if only it were her opinion instead of her summary of Virginia Woolf's understanding of what our moral reaction should be to photographs of the slaughter of non-combatants. Sontag (2003) asks, in reply, why should they only 'stimulate the repudiation of war'? 'Surely', she asks, could 'they not also foster greater militancy?' Sontag (2003) argues that all images need to be put into context. Against those who see 'war as generic' and feel we should be moved by images of 'anonymous, generic victims' Sontag (2003) cannot accept the idea that the photo can speak for itself. 'To the militant, identity is everything. All photographs wait to be explained or falsified by their captions' (Sontag 2003: 9).

But considering the image that I first presented, this seems overstated: confronted with that image, we know – and I suggest anyone who does not is not in our moral universe – that something is terribly wrong. We do not need a precise explanation to comprehend that. But is that image 'data' as traditional criminology has sought? No. Therefore criminology remains bounded and enfeebled. Criminology needs these as an archive and to reflect upon to become mature. To listen to Sontag (2003: 102):

> Someone who is perennially surprised that depravity exists (even incredulous) when confronted with evidence of what humans are capable of inflicting in the way of gruesome, hands-on cruelties upon other humans, has not reached moral or psychological adulthood .... No one after a certain age has the right to this kind of innocence, of superficiality, to this degree of ignorance, or amnesia.

But if these images were to become part of the criminological archive and terrain, what would be the effect? What is the normal and what is the deviant? I present three more images, connected with two staples of the criminological diet, trains (to go to conferences) and guilt.

Trains

> The idea which I shall present here came to me more or less out of the blue. I was on a train some five years ago, on my way to spend a day at Headingley and I was reading a book about the death camp at Sobibor .... The particular, not very appropriate, conjunction involved for me in this train journey ... had the effect of fixing my thoughts on one of the more dreadful features of human coexistence, when in the shape of a simple five-word phrase the idea occurred to me: The Contract of Mutual Indifference.
>
> (Norman Geras, 1998, book cover)

So the philosopher attempts to disturb what some have called the complacent abstraction of much contemporary theory. Geras (1998) focuses on the figure of the bystander – the bystander to the destruction of the Jews of Europe and the bystander to more recent atrocities – to consider the moral consequences of looking on without active response at persecution and great suffering. Mirroring some calls in criminology (Morrison, 2006), the tragedy of European Jewry ought to be centre place in political philosophy. He finds that the traditional concept of the social contract needs to be rethought with a triangular relation between perpetrators, victims and bystanders; the social contract entails indifference.[9] Could this be replaced by a universal duty to bring aid?

The artist/poet knows that the social contract involves indifference, and another train.

The train and the ramp have become the enduring symbols of the intermixing of power, excess and human indifference. Beside the ramp would be an ambulance, a false symbol of normalcy, but where was this place?

Figure 8.4 Take the Hell train

David Olère was a Polish-born French painter and sculptor who lived in Poland and Germany before moving to France in 1923. He was arrested early 1943 by French police during a round up of Jews in Seine-et-Oise and placed first in Drancy internment camp and later sent by train to Auschwitz. He survived because he was assigned to work and entered the Sonderkommando (forced prisoner labour details) at Birkenau, where he emptied gas chambers and burnt bodies. Most Sonderkommando were themselves killed after six months but Olere also helped SS guards write and decorate letters home. In this image the train towers above, its headlights (and light as symbol of the enlightenment) shine off into a vague distance, the Jews are lined up, transferred into the status of undermen, herded by the SS Supermen. In the holocaust the technological products of the enlightenment were used in part for a quasi-industrial manufacturing of corpses and muselemann (living corpses). In the classical tradition of art, the image was meant to represent the forms of nature, but Olere has been witness to things that should not have been and the ease with which the technology of 'progress' allowed 'humanity' to be split from itself. The polish poet Tadeusz Rozewicz, in his poem the professor's pen-knife has a professor remember a time where all that was normal was reversed, where his trip into the hell of the concentration camps began with a plan, normal train journey that passed fields of beautiful flowers, including forget-me-nots which always bring up for him the German word Vergissmeinnicht (forget-me-not) which is also the title of a song by Mozart. How can such beauty give rise to such horror? (discussed in the Introduction, 2011: 23).

Source: Cat. No. 2691, Art Collection, Ghetto Fighters' House Museum, Israel. Published in David Olère: L'Oeil du Témoin/The Eyes of a Witness. New York: The Beate Klarsfeld Foundation, 1989

Figure 8.5 Corpses lie in a row partially covered in preparation for reburial

On 19th April 1945, a freight train with nearly 4,500 prisoners from Buchenwald pulled onto the railroad siding at Nammering. The train had been destined for Dachau, but at Plattling it was diverted towards Nammering because of damage to the railroad caused by Allied bombing. Once in Nammering, some of the local inhabitants attempted to give the prisoners food and water, but these provisions were stolen by the 150 SS and police officers guarding the train. The commanding officer ordered during the halt that the bodies of the dead be removed from the train and cremated. This work proceeded too slowly for him, however, and prisoners were forced to carry the bodies of the dead to a nearby mass grave in a ravine roughly 500 yards from the train. There the prisoners carrying the corpses were shot by the guards and they were also buried in the grave. Altogether 524 prisoners were shot and nearly 800 were interred in the mass grave. The bodies were then covered with lime and the grave was flooded to speed up decomposition. The 3,100 prisoners who had remained on the train were sent on to Dachau, where they were liberated. After the discovery of the site by US troops on 28th April, captive SS men were required to exhume the corpses and lay them out on either side of the ravine above the mass grave. The inhabitants of Nammering were then ordered to walk through the gravesite, and the bodies were buried in the surrounding towns.

Source: Photograph date: Tuesday, May 1, 1945. Locale: Nammering, [Bavaria] Germany. Credit: United States Holocaust Memorial Museum, courtesy of Pam Feil.

The ramp has become increasingly alive with activity, increasingly noisy. The crews are being divided into those who will open and unload the arriving cattle cars and those who will be posted by the wooden steps .... Motorcycles drive up, delivering SS officers, bemedaled, glittering with brass, beefy men with highly polished boots and shiny, brutal faces. Some have brought their briefcases, others hold thin, flexible whips .... Some stroll majestically on the ramp, the silver squares on their collars glitter, the gravel crunches under their boots, their bamboo whips snap impatiently.... The train rolls slowly alongside the ramp. In the tiny barred windows appear pale, wilted, exhausted human faces, terror-stricken women with tangled hair, unshaven men. They gaze at the station in silence. And then, suddenly, there is a stir inside the cars, and a pounding against the wooden boards. 'Water! Air!'
(Borowski, 1976: 35–36, remembering watching the ramp at Auschwitz)

Borowski has as his narrator an inhabitant of the 'grey zone', a Sonderkommando (member of the forced labour units, who traded being alive for another six months for doing the horrid work of tricking the new arrivals into the gas chambers, taking out the bodies, extracting the gold teeth, cutting the hair, and then taking the corpses for burning; for their tortured accounts, see Greif, 2005).

He presents things as they are, since reality, outside the camps, no longer exists.

And guilt

In his opening story, Borowski has Tadeusz excited at the prospect of being assigned to help in the selection at the ramp and thus have access to remaining food and money that the transportees may have; he suddenly vomits and refuses to unload the rail cattle trucks, but then he works. (Contrast the following image, again by David Olère.)
After he has finished working, Borowski (1976: 48) rationalises his position:

I lie against the cool, kind metal and dream about returning to the camp, about my bunk, on which there is no mattress, about sleep among comrades who are not going to the gas tonight. Suddenly I see the camp as a heaven of peace. It is true, others may be dying, but one is somehow still alive, one has enough food, enough strength to work.

Borowski conjures in an art form a place and space which we respect in part because we know he was there .... We, thankfully, as individuals were not there. But we, as humans, were there, both as victims and perpetrators and as inhabitants of what Levi (1989) called 'the grey zone'. We must refashion the criminological tradition, change its referential frame, include the repressed, those hidden in the name of civilised space. In his poem *Beyond Words,*

Figure 8.6 Le vivre des morts pour les vivants/The food of the dead for the living
David Olère was deported from Drancy to Auschwitz, March 2, 1943, no. 106144.
This image is a self-portrait of Olère, one of the few to have survived being a Sonder-
kommando, but what is he doing? In the book in which this appears – translated into
English as *The Eyes of a Witness* – his son, writing the interpretations, labels this as
searching for food to throw over the fence to other inmates, but how do we know that
this was not a totally selfish foraging for provisions to be consumed by the
Sonderkommando?
Olère, David, oil on board. Gift of the Olère Family, Museum of Jewish Heritage – A
Living Memorial to the Holocaust, New York. Source: David Olère: *L'Oeil du
Témoin/The Eyes of a Witness*. New York: The Beate Klarsfeld Foundation, 1989,
p.86. Reprinted with permission.

Rozewicz (2011: 71) evokes the figures brought up from the black holes, figures of the atrocities of our age that we supress and yet, then, open up within
us an 'eyelid of a million shattered faces'. Let us remember their presence and
gain from them a critical energy. In another poem (*Posthumous Rehabilitation*, 2011: 78–79) he calls us to account, stating that the dead read our
books, scrutinize our lectures and thus we are 'guilty' who say nothing. Let us
remember, he asks, that 'the dead are taking stock of the living'.

Notes

1 At least he was spared the task of driving the bulldozers that pushed thousands of
corpses (hardly recognisable as human) into mass graves. It was only after he retired

from academic life that he wrote of his experiences; for a selection of letters, etc., see Hall Williams 1993.

2   For all the efforts of the contributors, neither 'war' nor 'genocide' appear in the index of this 550-page text published by Oxford University Press.

3   To foreshorten a long story, I agree with those who found human rights not on man as being in the image of God but on the political/normative task of the avoidance of atrocity (for example, Dershowitz, 2004). The question of the transcendent, however, remains.

4   To use this phrase 'War on the Jews' (the title of Lucy Dawidowicz's 1975 book) may appear controversial (the Jews after all were but a mythical and not real 'threat', had little defences and no army, etc.). But I follow Margaret Mead (1968: 215): 'warfare exists if the conflict is organised, and socially sanctioned and the killing is not regarded as murder'. *Pace* the illusions of criminology, Dawidowicz, although overstating the 'intentionalist' case, is useful in that she attacks the idea that the killing of the Jews was just one aspect of WWII; rather, she puts WWII in the context of the Nazi view in which it was (in large part) subsumed in a war against the Jews. The Nazi campaign was (as Raul Hilberg, 1979, argues) founded on law and bureaucracy and, as David Fraser (2005) brings out, never was anything but full of law. The mass face-to-face killings were structured by law in notions of obedience and acceptance of the right of the State to command, as were the labour and death camps.

5   The structure of the SS legal apparatus is laid out in Weingartner, (1983); see also Gross (2010: 193 Id., 489).

6   State Attorney Kugler: 'Did you investigate who was responsible for the gassings?' Former SS Judge Wiebeck: 'Back then that did not interest us. Those were supreme acts beyond justice (justizfreie Hoheitsakte)' (interaction during The Auschwitz Trial of 1963 in Germany, as from Hermann Langbein, *Der Auschwitz-Prozess*).

7   Weingartner, op. cit., 291; For other examples of Nazi legality in the midst of the killing machine, see Alfred M. de Zayas, 1989).

8   Daniel Heyman has produced a short book/collection of watercolours under the title *Bearing Witness*, in which he begins with his thoughts on a plane flying 'from the safe mental space of Philadelphia to the more exotic, foreign and unknown space of Istanbul, crossroads of the world as the literature repeatedly states.' Heyman reflectively ponders on borders and what he terms 'transgressions': did he really made the journey? Did his mind ever truly go that far? So his pictures are an attempt to show where he attempted to go, both physically and in terms of empathy, to viewers 'unaware that there is a journey here for all of us' (2009).

9   I am conscious that the kind of society that I am happy living within, and reasonably happy theoretically defending, has forms of 'indifference' at its core. Indifference, that is at the gender, skin colour, sexual preference, of those who share the space of the political entity. Contrast the *Volksgemeinschaft*. *Vergissmeinnicht*, German for forget-me-not. In his poem, *Mask*, of 1946, Czerniawski writes: 'Objects excavated in my country have small black/ heads sealed with plaster and horrible grins'. This appears in Tadeusz Rozewicz, *They Came To See a Poet*, (Selected Poems Translated by Adam Czerniawski) 3rd ed. revised and enlarged 2011. Anvil Press Poetry, London. www.anvilpresspoetry.com. Extract from *Mask* (2011: 38).

References

Aas, K. (2011) 'Visions of global control: cosmopolitan aspirations in a world of friction'. In M. Bosworth and C. Hoyle, (eds) (2011) *What is Criminology?*, Oxford: Oxford University Press.

Agamben, G. (1998) *Homo Sacer: Sovereign Power and Bare Life*. Trans. D. Heller-Roazen, Stanford, CA: Stanford University Press.

Alvarez, A. (2001) *Governments, Citizens, and Genocide: A Comparative and Interdisciplinary Approach*. Bloomington: Indiana University Press.

Arendt, H. (1973) *The Origins of Totalitarianism*. New York: Houghton, Mifflin, Harcourt.

Arendt, H. (1994) *Eichmann in Jerusalem: A Report on the Banality of Evil*, London: Penguin Books.

Baudrillard, J. (2008) *The Perfect Crime*, London: Verso.

Berger, J. (1965) *The Success and Failure of Picasso*, New York: Pantheon Books.

Borowski, T. (1976) *This Way for the Gas, Ladies and Gentlemen*. Selected and translated by Barbara Vedder, Introduction by Jan Knott, Harmondsworth: Penguin Books.

Bosworth, M. and Hoyle, C. (eds.) (2011) *What is Criminology?*, Oxford: Oxford University Press.

Bowling, B. (2011) 'Transnational criminology and the globalization of harm production'. In M. Bosworth and C. Hoyle (eds) *What is Criminology?* , Oxford: Oxford University Press, pp. 361–376.

Butler, J. (1990) *Gender Trouble*, London: Routledge.

Cunneen, C. (2010) 'Framing the crimes of colonialism: critical images of aboriginal art and law'. In K. Hayward and S. Presdee, (eds). *Framing Crime: Cultural Criminology and the Image*, Abingdon, Oxon: Routledge.

Daly, K. (2011) 'Shake it up baby: Practicing rock n'roll criminology'. In M. Bosworth and C. Hoyle (eds) (2011) *What is Criminology?*, Oxford: Oxford University Press.

Dawidowicz, L. (1975) *The War Against the Jews: 1933–45*, New York: Holt, Rinehart and Winston.

Dershowitz, A. (2004) *Rights From Wrongs: A Secular Theory of the Origins of Rights*, New York: Basic Books.

de Zayas, Alfred M. (1989) *The Wehrmacht War Crimes Bureau, 1939–1945*, Lincoln and London: University of Nebraska Press.

Fraser, D. (2005) *Law After Auschwitz: Towards a Jurisprudence of the Holocaust*, Durham, NC: Carolina Academic Press.

Freedberg, D. (1989) *The Power of Images: Studies in the History and Theory of Response*, Chicago: University of Chicago Press.

Friedrichs, D.O. (2011) 'The Crime of the last century – and of this century?' In Roth, D.L. and Mullins, C.W. (eds) *State Crime: Current Perspectives*, London: Rutgers University Press.

Friedländer, S. (2007) *Nazi Germany and the Jews, 1939–1945: The Years of Extermination*, New York: HarperCollins.

Geras, N. (1998) *The Contract of Mutual Indifference*, London: Verso.

Goldhagen, D. (1996) *Hitler's Willing Executioners: Ordinary Germans and the Holocaust*, London: Little, Brown.

Gottfredson, M., and Hirschi, T. (1990) *A General Theory of Crime*, Stanford CA: Stanford University Press.

Greif, G. (2005) *We Wept Without Tears: Testimonies of the Jewish Sonderkommando from Auschwitz*, New Haven: Yale University Press.

Gross, R. (2010) '"The ethics of a truth-seeking judge': Konrad Morgen, SS judge and corruption expert'. In Wiese, C. and Betts, P. (eds) *Years of Persecution, Years of*

Extermination: Saul Friedländer and the Future of Holocaust Studies, London and New York: Continuum.

Hall Williams, J.E. (1982) *Criminology and Criminal Justice*. London: Butterworths.

Hall Williams, J.E. (1993) *A Page of History in Relief*, York: Sessions Book Trust.

Hartouni, V. (2012) *Visualizing Atrocity: Arendt, Evil and the Optics of Thoughtlessness*, New York: New York University Press.

Heyman, Daniel. (2009) *Bearing Witness*, Philadelphia.

Hobbes, T. (1991 [1651]) *Leviathan*, Cambridge: Cambridge University Press.

Hursthouse, R. (1992) 'Truth and representation'. In Hanfling, O. (ed.) *Philosophical Aesthetics*, Cambridge: Blackwell in co-operation with the Open University.

Klee, E., Dressen, W. and Riess, V. (ed.) (1991) *'The Good Old Days': The Holocaust as Seen by Its Perpetrators and Bystanders*, Deborah Burnstone trans., New York: The Free Press.

Levi, P. (1989) *The Drowned and the Saved*, New York: Vintage International.

Mannheim, H. (1965) *Comparative Criminology*. New York: Hougton Mifflin.

May, L. (2011) *Global Justice and Due Process*, Cambridge: Cambridge University Press.

Mead, M. (1968) 'Alternatives to war'. In Fried, M., Harris, M. and Murphy, R. (ed.). *War: The Anthropology of Armed Conflict and Aggression*, Garden City, NY: Nat Hist Press.

Morrison, W. (1995) *Theoretical Criminology: From Modernity to Post-Modernism*. London: Cavendish.

Morrison, W. (2006) *Criminology, Civilisation and the New World Order*, Abingdon, Oxon: Routledge.

Nancy, J-L. (2007) *The Creation of the World or Globalization*, Francois Raffoul and David Pettigrew trans., Albany, NY.

Parmentier, S. (2011) 'The missing link: Criminological perspectives on dealing with the past'. In M. Bosworth and C. Hoyle (eds) (2011) *What is Criminology?*, Oxford: Oxford University Press.

Radnoti, M. (1972) 'Postcard 4', taken from the anthology, *Clouded Sky*, translated by Steven Polgar, Stephen Berg and S.J. Marks, New York: Harper & Row.

Rozewicz, Tadeusz. (2011) *They Came To See a Poet* (3rd edition), (selected poems translated by Adam Czerniawski), London: Anvil Press Poetry.

Schmitt, C. (1985) *Political Theology: Four Chapters on the Concept of Sovereignty*, Chicago: The University of Chicago Press.

Sontag, S. (2003) *Regarding the Pain of Others*, London: Penguin Books.

Struk, J. (2004) *Photographing the Holocaust: Interpretations of the Evidence*, London: I.B. Tauris.

Taffet, G. (ed.) (1945) *Extermination of Polish Jews: Album of Pictures* (ZagLada Zydostwa Poliskiego: Album Zdjec), Central Jewish Historical Committee in Poland (Centralna Zydowska Komisja Historyczna Polsce, Lodz).

Weingartner, J.J. (1983) 'Law and justice in the Nazi SS: The case of Konrad Morgen', *Central European History*, 16(3): 276–294.

Willett, J. (1998) *Dix: War, in Disasters of War: Callot Goya Dix, National Touring Exhibitions*, The South Bank Centre, London: Hayward Gallery and Arts Council Collection Publications.

9 Competing for the 'trace'

The legacies of war's violence(s)

Sandra Walklate and Ross McGarry

Introduction

The traces of the violences of war across history can be found in all societies. Sometimes those traces are concrete and deliberately maintained (for example, Oradour sur Glane in France); sometimes their presence is concrete but neglected (for example, the rural town of Belchite in Spain); sometimes their presence is stark (as in the rows of white tombstones or grey crosses across Northern France and Belgium); and sometimes they take the form of the war memorials found in many places across the world. More recent practices would point to the importance of the Internet and social media as creating both official and unofficial spaces of remembrance (Martinsen, 2013). Whatever their shape or form, the legacy of war's violences is there for all to see, for those who choose to look. Memorialisation to those dead, as a result of war, acts as a reminder to the living of the traces of these violences. Yet, embedded in these acts of memorialisation is a complex and ambiguous relationship between the state and the body. Fassin (2011: 288) suggests, 'As their voices are silences, it is their bodies that speak'. In the context of war it is the bodies of the dead that speak, and memorials arguably act as shorthand for their voices. The power of these traces of war is obvious, embodied poignantly during the wars in Afghanistan and Iraq in the military repatriations of the British war dead in the town of Royal Wootton Bassett. As one shop retailer from this town alludes to,

> When you see the lipstick kisses – you can see all the lipstick kisses on the windows of the hearse and smear marks of someone's tear-stained fingers down the window.
>
> (Retailer, Royal Wootton Bassett, November 2012)

War leaves a wide variety of traces above and beyond those to be found in sites of memorialisation. Our purpose in this chapter is to unwrap the multifaceted and multilayered nature of the traces of war in the context of one set of violences in particular: the past and present wars in Iraq and Afghanistan. Our central focus here is the legacy that these war's violences have had, and are having, on coalition military personnel. This is in no way intended to give primacy to these experiences above and beyond the horrors routinely experienced by civilians in the enduring 'War on Terror'. Indeed our intention is to place the experiences of the coalition military in the context of that bigger picture in order to elucidate some of the uncomfortable contradictions that arise as a result of them. In so doing we hope to articulate what kind of truth is being articulated – and by whom – from the state's engagement in this particular conflict, and what relevance this has for criminology. As shall be seen, focussing on the experiences of the military enables us to do this in a way that transgresses the borders of contemporary criminological engagement with war as an arena with which it might be concerned.

From Iraq and Afghanistan to Royal Wootton Bassett

Our interest in the traces of this specific conflict arises out of the confluence of a number of combined issues: contemporary criminological debates (about war), the political context of this conflict and our own personal research engagement. It will be useful to say a little about each of these in turn.

As this volume suggests, criminological engagement with war in general terms has, up until recently, been fairly limited and criminological engagement with this specific conflict even more so. Nonetheless, following on from the challenge laid down by Kramer and Michalowski (2005), the dilemmas posed for criminology by this conflict in particular and war more generally have grown (see, for example, Whyte, 2007; the special edition of *The British Journal of Criminology* edited by Hudson and Walters, 2009; and a further special edition discussing terrorism, edited by Karstedt *et al.*, 2010). This literature has been added to by the recent interventions of Braithwaite and Wardak (2013) (see also Wardak and Braithwaite, 2013). Moreover there has been an interesting juxtaposition between this rising curiosity within criminology and the increasing academic, political and policy awareness of the relationship between soldiering and criminality. This awareness has risen, not only in relation to the widely reported 'misdeamours' of war, as documented in the use of torture and other ceremonies of degradation as, for example, in Abu Ghraib (also see, The Red Cross, 2004; Lilly, 2007; Hamm, 2007) but also in relation to the more 'mundane' and 'ordinary' criminality committed in the course of soldiers 'doing their duty' (see for example, Jeffreys, 2007, on sexual violence directed towards male and female colleagues). These concerns have been added to by an increasing appreciation of the numbers of ex-service personnel found in the prison system and the reasons that lie behind this (see for example Napo, 2008; Treadwell, 2010a, Murray, 2013). In a survey conducted by The National Association of Probation Officers (Napo, 2009: 1) it was 'found that 12,000 former armed service personnel were under the supervision of the Probation Service in England and Wales on either community sentences or on parole', although other estimates have been more conservative.

In critiquing this kind of sociologising of war Jamieson (1999) was keen to point out that it is questionable whether war and the military are meaningfully perceived and understood in wider sociology or criminology. Indeed Treadwell (2010b: 74) has recently suggested, 'it would also be short-sighted to simply reduce the issue of ex-forces personnel in custody to a statistical counting exercise', given the latent impacts that war can have on British soldiers. Against this conventional criminological framing of 'deviant' military behaviour, and taken within the context of the dubious legal status of this particular conflict, there has also been some interest in developing an understanding of the rising socio-political framing of the soldier as victim (see inter alia King, 2010; McGarry and Walklate, 2011). Framing the soldier as victim (considered in more detail below) is the juncture at which appreciating the political context of this particular conflict becomes salient.

It is evident that British soldiers deployed in Iraq and Afghanistan have been party to an ambiguous construction and reception of their role. This stands in stark contrast with their articulation as 'heroes' in the First and Second World Wars. Dubbed as the 'risk wars' (Beck, 2009), this experience of ambivalence in relation to Iraq and Afghanistan has not necessarily been manifest in the same way and to the same degree for all of the NATO participants to this conflict (see Martinsen, 2013, ch. 5). In the context of the UK, however, it must be remembered that the conflict in Iraq was executed without the support of the United Nations or the international community, and its legality has always been in question (see Green and Ward, 2009). This uncertainty was embodied by an unprecedented number of people – estimated at over a million – taking to the streets of London to march against British military action in this war. Over time public support for the Iraq war has become more clearly defined as the wrong course of action to have been taken by the US and UK coalition forces (see Gribble *et al.*, 2012). Given the protracted nature of this conflict (now over ten years old), the economic cost to a state seeking to cut back on expenditure, the admission that such conflicts are 'unwinnable' and with none of the political targets achieved (and arguably those advances in health and education that have been put in place likely to be unsustainable), this wider political context is one that still requires negotiation and management on the part of those in power. Whilst such governmental management practices vary (see Martinsen, 2013), in the UK the dubious legal status of this conflict has left its mark in a number of ways. Two are particularly telling for our discussion here. First, a debate has ensued, and still ensues, about the extent to which, had soldiers been better equipped, fewer fatalities would have occurred (discussed more fully below). Second, and this is where our own personal research interests become pertinent, the process of the repatriation of dead military personnel, particularly through the Wiltshire town of Royal Wootton Bassett, arguably captured the public imagination and the thereby wider multilayered socio-political traces of this conflict.

Presented as an 'ethnography at long and short range' (McGarry, *forthcoming*), our interest in Royal Wooton Bassett began in the classroom at the University of Liverpool. Here we posed a simple question for seminar discussion: 'What is Wootton Bassett about?' To explore this question we used several photographs taken of a military repatriation at Royal Wootton Bassett by an independent professional photographer (and colleague)[1] accompanied by a range of journal articles that were intended to facilitate different ways of interpreting each image. Having offered our own interpretations during the seminars, we asked students to document their own ideas of what they thought 'Wootton Bassett was about'. Some of their responses included:

> Displays of peace and solidarity to bring calm back to the community and country after soldiers have lost their lives in the war. It is a time of reflection.
> Grieving as a nation.
> Respect for British soldiers – a place where people can offer tributes to those that have died.
> Honouring fallen soldiers.
> Collective interests.

Although none of these statements accurately reflected the content of the articles provided to the students, they did reflect a general normative understanding of what the military repatriations comprised and elicited from the photographs. These perhaps fed into some commonsense understandings of military losses and conduct of funeral processions: respect, grief, reflection and commemoration. In an attempt to begin shaping a cultural understanding of the military repatriations, we proposed a victimological analysis of these photographs and suggested that they could be understood to represent different frames of meaning: as a public outlet for privatised grief, as evidence of dark tourism (Foley and Lennon, 1996) or as displays of apolitical resistance against the wars in Afghanistan and Iraq (see Walklate *et al.*, 2011). Since this publication, a range of other literature has emerged concerned with a conceptual analysis of the dead body of the solider (see, for example, Drake, 2011, 2013a, 2013b). In addition Jenkings *et al.* (2012) have provided a useful timeline of the media coverage of these repatriations. Our work in 'Bassett' is ongoing, although we shall draw upon some of its findings as this chapter unfolds.

The juxtaposition of these three influences forms the backcloth to the concerns developed here. In particular we want to consider the ways in which the state's monopoly over its legitimate recourse to violence, in return for providing protection to its citizens (qua Weber), is simultaneously compromised by that same recourse to violence. We centre the soldier in this analysis as illustrative of such a compromise. Within it we are concerned to explore, theoretically and empirically, the traces that power, and in this particular case the use of violence as a feature of power, leaves on the bodies of those so afflicted. Our concern in centring these bodies is not with their literal physical form, in and of themselves, but how their presence makes recursive demands on the state. In this way, we are all asked to reflect upon the truth that these traces speak of. Who and what is listened to, and who and what is denied: perhaps emotively reflected in the comment at the start of this chapter, 'the lipstick kisses on the windows of the hearse'. However, none of the above is doable without some sense of the wider costs of this conflict.

Tracing the bodies: counting the cost

On 1st February 2014, the iraqbodycount.org reported 184,000 deaths (including combatants) as a consequence of the different violences that have taken place in Iraq since the invasion by US and coalition forces in 2003. By far the majority of those deaths have been civilian. In a review of the health consequences of the Iraq war, Levy and Sidel (2013: 949) add that 'Many Iraqi civilians were injured or became ill because of damage to the health-supporting infrastructure of the country, and about 5 million were displaced'. Moreover they go on to add that, '31,000 U.S. military personnel were injured and a substantial percentage of those deployed endure post-traumatic stress disorder, traumatic brain injury, and other neuropsychological disorders' (Levy and Sidel, 2013). The economic costs of this conflict add a further level of harm suffered as a result. Stiglitz and Bilmes (2008) referred to this as the 'three trillion dollar war': a figure that encompasses all the costs to the United States, including rebuilding projects in Iraq and Afghanistan. These total costs to the US have recently been revised by Bilmes (2013) and are now projected to reach somewhere between 4 and 6 trillion dollars. In addition, the US Department of Veteran Affairs stated that it expected to spend 57 billion dollars on disability payments alone in 2012, nearly four times the amount spent per year before this particular conflict began. In a unique study of the economic and social costs to the Iraqi country as a whole, Hagan *et al.* (2012) estimate them to be somewhere in the region of 239 billion dollars, some of which has been disproportionately experienced by Sunni groups. Taking the loss of life and economic costs together, it is hard to disagree with Hagan *et al.*'s (2012: 481) assessment that, 'These losses were widespread and systematic, the hallmarks of crimes against humanity'. If we add to this the estimated 12 billion dollars appropriated and unaccounted for by the coalition forces in Iraq (Whyte, 2007), then the potential for criminological interest in the state's engagement with criminal activity is tellingly obvious.

Against this larger picture, there have, of course, also been specific costs to coalition forces in terms of deaths and injuries. According to the American Bureau of Labor Statistics, by 2012, 4,500 American troops had been killed in Iraq and 1,800 in Afghanistan, with some 633,000 veterans from this conflict having a service-connected disability. In the UK, as of December 2013, 447 military and civilian personnel have lost their lives in Afghanistan, with a further 7,186 field hospital admissions. In the light of the costs presented above, these figures may not appear to be particularly large or significant. They nonetheless constitute 'adverse health consequences' (Levy and Sidel, 2013); it is aspects of these consequences, and the traces of war's violences within them, that we wish to explore in greater depth. In order to do this we return to framing the 'soldier as victim' (McGarry and Walklate, 2011).

Making the bodies count: the soldier as victim?

The graphic images associated with the atrocities of Mai Lai brought home to a generation the potential criminality endemic in soldiering. For some this particular event, and the Vietnam War more generally, constituted the turning point in the recognition of Post Traumatic Stress Disorder (PTSD) for soldiers who both perpetrated and witnessed atrocities (Fassin and Rechtman, 2009). The images from Abu Ghraib, and the increasing awareness of the problematic behaviour of soldiers in Iraq (referenced above), raise similar questions about the criminality inherent in these more recent conflicts. Whilst there has been a rising interest in this kind of criminality and the extent to which military service, in and of itself, acts as a bridge to criminal behaviour in other spheres of their life or as veterans (see Jamieson, 1998 and above), framing the soldier as victim, on whom war leaves other kinds of traces, has much less visibility.

Historically, the First World War saw the beginnings of appreciation for the trauma experienced by soldiers at war (Prestwich, 2003; Fassin and Rechtman, 2009) with Keegan and Holmes (1985) making explicit the ambivalent nature of the soldiers' experiences. They state 'the soldier is both victim and executioner. Not only does he run the risk of being killed and wounded himself, but he also kills and wounds others' (Keegan and Holmes, 1985: 266). Indeed, Barker (1992: 115) goes on to remind us that, 'as soon as you accepted that the man's breakdown was a consequence of his war experience rather than his own innate weakness, then inevitably the war became the issue'. The idea of the soldier as victim became increasingly common in the UK media reporting during the Iraq and Afghanistan conflict (see McGarry and Ferguson, 2012). For example, in the British press the death of the 126th British soldier in Afghanistan in November 2008 was described as a 'Helmand victim' (Cramb, 2008: 10); the most senior officer to be killed in Afghanistan, Lieutenant Colonel Thorneloe, was named as one of the 'many victims of the Taliban' (Steele, 2009: 11); and a soldier killed in Afghanistan during June 2010 was displayed on the front of The Sunday Telegraph below the title '299th victim' (Hennessy, 2010: 1). This victim imagery has also been regularly captured by television documentaries. Such programmes often presented the range of harms experienced by male soldiers including the pains of family separation, the social consequences of war post-conflict and its long-term psychological effects. Such has been the popularity of these types of programmes, that *Wounded* (see Aldous, 2009) – a documentary of the recovery of two young, white, male amputee British soldiers from Afghanistan – won a BAFTA for Best Single Documentary in 2010. This shift toward identifying the soldier as a victim is also reflected in political exchanges and enshrined in law. In 2006 The *Daily Telegraph* led with the story of British soldiers being defined as 'victims of crime' for compensation purposes when injured in Afghanistan and Iraq due to the asymmetrical tactics being employed on them by insurgents which fall outside the confines of 'just war' tactics (Rayment, 2006).

However, framing the soldier as victim poses a number of conundrums and contradictions. Certainly the social and cultural expectations traditionally associated with soldiering do not lend themselves easily to the connotations of victimisation that imply vulnerability, weakness and passivity (Rock, 2007). A soldier is the epitome of normative heterosexuality: very much a 'non-victim' endowed with the capacity for the use of brute force and resilience. However, men in general constitute the 'other' of mainstream victimological thought (Walklate, 2007a); outside the conceptual framework of victimhood, though not necessarily outside the experience of victimisation. Thus the harms that males experience in general are frequently reduced to a 'latent invisibility' (Walklate, 2007b), perhaps paralleling the experiences of personnel from the predominantly male, British armed forces. This being said, it is clear that the harms faced by modern soldiers in Afghanistan and Iraq are far from hidden or invisible, which is evident from the newspaper reports documented above and the public and political attention that Royal Wootton Bassett attracted. The harms with which we are concerned here in particular are the psychological and the physical. We have separated these out as a heuristic device only: experientially it is fair to assume that they are unlikely to be separable or separate processes.

Soldiers as victims: the psychological trace?

> Accept it and forget it. There, there was time to grieve and time to think about it later on, err that wasn't the time ... there was too many other things to think about ... you don't think about it then, you think about it later, err and I, and I think that's probably one of the post traumatic stress things.
>
> (Participant D, in McGarry, 2010: 172)

Although not his words, the soldier in Figure 9.1 captures a telling portrait of 'accept it and forget it' from the extract above. He sits, possibly at home but nonetheless comfortable next to a cushion covered by the union flag, impeccable in his uniform, but showing signs of emotional relief of some kind. We are not in a position to second-guess whether or not behind his eyes are tears of joy or sadness, or just the mixed emotions of being in a place now that stands in stark contrast to where he has been: a contrast he more than likely feels unable to communicate or share with those around him. Whilst in no way implying that this particular soldier is having anything other than a normal emotional response to his surroundings, perhaps the most dominant

Figure 9.1 Iraq war veteran, who was injured in a 'friendly fire' incident sits in his living room, Bolton UK[2]

representation of harm suffered to British soldiers serving in Afghanistan and Iraq is impairments to their mental health. Since 2004 there has been a groundswell of research investigating a range of psychological impacts on British soldiers resulting from conflict. These include PTSD (see for example, Hoge and Castro, 2006; Rona *et al*, 2006; Iversen *et al*, 2008), alcohol misuse and anxiety disorder (see Jones *et al*, 2006; Iversen and Greenberg, 2009), and incidents of suicide (Fear, 2003), to name but a few. In criminology, the psychological impact of their experiences in conflict, in particular the 'hidden wound' of PTSD (Treadwell, 2010b: 76), is seen as the key push factor leading male British veterans into the criminal justice system. Whilst the psychological problems faced by ex-service personnel have long been known (Fassin and Rechtman, 2009), obtaining recognition of, and an appropriate response to, these and other difficulties encountered by veterans is still fraught with problems despite the development and adoption of the 'military covenant' (see Ministry of Defence 2001, 2005) and the Armed Forces Covenant (see Ministry of Defence, 2011). Moreover, Treadwell (2010b: 73) reminds us:

> the other casualties of war are, perhaps, those soldiers who return seemingly physically healthy after military service, and the unfortunate

people who, at some unspecified point in the future will become victims of their crime.

Such an observation is, of course, speculative. What is less speculative is the length of time some of these psychological problems take to manifest themselves (Combat Stress, 2010) and the recognition, within the Military Covenant itself, of their potential occurrence,

> Military action in the land environment is usually 'up close and personal', where the killing and destruction cannot be left behind: the smell, noise and feel are personally felt and never forgotten. There is no easy detachment from the consequences of using or facing force.
>
> (Ministry of Defence, 2010: 3–5, para. 0303)

That same action can and does, of course, take its toll on military personnel physically.

Soldiers as victims: the physical trace?

As has been intimated above, the coalition forces in Iraq and Afghanistan have sustained significant losses in terms of fatalities and injuries (see also Martinsen, 2013); for the UK these wars mark the largest loss of military life since the much shorter-lived Falklands War of the early 1980s. Within this casualty list there have been over 7,000 field hospital admission as of December 2013 with a similar number air lifted back to the UK. In many ways the picture below speaks for itself. Two legs, seriously damaged, now repaired: a testimony to the medical interventions now available to those injured in combat: injuries that at one time would have left them even more severely disabled or dead.

There are, however, two other observations to make about the nature and extent of the injuries received in Iraq, Afghanistan and elsewhere. First is their complexity, arguably a result of the nature of the combat being engaged in and the kinds of weapons being used. Second is the sophistication of the medical response to these injuries and the speed with which they are attended to, meaning that many of those who survive their injuries in present times would not have done so in the past. These observations are intimately connected with the nature and availability of appropriate protective equipment for those soldiers on the ground. This issue has been hotly disputed in the context of the UK engagement in this conflict and adds a further dimension to the victimhood of soldiers (see McGarry *et al*, 2012).

The Military Covenant, referenced above, bestows 'unlimited liability' on British soldiers during their service, to forsake their Right to Life for the good of others. Obviously, as serving personnel, military objectives dictate that soldiers often have to work in dangerous and hostile environments

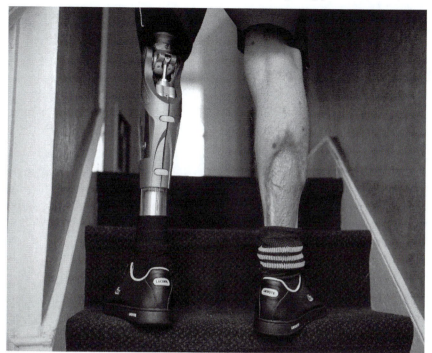

Figure 9.2 Iraq war veteran walking the stairs of his mother's home, London UK[3]

(Woodward and Jenkings, 2011). Nevertheless, Tipping (2008) observes that, 'unlimited liability' infers a moral exchange: in return for forfeiting many of their rights in the line of their duties, in particular their Right to Life, the British government has an obligation to provide members of the British military with the 'enthusiasm to fight' as 'a product of training, confidence in equipment, effective leadership and management [and]... fair terms of service' (Ministry of Defence, 2010: 2–26, para. 0240). The extent to which these tenets have been met in practice is a moot point.

General evidence about the effectiveness of equipment and support was provided by Air Chief Marshall Sir Jock Stirrup (2010) who informed the Chilcot Inquiry of the logistical inadequacies of resources prior to, and during, the war in Iraq. These comments echoed a long-standing dissatisfaction with equipment from British service personnel, well documented in the Armed Forces Continuous Attitudes Survey. This survey has previously reported that over half of all service personnel were dissatisfied with the standard of equipment and resources available to them to do their jobs (Ministry of Defence, 2008: 14). Dissatisfaction of this nature, whilst seemingly trivial, can have fatal consequences for British soldiers,

> Throughout the (Iraq) conflict I had one plate for my vest (body armour), so you had to decide whether you were getting shot in the front or shot in the back.
>
> (Participant B, in McGarry *et al.*, 2012: 1188)

Nicol (2005: 65) adds weight to the kinds of preventable risks documented by the respondent above. In the early stages of the Iraq war, British Army Sergeant Steven Roberts gave his body armour to 'frontline' soldiers whom senior commanders deemed to be more at risk and lost his life as a consequence. It later transpired that Sergeant Roberts had attempted to build his own makeshift body armour by stuffing padding down his uniform and taping it into place (Herbert, 2006). At his inquest coroner Andrew Walker (cited in Herbert, 2006: 2) stated that such failures were 'unforgivable and inexcusable and represent a breach of trust that the soldiers have in those in government'.

Of course, by no means all of the physical injuries sustained in this conflict can be, or have been attributable to equipment failures. It is, however, worth considering whether such issues would have received such public, high-profile attention if the conflict itself had been more widely accepted. As some of the data referred to above indicates, whilst there has been widespread sustained public reluctance to endorse this conflict, this does not mean that soldiers themselves have been treated with the same lack of support (Gribble *et al*, 2012). This is not only evidenced in public attitudes in general, but also in more concrete terms. As one of our respondents from the Royal Wootton Bassett case study observes,

> there's a lot of evidence out there saying that charities are going through a really rough time and their income is decreasing significantly, we've held ours and a slight increase, the Army Benevolent Fund have done the same, now why, you know and Help for Hero's as well, they've (had) a lot of money off people .... I think people have donated to Help for Heroes in the past because of the erm, very visible presence, perhaps created by the repatriations, by the press by whatever, erm, as opposed to what Help for Heroes is really set up for which is helping the injured coming back from, from Afghanistan ... but would that have worked if it hadn't been for Bassett, possibly, but, I don't know.
>
> (Male interview respondent, January 2013)

This respondent is clearly identifying a potential link between the wider coverage given to the repatriations through Royal Wootton Bassett with increased willingness to give to military charities that he observed taking place, tight economic times notwithstanding. Indeed, even the banks (well one banking group in particular[4]) have made distinct efforts to offer soldiers, especially those with disabilities, support, adding some weight to our respondents' observations. The question remains: what does this amount to in terms of understanding the traces of war and/or criminology's capacity for making sense of these traces?

Soldier as criminal or soldier as victim: competing for the trace?

What our discussion has intimated so far is a rising recognition of the contradictory place in which soldiers can find themselves and in which they are to be found within criminological/victimological discourses. A place that is arguably refracted through, and reflected in, the contemporary ambivalent position in which soldiers find themselves in relation to the wider socio-political climate of the Iraq and Afghanistan conflict. In all of this, soldiers are clearly not neglected as bodies in need of treatment, whether that be psychological or physical, neither are they neglected as bodies who may be in need of support, whether that be financial or again psychological. However, where they are neglected is within our capacity to understand either their criminality or their victimhood as a product of not just the traces of war's violences on them as individuals (and the discussion in this chapter so far alludes to the problems inherent in our understandings of them even at this level) but as a product of the traces of the violences of war that maybe perpetrated by them but on behalf of the state. It is at this juncture that we are returned to the observations of Fassin (2011: 284), who states, 'If power leaves traces on bodies, what sort of truth does the state – and more generally society – extract from them?' We shall illustrate this analytical neglect by reference to two (on the surface) unrelated events that actually share a deep connection.

On 22nd May 2013 a young British soldier, Fusilier Lee Rigby, was publicly murdered on the streets of Woolwich, London by two British-born males: Michael Adebowale and Michael Adebolajo. Their motives for this attack were stated as the involvement of the British Government in the wars in Afghanistan and Iraq. In its aftermath, the British media caused the binaries potentially inherent in this event to be presented as banal: Fusilier Rigby was the victim; Adebowale and Adebolajo are 'terrorists' responsible for murder. Although linear in appearance, as Kauzlarich *et al.*, (2001) have suggested, by focussing on the victim we are able to question what harm has been caused to whom, and – importantly – *why*. It has since come to light following the murder trial that Fusilier Rigby was targeted specifically as a member of the British military, identified by wearing a camouflaged backpack in the vicinity of Woolwich barracks (BBC News, 2013). So this soldier was targeted as a symbolic representative of British foreign policy at war (see McGarry, 2014 for an extended discussion of this).

The personal circumstances of Adebowale and Adebolajo, the perpetrators of this attack, are fairly complex. Both men are from lower socio-economic, minority ethnic groups in London, but they had differing successes at college and university. The older of the two men (Adebolajo, 29) converted to Islam whilst studying at university at the height of the British military involvement in the Iraq war. The younger of the two men (Adebowale, 22) emerged from a troubled background involving bullying and 'gang activity'. He had previously been hurt in a violent attack involving drugs resulting in the death of one of his friends and serious injury to another. Following being a witness in the murder trial, Adebowale was diagnosed with a mental illness, 'disappeared' for a while and returned having converted to Islam (see McGarry, 2014 for an extended discussion of this).

As McGarry (2014) has argued, the Woolwich attack illustrates the coming together of broad issues impacting upon the UK relating to crime, disorder, social inequality and war: as he says 'this was not terrorism "pure and simple"' (McGarry, 2014: 29). The traces of the war in Iraq and Afghanistan are clearly evident in the links between the soldier so targeted and the depiction of the offenders as terrorists. However, there is one elephant in this particular room with two trunks. That elephant is the role of the state in perpetrating the violence of Iraq and Afghanistan, and the role of the state in creating, targeting, and making sense of who is to be suspected in relation to this violence (see Walklate and Mythen, 2014: ch. 5).

If Fusilier Rigby was a victim, it is without doubt that Royal Marine Sergeant Alexander Blackman (Marine A) has been marked out as an offender. He was stripped of his rank and given a ten-year prison sentence in December 2013 for the murder of a seriously wounded member of the Taliban in Afghanistan. Throughout his trial Sergeant Blackman never denied his actions and nor could he given the recording available from his helmet camera capturing the murder on film. Perhaps what is at issue here is, what murder might mean in the context of war in general and this conflict in particular. Soldiers, particularly Royal Marines, are expected and trained to kill; despite the validity or otherwise of the particular actions of Marine A, murder requires intent. Did his training provide him with intent or was he engaged in an intent to kill outwith the expectations of him in his role at that particular moment in time? Perhaps these questions need to be put in context. The report by Terrill (2013) achieves some of this. He offers the following assessment,

> Soldiers are not automatons. They are flesh-and-blood human beings with frailties and vulnerabilities like all of us. They are ordinary people doing extraordinary things on our behalf; risking their lives in combat and having to make difficult and morally confusing judgments in the heat of battle. They don't always get it right because, sometimes, the stakes are just too high for any one man to cope with. I believe that if Marine A is a criminal of war, then he is also a casualty of war.

Sergeant Blackman has been tried and convicted for his actions. In many ways he fits well with a conventional criminological account of the route from legitimate behaviour in war to illegitimate behaviour in war. However who draws the line between the one and the other? Who really understands the pressures presented for soldiers fighting an ambivalent conflict, losing their comrades in the process, being under threat for their own lives minute by minute, but being monitored by cameras all at the same time? These, too, constitute the traces of war's violences, but in this room the elephant has but one trunk. The state both expects the soldier to kill and put their own lives at risk, but at the same time expects them to do that within the confines of the shifting sands of the state's definition of what counts as the legitimate means by which to do that.

Both of the cases referred to above illustrate the slippery nature of labels and the problems of consigning soldiers into one category or another. This much might be said of a wide range of events and processes in which individuals may transcend the criminal/victim binary. It is a problem increasingly recognised within the wider criminological literature. However, what these two examples also illustrate very well is the hand of the (invisible) state in contributing to the victims and offenders that we see, along with those that we fail to see. These are the (in)visible traces of war's violences.

Conclusion: the (in)visible traces of war?

In this chapter we have used the concept of the 'trace' to try and unwrap the different layers to the traces of the violences of war. In so doing we have, by implication, alluded to those violences that are readily seen and commented on and those that are not. Criminology, like other arenas of analytical comment, is not averse to seeing some of these traces over and above others. We have centred the soldier in this analysis not by way of lessening the importance of the other harms done in war, but by way of illustrating how the traces of war, in all their manifestation, can be made visible through the lens of hegemonic masculinity. Crucial to the analysis offered here is not so much the visible traces of war's violences on soldiers' bodies but the invisible traces. Those traces are the ones left by the state. Following Sykes and Matza (1957), two 'techniques of neutralization' become apparent here. The first is 'denial of responsibility'. Harms done as a result of state negligence become constituted as part of the costs of war and beyond the control of the State itself, as in the debate over the adequacy of equipment. Second is 'denial of the victim'. Soldiers cannot be victims because of the contract that they make with the state in the course of doing their duty. What underpins these obvious denials are, of course, further layers of denial: from the dubious status of this particular conflict, to the role of domestic policy in creating suspect populations as contributing to the problems inherent in this conflict, to the crimes against humanity perpetrated in the name of this conflict. Taken together, these suggest a 'culture of denial' by the state, in which immoral actions are concealed via misinformation and refutation (Cohen, 2003). However, the traces of war's violences inevitably expose this culture for what it is. The kind of truth extracted from these traces is the kind of truth that cannot be denied. It lies in the traces of lipstick on the windows of military hearses.

Notes

1 The colleague who provided these images of Royal Wootton Bassett is Stuart Griffiths, who is the same independent photographer who provided the image for the cover of this book and also the images presented within this chapter.
2 Photograph from the series 'Closer', courtesy of Stuart Griffiths (http://stuartgriffiths.net).
3 Photograph from the series 'Closer', courtesy of Stuart Griffiths (http://stuartgriffiths.net).
4 See www.mybarclays.co.uk/AFTER.

References

Aldous, J. (2009 September 25) *Wounded*, [BBC One], London: BBC.

Barker, P. (1992), *Regeneration*, London: Penguin Books.

Beck, U. (2009) *World at Risk*, Cambridge: Polity.

Bilmes, L.J. (2013) 'The Financial Legacy of Iraq and Afghanistan: How Wartime Spending Decisions Will Constrain Future National Security', Budgets Faculty Research Working Paper Series, Harvard: University of Harvard.

Braithwaite, J. and Wardak, A. (2013) 'Crime and War in Afghanistan Part 1: The Hobbesian Solution', *British Journal of Criminology*, 53(2): 179–196.

Cohen. S. (2003) 'Human Rights and Crimes of the State: The Culture of Denial'. In McLaughlin, E. Muncie, J. and Hughes, G. (eds) *Criminological Perspectives: Essential Readings*, London: Sage.

Combat Stress. (2010) *Annual Review 2010*. Available from: www.combatstress.org.uk/data/files/cs.annualreview.fin.pdf.

Cramb, A. (2008) 'Helmand Victim Was Due To Be Married', *The Daily Telegraph*, 26th November.

Drake, M. (2011) 'The Returns of War: Bodies, Images and Invented Ritual in the War on Terror'. In Karatzogianni, A. (ed.) *Violence and War in Culture and the Media*, Oxon: Routledge, pp.131–147.

Drake, M. (2013a) 'Commemorating Fatalities of War and National Identity in the Twenty-first Century'. In Ogden, C.A. and Wakeman, S. (eds) *Corporeality: the Body and Society. Issues in the Social Sciences: 8*, Chester: University of Chester Press, pp. 121–132.

Drake, M. (2013b) 'The War Dead and the Body Politic: Rendering the Dead Soldier's Body in the New Global (Dis)order'. In McSorley, K. (ed.) *War and the Body: Militarisation, Practice and Experience*. Oxon: Routledge, pp. 210–224.

Fassin, D. (2011) 'The Trace; Violence, Truth and the Politics of the Body', *Social Research*, 78(2): 281–298.

Fassin, D. and Rechtman, R. (2009) *The Empire of Trauma: An Inquiry into the Condition of Victimhood*, Princeton, NJ: Princeton University Press.

Fear, N. (2003) *Suicide and Open Verdict Deaths Among Males in the UK Civilian Population and the UK Military*, London: Defence Analytical Service Agency. Available: www.dasa.mod.uk/publications/pdfs/suicide/suicide03.pdf.

Foley, M. and Lennon, J. (1996) 'JFK and Dark Tourism: A Fascination with Assassination', *International Journal of Heritage Studies*, 2: 198–211.

Green, P. and Ward, T. (2009) 'The Transformation of Violence in Iraq', *British Journal of Criminology*, 49(5): 609–627.

Gribble, R., Wessely, S., Klein, S. and Alexander, D.A. (2012) *The UK's Armed Forces: Public Support for the Troops But Not Their Missions?* Available: www.bsa -29.natcen.ac.uk.

Hagan, J., Kaiser, J., Rothenberg, D., Hanson A. and Parker, P. (2012) 'Atrocity Victimization and the Costs of Economic Conflict Crimes in the Battle for Baghdad and Iraq', *European Journal of Criminology*, 9(5): 481–498.

Hamm, M. (2007) '"High Crimes and Misdemeanors": George W. Bush and the Sins of Abu Ghraib', *Crime Media Culture*, 3(3): 259–284.

Hennessy, P. (2010) '299th Victim', *The Sunday Telegraph*, 20th June, p. 1.

Herbert, I. (2006) 'Coroner in Blistering Attack on Ministers at Inquest', *The Independent*, 19th December, p. 2.

Hoge, C. W. and Castro, C. A. (2006) 'Post-Traumatic Stress Disorder in UK and US Forces Deployed in Iraq', *The Lancet*, 368: 837.

Hudson, B. and Walters, R. (ed.) (2009) 'Criminology and the War on Terror', *British Journal of Criminology Special Issue*, 49(5): 603–617.

Iversen, A.C. and Greenberg, N. (2009) 'Mental Health of Regular and Reserve Military Veterans', *Advances in Psychiatric Treatment*, 15(2): 100–106.

Iversen, A.C., Fear, N. T., Ehlers, A., Hacker Hughes, J., Hull, L., Earnshaw, M., Greenberg, N., Rona, R., Wessely, S. and Hotopf, M. (2008) 'Risk Factors for Post-Traumatic Stress Disorder Among UK Armed Forces Personnel', *Psychological Medicine*, 38(4): 511–522.

Jamieson, R. (1998) 'Towards a Criminology of War in Europe', in South, N., Ruggiero, V. and Taylor, I. (eds) *The New European Criminology*, London: Routledge, pp. 480–506.

Jamieson, R. (1999) 'Councils of War', *Criminal Justice Matters*, 34: 25–26.

Jeffreys, S. (2007) 'Double Jeopardy: Women, the US Military and the War in Iraq', *Women's Studies International Forum*, 30(1): 16–25.

Jenkings, K.N., Megoran, N., Woodward, R. and Bos, D. (2012) 'Wootton Bassett and the Political Spaces of Remembrance and Mourning', *Area*, 44(3): 356–363.

Jones, M., Rona, R. J., Hooper, R. and Wessley, S. (2006) 'The Burden of Psychological Symptoms in UK Armed Forces', *Occupational Medicine*, 56(5): 322–328.

Karstedt, S., Levi, M., and Ruggiero, V. (eds) (2010) 'Terrorism: Criminological Perspectives', *British Journal of Criminology Special Issue*, 50(4): 617–793.

Kauzlarich, D., Matthews, R. A. and Miller, W. J. (2001) 'Toward a Victimology of State Crime', *Critical Criminology*, 10(3): 173–194.

Keegan, J. and Holmes, R. (1985) *Soldiers: A History of Men in Battle*, London: Guild Publishing.

King, A. (2010) 'The Afghan War and "Postmodern" Memory: Commemoration and the Dead of Helmand', *British Journal of Sociology*, 61(1): 1–25.

Kramer, R.C. and Michalowski, R.J. (2005) 'War, Aggression and State Crime: A Criminological Analysis of the Invasion and Occupation of Iraq', *British Journal of Criminology*, 45(4): 446–469.

Levy, B.S., and Sidel, V. W. (2013) 'Adverse Health Consequences of the Iraq War', *The Lancet*, 381: 949–958.

Lilly, R.J. (2007) 'COUNTERBLAST: Soldiers and Rape: The Other Band of Brothers', *The Howard Journal*, 46(1): 72–75.

McGarry, R. (2010) 'Accept it and Forget it: Disintegration, Reintegration and the Military Homecomer'. In Ferguson, N. (ed.) *Post-Conflict Reconstruction*, Cambridge: Cambridge Scholars Press, pp. 165–180.

McGarry, R. (2014) 'Dismantling Woolwich: Terrorism "Pure and Simple"?', *Criminal Justice Matters*, 91(1): 28–29.

McGarry, R. and Walklate, S. (2011) 'The Soldier as Victim: Peering Through the Looking Glass', *British Journal of Criminology*, 51(6): 900–917.

McGarry, R. and Ferguson, N. (2012) 'Exploring Representations of the Soldier as Victim: from Northern Ireland to Iraq'. In Gibson, S. and Mollan, S. (ed.). *Representations of Peace and Conflict*. Basingstoke: Palgrave, pp. 120–142.

McGarry, R., Mythen, G., and Walklate, S. (2012) 'The Soldier, Human Rights and the Military Covenant: A Permissible State of Exception?' *International Journal of Human Rights*, 16(8): 1182–1195.

McGarry, R., (forthcoming) 'Conducting "Community Orientated" Military Research.', in Williams, A.J., Woodward, R., Jenkings, K.N. and Rech, M. (eds) Ashgate Research Companion to Military Research Methods, Surrey: Ashgate, pp. TBC..

Martinsen, K.D. (2013) *Soldier Repatriation: Popular and Political Responses*, London: Ashgate.

Ministry of Defence. (2001) *Soldiering: The Military Covenant ADP Vol. 9*. Available: www.army.mod.uk/join/terms/3111.aspx.

Ministry of Defence. (2005) *Army Doctrine Publication: Land Operations*, London: Directorate General of Development and Doctrine. Available: www.da.mod.uk/jscta/preparation/adp_land_ops.pdf.

Ministry of Defence. (2008) *Armed Forces Continuous Attitudes Survey 2007: Results*, London: Ministry of Defence. Available: www.dasa.mod.uk/applications/newWeb/www/index.php?page=67&pubType=0&thiscontent=700&date=2011-03-31.

Ministry of Defence. (2010) *Army Doctrine Publication: Operations*, Swindon: Development, Concepts and Doctrine Centre. Available: www.mod.uk/NR/rdonlyres/41903E11-B6F4-4351-853B-2C1C2839FE1B/0/ADPOperationsDec10.pdf.

Ministry of Defence. (2011) *The Armed Forces Covenant*, London: Ministry of Defence. Available: www.mod.uk/NR/rdonlyres/4E9E2014-5CE6-43F2-AE28-B6C5FA90B68F/0/Armed_Forces_Covenant.pdf.

Murray, E. (2013) 'Post-army Trouble: Veterans in the Criminal Justice System', *Criminal Justice Matters*, 94(1): 20–21.

Napo. (2008) 'Ex Armed Forces Personnel and the Criminal Justice System', Briefing Paper. Available:www.napo.org.uk/templates/assetrelay.afm?frmAssetFileID=317.

Napo. (2009) 'Armed Forces and the Criminal Justice System', Briefing Paper. Available: www.napo.org.uk/templates/assetrelay.cfm?frmAssetFileID=319.

Nicol, M. (2005) *Last Round: The Red Caps, the Paras and the Battle of Majar*, London: Cassell Military Paperbacks.

Prestwich, P.E. (2003) '"Victims of War"? Mentally-Traumatized Soldiers and the State, 1918–1939', *The Western Society for French History*, 31: 243–254.

Rayment, S. (2006) 'Wounded Troops to get Millions in Compensation', *The Sunday Telegraph*, 10th December: 1.

Rock, P. (2007) 'Theoretical Perspectives on Victims and Victimisation'. In Walklate, S. (ed.) *Handbook of Victims and Victimology*, London: Routledge-Willan, pp. 37–61.

Rona, R. J., Hooper, R., Jones, M., Hull, L., Browne, T., Horn, O., Murphy, D., Hotopf, M. and Wessely, S. (2006) 'Mental Health Screening in the Armed Forces Before the Iraq War and Prevention of Subsequent Psychological Morbidity: Follow-up Study', *British Medical Journal*. Available: http://bmj.com/cgi/content/full/333/7576/991.

Steele, J. (2009) 'Taliban Kill most Senior Officer so Far', *Metro*, 3rd July, p. 11.

Stiglizt, J. and Bilmes, L. (2008) *Three Trillion Dollar War: The True Cost of the Iraq Conflict*, New York: W.W. Norton.

Stirrup, J. (2010) *Air Chief Marshal Sir Jock Stirrup Transcript*. Available: www.ira qinquiry.org.uk/media/45320/20100201am-stirrup-final.pdf.

Sykes, G.M. and Matza, D. (1957) 'Techniques of Neutralization: A Theory of Delinquency', *American Sociological Review*, 22(6): 664–670.

Terrill, C. (2013) 'Marine A; Criminal or Casualty?', *The Daily Telegraph*, 1st December.

The Red Cross. (2004) 'Report of the International Committee of the Red Cross (ICRC) on the Treatment by the Coalition Forces of Prisoners of War and Other Protected Persons by the Geneva Conventions in Iraq During Arrest, Internment and Interrogation'. Available: www.globalsecurity.org/military/library/report/2004/ icrc_report_iraq_feb2004.pdf.

Tipping, C. (2008) 'Understanding the Military Covenant', *RUSI*, 153(3): 12–15.

Treadwell, J. (2010a) 'Are Today's Heroes Tomorrow's Prisoners?', *Criminology in Focus*, 5: 8.

Treadwell, J. (2010b) 'COUNTERBLAST: More than Casualties of War?: Ex-Military Personnel in the Criminal Justice System', *The Howard Journal*, 49(1): 73–77.

Walklate, S. (2007a) *Imagining the Victim of Crime*, Maidenhead: Open University Press.

Walklate, S. (2007b) 'Men, Victims and Crime'. In Davies, P., Francis, P. and Greer, C. (ed.), *Victims, Crime and Society*, London: Sage, pp. 87–98.

Wardak, A. and Braithwaite, J. (2013) 'Crime and War in Afghanistan Part 2: A Jeffersonian Alternative?', *British Journal of Criminology*, 53(2): 197–214.

Walklate, S. and Mythen G. (2014) *The Contradictions of Terrorism*, London: Routledge.

Walklate, S., Mythen, G. and McGarry, R. (2011) 'Witnessing Wootton Bassett: An Exploration in Cultural Victimology', *Crime Media Culture*, 7(2): 149–166.

Whyte, D. (2007) 'Crimes of the Neo-Liberal State in Occupied Iraq', British Journal of Criminology, 47(2): 177–195.

Woodward, R. and Jenkings, N. (2011) 'Military Identities in the Situated Accounts of British Military Personnel', *Sociology*, 45(2): 252–268.

Postscript

From the criminalisation of war to the militarisation of crime control

John Lea

War, crime and politics

The distinction between war and crime is a product of the evolution of the modern state. Before the consolidation of the modern system of nation states there were only really varieties of war: war between kings and princes, feuds and vendettas between communities and interpersonal disputes settled in various ways. Even in the early stages of development of the modern European state, serious crime, as Foucault (1977) famously showed, was seen as a variety of rebellion or war on the Sovereign and punishment a variety of revenge on the body of the offender.

From the Westphalian settlement of 1648 onwards the distinction between affairs within the territorial nation state and relations between nation states is consolidated. The terrain of the nation state is the locus for most of the development of personal restraint (Elias, 2000) and the concentration of legitimate coercion in the state apparatus. Citizens hand over their conflicts to the state (Christie, 1977) and remain, unless called to give evidence, passive observers. Their conflicts become crime and are regarded as offences against the public peace, rather than simply a violation of the victim. The state courts decide the identity of, and indeed the categories of, victim and offender through a legal procedure which, in its modern variant, recognises civil rights pertaining to both victim and accused. Police, the (usually armed) force of the territorial state concentrate on containing public disturbances, gathering evidence on crimes and bringing offenders before the courts. This is done in accordance with a set of legal rules of restraint the violation of which may invalidate the prosecution case. Prosecution and trial is similarly rule-governed with recognition of the rights of the accused, the status of evidence and the guarantee of fair trial. This description is of course an ideal type of the modern liberal democratic state. Not all states adhere to such norms.

Warfare remained as a possible form of relations between nation states. It was famously defined as the continuation of politics by other means (Clausewitz, 1989). The target of warfare is not criminal offenders but the uniformed military of the opposing state. There is no higher authority – no world state – that can define the illegality of the act or the identities of victim and offender.

These, insofar as they are at all deployed as categories, are determined purely by the outcome of the conflict and the nature of peacemaking or surrender in each case. Warfare classically combines both organised violence and the attempt to suppress the organised violence of the enemy state. War is both 'crime' and 'criminal justice', merged into a single process.

The work of the military is quite different to that of police. Careful restraint and the gathering of evidence for prosecution is replaced by the continuation of the martial spirit or 'killing mood' (Cohen, 2001; Bourke, 1999). The aim is not arrest of the guilty but the identification of targets and pre-emptive neutralisation of enemy assets. Captured enemy soldiers are not regarded as criminal suspects. Soldiers who die in battle are not normally regarded as victims of crime. There is, however, a concept of war crime: the various Geneva conventions which, dating from the mid-nineteenth century with subsequent elaborations, establish rules for the appropriate conduct of war rather than attempting to outlaw war as such. Contending states, even when at war, might be seen to have a mutual interest in such matters as treatment of prisoners, wounded, refugees and even the non-use of weapons of mass destruction. Under various conventions violation of these rules has the status of war crime. The study of war crime might still seem a more legit-imate, though sparsely researched, area for criminology than war itself (Mullins, 2011).

Finally, the conduct of war diverges radically from the conduct of criminal justice. The latter is a normal day-to-day feature of life in the modern state which rarely concerns the average citizen. The former is episodic and, in its modern industrial form, as epitomised by the two World Wars, requires a diversion of all social and economic resources to the 'war effort'. This may also involve the suspension of normal liberties of the citizen for the duration of the conflict. Wide ranges of activities perceived by political and military elites as likely to undermine morale are likely to be criminalised, while groups, such as refugees from the enemy state, are likely to be regarded as a 'risk group' and incarcerated on that basis for the duration of hostilities. Thus, during the second world war in the UK Order 18b of the Defence Regulations enabled the authorities to incarcerate anyone deemed likely to be a Nazi sympathiser. Churchill, mindful of the resources and time necessary to interrogate and determine culpability of individual German and Italian citi-zens living in the UK issued the famous order to 'collar the lot'. The con-sequent mass internment irrespective of actual involvement in sabotage or enemy sympathies was an early example of 'actuarial justice' at work (Gillman and Gillman, 1980; Simpson, 1992).

The changing relationship between war and crime

The Second World War was the last war between advanced industrial nation states. A strong body of opinion suggests that such industrialised total war with its attendant carnage is never likely to recur. The very fact of nuclear weapons makes the likely Armageddon unthinkable. This has been reinforced by the emergence in the West of a post-military society (Shaw, 1991). Military elites have become smaller and politically marginalised, while mass conscription has been replaced by small professional armies. Mass nationalism and religious fervour have been in serious decline in the global north. Most who choose a military career are less motivated by service to 'Queen and Country' than the transferability to later civilian life of technical skills acquired. War has become something of limited duration normally occurring in faraway areas of the global south or Eastern Europe, and its images, transmitted by global media, have become a variety of spectator sport (Mann, 1988). Under such circumstances the type of wars that northern industrial states can mount are 'risk-transfer' wars (Shaw, 2005), which prioritise force protection and transfer of casualty risks to the enemy, a strategy which unravelled disastrously in Iraq and Afghanistan and has crippled the ability of powerful states to rally public support for anything but bombing raids and robot-controlled 'warfare at a distance' by pilotless drones.

The decline of nationalism seems to have been replaced by increased empathy for suffering and poverty and a concern with human rights. The carnage of the Second World War, the Holocaust in particular, revived the dormant concern with human rights which, a product of the eighteenth century, had been suppressed by the racism and nationalism of the late nineteenth and early twentieth centuries (Hunt, 2008; Ishay, 2008). The Nuremberg trials of Nazi leaders provided a context for elaboration of conceptions of war crimes, crimes against humanity and genocide. The United Nations Charter of 1945, with more success than its predecessor, the League of Nations, prohibited unilateral recourse to armed force by member states and was followed in 1948 by the Universal Declaration of Human Rights. The model for legitimate armed intervention by all states in the affairs of other states was henceforth only as 'cosmopolitan law enforcement' (Kaldor, 1999: 11).

If military action was now legitimate, not as the continuation of politics by other means but as police action in defence of human rights on behalf of the United Nations, most armed conflict in various parts of the world was assuming a character more resembling crime than classic inter-state war. The 'new wars' thesis popularised by Kaldor (1999) and others (Holsti, 1996; Van Creveld, 1991; Munkler, 2005) saw most warfare not as inter-state but intrastate and fought in the context of state collapse. Participants in such conflicts were not the organised militaries of rival states but a 'disparate range of different types of groups such as paramilitary units, local warlords, criminal gangs, police forces, mercenary groups and also regular armies including breakaway units of regular armies' (Kaldor, 1999: 8). Funding was derived less from national state taxation and 'war effort' than through the contributions of diaspora communities, organised criminal protection rackets, drugs and arms trafficking (Schlichte, 2003; Strazzari, 2003). Finally, much more than in classic interstate warfare, the aim of conflict is 'ethnic cleansing' and direct targeting of civilian populations, often taking violent and sadistic forms such as organised rape and, finally, genocide (Shaw, 2003, 2013). It is possible to regard such conflicts, by contrast with traditional inter-state war, as straightforward criminal violations of human rights and certainly to see in such conflicts the collapse of the distinction between war as such and war crime.

The contrast between a global south vulnerable to poverty, state failure and armed conflict and a global north of strong states able to function as aid donors or police is a reflection of the massive inequalities, both within and between states, associated with globalisation (Arrighi and Silver, 1999; Therborn, 2013). Reinforced by climate change and resource erosion, these changes lie behind new wars, terrorism and rural rebellions stretching across the global south (Abbott, *et al.*, 2007; Brock, 2014). Where the global economy and the social policies of states no longer focus on social inclusion and integration but at the same time spread the message of Western values and consumption, then the marginalised will develop forms of expression, not to say rage, and innovatory ways of combating their exclusion.

Problems of international criminal justice

The notion of military intervention under UN authority as police action requires some qualification. Most such action is of a peacekeeping variety, oriented to protection of civilians, refugees, aid convoys, etc. The main aim is not the arrest of offenders. The analogy is with public order policing rather than detective work. Nevertheless the arrest sanction is necessary if criminalisation is to be anything other than rhetoric. This requires some sort of functioning criminal justice system. In the absence of a global state, all variants of international law rest on the mutual agreement of states. The emergence of a system of tribunals culminating in the establishment of the International Criminal Court (ICC) in 2002, notwithstanding that not all states are signatories, is testimony to the legitimacy of the United Nations under whose auspices it acts with authority to try individuals, including heads of state, for war crime, crimes against humanity and genocide.

However, there are two important obstacles to any straightforward criminalisation of war through the ICC. The first is that, despite the authority of the UN the ICC is vulnerable to the machinations of the most powerful states. In fact a number of powerful states including the US itself, China and India and several smaller states are not even signatories to the ICC. The fact that powerful states no longer resort to armed force to settle disputes among themselves does not imply the absence of national interests (as defined by ruling elites) in each state nor that force will not be used against weaker states or that proxy wars, including 'new wars', will not be promoted in furtherance of national interests. The invasion of Iraq, a weaker state, by the US-led coalition in 2003 in blatant violation of the UN Charter and international law can be regarded as state crime (Kramer and Michalowski, 2005). The US and its allies were quite determined to pursue their own national interests even if that meant violating the UN itself.

The ICC and similar specialist UN tribunals established to deal with particular conflicts such as Yugoslavia or Rwanda have in the main indicted very few individuals and, apart from Yugoslavia, most of these are from weak African states. The likelihood of the US or the UK being indicted over the invasion of Iraq or Afghanistan or the bombing of Libya remains remote. In the current protracted civil war in Syria, elements of new war – mainly Islamic Jihadist irregulars, including Al Qaeda, fighting the severely weakened regime of Bashar al-Assad – appear as proxy war, reminiscent of the Cold War period, sustained on one side by the US and its allies and on the other by Russia and Iran. In May 2014 the UN Security Council attempt to refer the conflict to the ICC was vetoed by Russia and China. In this case the US was supportive of the ICC, even though not a signatory. Critics argue that it is difficult to see what role the ICC can play where warfare is so obviously the continuation of politics by other means, and the only feasible solution is either the victory of one party or a process of political compromise (Cronin-Furman, 2013, 2014). Even in weak states the ICC is dependent for evidence gathering on forms of local political compromise which threaten to make it a tool of the contending parties rather than an impartial court (Cadman, 2012).

The second obstacle concerns the role of criminal justice as a method of settling disputes between parties. In domestic criminal justice systems, crime is ultimately a violation of the public peace. The victim is the vehicle of that violation. Even in intra-state 'new wars' the most immediate issue may not be that war crimes or even crimes against humanity have been committed, but that communities, ethnic groups, or warlord-led armies are in conflict. The aim of any realistic outside intervention is to establish the basis of compromise and reconciliation. From such a standpoint the ICC and similar tribunals (such as those devoted to the conflicts in former Yugoslavia or Rwanda) may be either irrelevant to, or indeed barriers to, the processes of political compromise between communities which are a necessary part of state-building in post-conflict situations (Chandler, 2006; Steele, 2008; Lea, 2010; Abrams, 2012).

These obstacles may be less important than they appear. If it is accepted that entities like the ICC are inevitably assimilated to the development agendas of powerful states, then the question is, what role can they play in that context? If the aim is simply state-building and national reconstruction, then criminal prosecution may well be counter-productive to community reconciliation. But, if the agenda is rather the management of conflicts (whether at state or sub-state level) to the advantage of powerful states and transnational corporations, then a variety of additional strategies can be useful, ranging from Western-funded NGOs channelling development aid direct to local communities (rather than via a non-existent local state apparatus), through negotiations with local warlords in conflict zones to guarantee access to mineral deposits, to cosmopolitan law enforcement. In this more flexible context, the role of the ICC as a tactical device to 'take out' particularly troublesome local leaders through war crime indictments might be useful. Even so, in its present guise the ICC is cumbersome and expensive, with few successfully concluded prosecutions to its credit. Whether any strategy or combination of strategies – criminal justice, warfare, development aid – will be sufficient to resolve the global crises of poverty and marginalisation is another matter (Rogers, 2010).

Terrorism and the militarisation of criminal justice

The inequality, poverty, armed violence and shadow economies of the conflict zones of the global south make their way to northern industrial cities through global terrorist and organised crime networks, undocumented migrations and internet communications. But such conditions are already present in many large cities, both north and south. Paramilitary policing is already well established in Los Angeles or Rio de Janeiro as much as in Beirut or Mogadishu (Davis, 2006; de Almeida, 2010). Various mixtures of criminal justice, aimed at arrest and prosecution, and military action, aimed at containment and neutralisation of equally militarised gangs and criminal militias, prevail, depending on context.

In relatively peaceful liberal democracies such as the UK with no modern tradition of 'internal war' there is nevertheless a discerned movement in the opposite direction to the criminalisation of war discussed so far. At present it is represented less in the overt militarisation of policing than in legal and regulatory changes evident particularly in anti-terrorist legislation enacted following '9/11'. After 2001 focus shifted to globalised 'network terrorism' (Stepanova, 2008) and new forms of state response blurring the boundaries between crime control and warfare (Degenhardt, 2010, 2013).

The US response to Al Qaeda-inspired terrorism took the form of the now exhausted 'war on terror' which, fuelled by unique traditions of 'frontier justice' (Steinert, 2003), culminated in alleged practices of torture and rendition with incarceration in Guantanamo Bay. The latter appeared as the ultimate hybrid institution whose inmates, neither prisoners of war nor criminal suspects but 'unlawful combatants' (Megret, 2006), have for many years been subject to gross violations of both statuses.

European jurisdictions attempted to maintain criminal justice orientations to terrorism as they had during the 1970s and '80s with Red Army Faction in Germany and the Red Brigades in Italy. In the UK, by contrast, internment without trial in Northern Ireland of IRA terrorist suspects from 1971 to 1975, accompanied by what the European Court of Human Rights described as inhuman and degrading treatment of internees, was a major step in the direction of deployment of wartime emergency (Hillyard, 1993). The response to Al Qaeda-inspired terrorism has seen nothing on the scale, nor the degrading treatment, of the 1970s internment. Nevertheless, some similar principles have been applied with Control Orders (enacted in 2005), replaced in 2011 by Terrorism Prevention and Investigation Measures. In both cases restrictions of liberty, imposed by government authority without conviction in the courts, based on police or security service intelligence which the accused cannot challenge in open court, are maintained.

Such measures, and the associated notions of national emergency that accompany them, are generally argued for on the basis of risk. The 'war on terror' comes to be seen as a variety of risk management (Heng, 2005). The risk argument relies on the contrast between on the one hand the grave consequences of a successful audacious terrorist incident and, on the other, the fact that available intelligence information of the conspiracy may fall far short of that required for successful criminal prosecution. This, in the words of a former Director of the UK security service, MI5, creates the 'central dilemma, how to protect our citizens within the rule of law when intelligence does not amount to clear cut evidence' (Manningham-Buller, 2005).

This fostered a militarisation of criminal justice in two senses. First, the emphasis inevitably shifts from gathering evidence sufficient for prosecution to the identification of targets on the basis of risk calculations derived from techniques such as profiling, surveillance of communications meta-data and other sources of intelligence. The aim then becomes that of pre-emptive neutralisation of risky individuals before they can do any damage, despite evidence being insufficient to sustain a conspiracy prosecution: 'The central question to be asked in the context of a possible intervention becomes not "has this individual committed a crime?" but, rather, "does this person constitute a risk?"' (Hörnqvist, 2004: 37). The principles of wartime emergency reminiscent of internment of enemy aliens as 'likely' threats to security begins to gain a foothold. This time the emergency is permanent. There is no point at which the enemy surrenders and peace is restored. The emergency measures are initially directed at communities of similar ethnic or religious background to the suspected terrorists. These communities thereby become new 'suspect communities' (Pantazis and Pemberton, 2009, 2012). Second, the police themselves begin to militarise, not just in the use of technology (Graham, 2010b) but also arguably adopting military methods of neutralising targets rather than making arrests. The shooting by police in London of the entirely innocent Brazilian, Jean Charles de Menezes, in July 2005 gave rise to the suspicion that in certain circumstances a 'shoot to kill' policy was now legitimate in mainland UK (Kennison and Loumansky, 2007).

Once established, such principles and methods of work set up a trickle-down and contamination effect on other areas of criminal justice and state security. The methods developed in anti-terrorism strategies are applied to other types of criminal offenders regarded as sufficiently dangerous to require a more pre-emptive response. Restrictions on travel, communications and other activities similar to restrictions on terrorist suspects as well as asset forfeiture irrespective of criminal conviction may apply to those suspected of involvement in organised crime. Serious Crime Prevention Orders (SCPOs) were introduced in the UK in 2007 and asset forfeiture without criminal conviction in 2002 (Lea, 2004; H.M. Government, 2013). Illegal migrants as non-citizens are immediately vulnerable to incarceration and deportation with little recourse to due process of law. A general principle of anticipatory or pre-emptive criminalisation is established which gradually permeates the criminal justice and other agencies of social control and begins to move from the social periphery – of terrorists, traffickers and illegal migrants – to the core population (Hallsworth and Lea, 2011).

An aspect of this was revealed in the indiscriminate programme of covert mass surveillance of personal communications revealed by Edward Snowden (Greenwald, 2014; Harding, 2014). Undertaken in the UK by the Government Communications Headquarters (GCHQ) (and in the US by the National Security Agency), the activity has dubious legality (Hopkins, 2014a, 2014b), yet is defended by senior security officials as essential to combatting terrorism. Even if this were the aim, the Orwellian scope of covert surveillance is far wider than a focus that terrorism might conceivably justify (Taylor and Hopkins, 2013). Terrorism in recent years has expanded to embrace vaguely defined 'domestic extremism', which usually indicates animal rights or ecological activist groups.

Governing through security

Meanwhile, similar principles are increasingly applied to the general management of the poor through an apparatus of pre-emptive criminalisation, overwhelmingly of young people in deprived urban areas, through curfew orders, dispersal zones and anti-social behaviour orders (ASBOs) (Crawford, 2009) (replaced in 2014 by Injunction to Prevent Nuisance and Annoyance) and Public Space Protection Orders which effectively eliminate unsurveyed public space in the UK following similar developments in the US (Appleton, 2014).

At the same time, military surveillance techniques are finding their way into normal urban design at an alarming pace. The military strategy of identification of targets and intruders via CCTV is supplemented by technology with military origins such as use of unmanned drones in urban surveillance; Steve Graham (2010a, 2010b) has coined the term 'military urbanism'. The end result is the urban dystopia of militarised and surveyed public space on the one hand and fortified, gated middle-class residential communities, shopping and business precincts on the other described by Mike Davis (1990) in Los Angeles over two decades ago. Alongside this is the merging of terrorist suspects, undocumented migrants, traffickers and unemployed youth into 'an entire "enemy population"', rather than individual offenders, against whom security initiatives are targeted' (Zedner, 2000: 211. See also Zedner, 2010; Fekete and Webber, 2010; Krasmann, 2007). In this process the notion of war as in 'war on crime/drugs/anti-social behaviour' becomes, as Steinert (2003) observed, a 'populist moment'. It makes possible a variety of 'war effort' against an amalgam of enemies.

Although anti-terrorist policy is an ingredient of such developments, notions of trickle-down are inadequate. Just as important is 'trickle-up' based on the militarised techniques developed for the surveillance of the poor. The ASBO, the dispersal zone, the Public Space Protection Order creates an environment legitimising the anti-terrorist Control Order as much as the reverse. Expanding urban surveillance and access to individual citizens' communication data by police, local authorities and other bodies creates a normalising environment in which the security services see covert mass surveillance as justifiable, even if illegal.

These forms of urban social control spreading through the deprived urban areas of otherwise strong states in the global north are ultimately rooted in the same social and economic forces that have wreaked such havoc in the global south. The same dynamics of globalisation and inequality that lie behind state collapse and new wars in the global south lie behind the collapse of the old welfare state society which aspired to universalist 'welfare citizenship', defined the poor as fellow citizens to be assisted and rehabilitated, and which organised domestic politics around a carefully calibrated compromise between social classes. The neoliberal successor regime sees the poor as responsible for their own fate, to choose whether to join a precariat of flexible low-wage labour or remain unemployed. Meanwhile the welfare state morphs into a workfare state designed to coerce the poor to make the 'correct choice' of low-wage work while the middle classes are encouraged to resort to private provision. Politics becomes increasingly a conversation between the political elite, finance capital and the asset-rich middle class, with little role for political compromise with a weak, socially excluded, de-industrialised working class. As a consequence politics becomes increasingly a 'hollowed out' conversation among the elite. The poor are no longer effectively represented in the decision-making organs of the state but are regarded as a risk group to be managed, surveyed and kept bottled up in their zones and ghettos where they are vulnerable to their own variety of 'new wars' in the form of gang conflicts and periodic riot. If the welfare state aspired to end poverty, the security state works to 'criminalize poverty via the punitive containment of the poor' (Wacquant, 2007: 277).

Convergence: the security paradigm

The question is how best to defeat or neutralise the enemy. Whether this is to be done by fortifications and exclusion zones, surveillance, public order maintenance, riot control, arrest and prosecution becomes a matter of simple policy choices to be made as the situation demands; criminal justice, with its rules of evidence and guarantee of rights for the suspect to a fair trial, is not abolished. It is rather eaten away at the edges by a spectrum of other measures which are not so focused on guaranteeing those rights. At the other end of the continuum lies warfare, which is manifestly not concerned with these rights but with targets and neutralisation. The issue is to prevent the slippage along that continuum to the nightmare scenario of urban armed conflict. Some time ago Mike Davis (2006: 203 from Peters, 1996) quoted a retired but prescient US military officer:

> The future of warfare lies in the streets, sewers, high-rise buildings, industrial parks, and the sprawl of houses, shacks, and shelters that form the broken cities of our world .... Our recent military history is punctuated with city names – Tuzla, Mogadishu, Los Angeles, Beirut, Panama City, Hue, Saigon, Santo Domingo – but these encounters have been but a prologue, with the real drama still to come.

Intervention in internal warfare in collapsed states with the aim of stabilisation rather than military conquest shifts the military paradigm in the direction of policing. But at the same time intervention to contain marginalised populations in large cities pushes the police paradigm in the direction of militarisation. The two paradigms meet halfway where they construct a new amalgam – the security paradigm. At an operation level – how police or military or paramilitary forces conduct themselves – this takes from the military the focus on control of populations, rather than individuals, and an enthusiasm for the pre-emptive neutralisation of targets. It takes from the policing paradigm a certain respect for the individual rights of suspects, the gathering of evidence where necessary and the prioritisation of peaceful containment over the use of indiscriminate deadly force. In particular contexts the paradigm may shift in one direction or another along the police–military continuum.

In certain contexts, such as guaranteeing a peaceful terrain for state-building and social reconstruction following a new war, this operational mix can have a progressive role (Friesendorf, 2010). But this is only one part of the amalgam. It depends what else is going on. In neoliberal social policy in the global north, it is likely to be accompanied by massive surveillance, the zoning of the poor out of the consumption and business areas of the city, the decimation of employment and the collapse of welfare systems into coercive workfare and low-wage precarious employment. In this context it becomes pure containment, the management of risk. In zones in the global south where armed conflict is perpetual and long term and any central state is absent, it is likely to become a question of the protection of Western assets – access to mineral deposits, fortified aid bases and refugee camps – a force to keep warring factions apart and generally an aspect of what Duffield (2014) called the securitisation of development.

References

Abbott, C., Rogers, P. and Sloboda, J. (2007) *Beyond Terror: The Truth About the Real Threats to Our World*, London: Rider.

Abrams, E. (2012) 'Pressure Points Thinking About the International Criminal Court', Council on Foreign Relations – Pressure Points. Available: http://blogs.cfr.org/abram s/2012/07/10/thinking-about-the-international-criminal-court.

Appleton, J. (2014) 'The End of Public Space: One Law To Ban Them All', open-Democracy.   Available: www.opendemocracy.net/ourkingdom/josie-appleton/ end-of-public-space-one-law-to-ban-them-all.

Arrighi, G. and Silver, B.J. (1999) *Chaos and Governance in the Modern World System*, Minneapolis: University of Minnesota Press.

Bourke, J. (1999) *An Intimate History of Killing: Face-to-face Killing in Twentieth-century Warfare*, London: Granta.

Brock, H. (2014) 'Marginalisation of the Majority World: Drivers of Insecurity and the Global South', Oxford Research Group: Building Bridges for Global Security. Available from: www.oxfordresearchgroup.org.uk/publications/briefing_papers_and_ reports/marginalisation_majority_world_drivers_insecurity_and_globa (accessed 20 May 2014).

Cadman, T. (2012) 'The International Criminal Court's Many Flaws Can't Simply Be Glossed Over', *The Guardian*, 28th June. Available from: www.theguardian.com/ commentisfree/2012/jun/28/international-criminal-courts-flaws-overlooked (accessed 24 May 2014).

Chandler, D. (2006) *Empire in Denial: The Politics of State-Building*, London: Pluto.

Christie, N. (1977) 'Conflicts as Property', *British Journal of Criminology*, 17: 1–15.

Clausewitz, C.V. (1989) *On War* (new edition), Princeton, NJ: Princeton University Press.

Cohen, E. (2001) 'Kosovo and the New American Way of War' in Cohen, E. and Bacevitch, J. (eds) *War Over Kosovo*, New York: Columbia University Press.

Crawford, A. (2009) 'Governing Through Anti-Social Behaviour: Regulatory Challenges to Criminal Justice', *British Journal of Criminology*, 49: 810–831.

Cronin-Furman, K. (2013) 'Managing Expectations: International Criminal Trials and the Prospects for Deterrence of Mass Atrocity', *International Journal of Transitional Justice*, 7(3): 434–454.

Cronin-Furman, K. (2014) 'Would an ICC Referral Have Helped Syria?' *Washington Post*, 22nd May. Available from: www.washingtonpost.com/blogs/monkey-cage/wp/ 2014/05/22/would-an-icc-referral-have-helped-syria.

Davis, M. (1990) *City of Quartz: Excavating the Future in Los Angeles*, London: Verso.

Davis, M. (2006) *Planet of Slums*, London: Verso.

de Almeida, R. (2010) 'Brazil: The Shadow of Urban War', openDemocracy. Available from: www.opendemocracy.net/article/brazil_shadow_urban_war.

Degenhardt, T. (2010) 'Representing War as Punishment in the War on Terror', International Journal of Criminology and Sociological Theory, 3(1): 343–358.

Degenhardt, T. (2013) 'The Overlap Between War and Crime: Unpacking Foucault and Agamben's Studies Within the Context of the War on Terror', Journal of Theoretical and Philosophical Criminology, 5(2): 29–58.

Duffield, M.R. (2014) *Global Governance and the New Wars: The Merging of Development and Security* (new edition), Zed Books Ltd.

Elias, N. (2000) *The Civilizing Process*, Oxford and Malden, MA: Blackwell Publishers.

Fekete, L. and Webber, F. (2010) 'Foreign Nationals, Enemy Penology and the Criminal Justice System', Race & Class, 51(4): 1–25.

Foucault, M. (1977) *Discipline and Punish: The Birth of the Prison*, London: Allen Lane.

Friesendorf, C. (2010) *The Military and Law Enforcement in Peace Operations: Lessons from Bosnia-Herzegovina and Kosovo*, Lit Verlag.

Gillman, P. and Gillman, L. (1980) *Collar the Lot! How Britain Interned and Expelled its Wartime Refugees*, (new edition), London: Quartet Books.

Graham, S. (2010a) *Cities Under Siege: The New Military Urbanism*, Verso Books.

Graham, S. (2010b) 'From Helmand to Merseyside: Unmanned Drones and the Militarisation of UK Policing', openDemocracy. Available from: www.opendemocracy.net/ourkingdom/steve-graham/from-helmand-to-merseyside-military-style-drones-enter-uk-domestic-policing.

Greenwald, G. (2014) *No Place to Hide: Edward Snowden, the NSA and the Surveillance State*, London: Hamish Hamilton.

Hallsworth, S. and Lea, J. (2011) 'Reconstructing Leviathan: Emerging Contours of the Security State', *Theoretical Criminology*, 15: 141–157.

Harding, L. (2014) *The Snowden Files: The Inside Story of the World's Most Wanted Man*, Chatswood, NSW: Guardian Faber Publishing.

Heng, Y-K. (2005) *War as Risk Management: Strategy and Conflict in an Age of Globalised Risks*, London: Routledge.

Hillyard, P. (1993) *Suspect Community: People's Experiences of the Prevention of Terrorism Acts in Britain*, London: Pluto Press.

H.M. Government. (2013) *Serious and Organised Crime Strategy*, London: The Stationery Office.

Holsti, K.J. (1996) *The State, War, and the State of War*, Cambridge: Cambridge University Press.

Hopkins, N. (2014a) 'GCHQ's Cover for Optic Nerve Provided by Legislation Introduced in 2000', *The Guardian*, 27th February. Available from: www.theguardian.com/world/2014/feb/27/gchq-insists-optic-nerve-program-legal-legislation-2000.

Hopkins, N. (2014b) 'Huge Swath of GCHQ Mass Surveillance Is Illegal, Says Top Lawyer'. *The Guardian*, 28th January. Available from: www.theguardian.com/uk-news/2014/jan/28/gchq-mass-surveillance-spying-law-lawyer.

Hörnqvist, M. (2004) 'The Birth of Public Order Policy', *Race and Class*, 46: 30–52.

Hunt, L. (2008) *Inventing Human Rights: A History*, W.W. Norton & Company.

Ishay, M.R. (2008) *The History of Human Rights from Ancient Times to the Globalization Era* (2nd edition), Berkeley, CA: University of California Press.

Kaldor, M. (1999) *New and Old Wars: Organized Violence in a Global Era*, Cambridge: Polity.

Kennison, P. and Loumansky, A. (2007) '"Shoot to Kill": Understanding Police Use of Force in Combatting Suicide', *Terrorism, Crime, Law and Social Change*, 47: 151–168.

Kramer, R.C. and Michalowski, R.J. (2005) 'War, Aggression and State Crime. A Criminological Analysis of the Invasion and Occupation of Iraq', *British Journal of Criminology*, 45(4): 446–469.

Krasmann, S. (2007) 'The Enemy on the Border: Critique of a Programme in Favour of a Preventive State', *Punishment and Society*, 9: 301–318.

Lea, J. (2004) 'Hitting Criminals Where it Hurts: Organised Crime and the Erosion of Due Process', *Cambrian Law Review*, 35: 81–96.

Lea, J. (2010) 'Left Realism, Community and State-building', *Crime, Law & Social Change*, 54(2): 141–158.

Mann, M. (1988) *States, War, and Capitalism: Studies in Political Sociology*, Basil Blackwell.

Manningham-Buller, E. (2005) 'The International Terrorist Threat and the Dilemmas in Countering It, Security Service MI5'. Available from: https://www.mi5.gov.uk/home/about-us/who-we-are/staff-and-management/director-general/speeches-by-the-director-general/director-generals-speech-to-the-aivd-2005.html.

Megret, F. (2006) 'From "Savages" to "Unlawful Combatants": A Postcolonial Look at International Law's "Other"' in Orford, A. (ed.) *International Law and its Others*, Cambridge: Cambridge University Press.

Mullins, C.W. (2011) 'War Crimes in the 2008 Georgia–Russia Conflict', *British Journal of Criminology*, 51(6): 918–936.

Munkler, H. (2005) *New Wars*, Cambridge: Polity.

Pantazis, C. and Pemberton, S. (2009) 'From the "Old" to the "New" Suspect Community Examining the Impacts of Recent UK Counter-Terrorist Legislation', *British Journal of Criminology*, 49(5): 646–666.

Pantazis, C. and Pemberton, S. (2012) 'Reconfiguring Security and Liberty Political Discourses and Public Opinion in the New Century', *British Journal of Criminology*, 52(3): 651–667.

Peters, R. (1996) 'Our Soldiers, Their Cities', *Parameters*, 26(Spring): 43–50.

Rogers, P. (2010) *Losing Control: Global Security in the 21st Century*, London: Pluto.

Schlichte, K. (2003) 'State Formation and the Economy of Intra-state Wars' in Jung, D. (ed.) *Shadow Globalization, Ethnic Conflicts and New Wars: A Political Economy of Intra-state War*, London: Routledge.

Shaw, M. (1991) *Post-military Society: Militarism, Demilitarization and War at the End of the Twentieth Century*, Cambridge: Polity.

Shaw, M. (2003) *War and Genocide: Organized Killing in Modern Society*, Cambridge, UK, Malden, MA: Polity Press.

Shaw, M. (2005) *The New Western Way of War: Risk-transfer War and Its Crisis in Iraq*. Cambridge: Polity.

Shaw, M. (2013) *Genocide and International Relations: Changing Patterns in the Transitions of the Late Modern World*, New York: Cambridge University Press.

Simpson, A.W.B. (1992) *In the Highest Degree Odious: Detention Without Trial in Wartime Britain*, Oxford: Oxford University Press.

Steele, J. (2008) 'The ICC Should Not Indict Omar al-Bashir', *The Guardian*, 11th July, Available from: www.theguardian.com/commentisfree/2008/jul/11/sudan.unitednations.

Steinert, H. (2003) 'The Indispensible Metaphor of War', *Theoretical Criminology*, 7: 265–291.

Stepanova, E. (2008) *Terrorism in Asymmetrical Conflict: Ideological and Structural Aspects. SIPRI Research Report No. 23*, Oxford: Oxford University Press.

Strazzari, F. (2003) 'Between Ethnic Collusion and Mafia Collusion: The "Balkan Route" to State-Making' in: Jung, D. (ed.) *Shadow Globalisation, Ethnic Conflicts and New Wars: A Political Economy of Intra-state War*, London: Routledge.

Taylor, M. and Hopkins, N. (2013) 'GCHQ Mass Surveillance Putting Right To Challenge State at Risk, Say Lawyers', *The Guardian*, 13th October. Available from: www.theguardian.com/law/2013/oct/13/gchq-surveillance-right-challenge-state-law.

Therborn, G. (2013) *The Killing Fields of Inequality*, Polity Press.

Van Creveld, M. (1991) *The Transformation of War*, New York: Free Press.

Wacquant, L. (2007) *Urban Outcasts: A Comparative Sociology of Advanced Marginality*, Cambridge: Polity.

Zedner, L. (2000) 'The Pursuit of Security' in Hope, T. and Sparks, C. (ed.) *Crime, Risk and Insecurity: Law and Order in Everyday Life and Political Discourse*, London: Routledge.

Zedner, L. (2010) 'Security, the State, and the Citizen: The Changing Architecture of Crime Control', *New Criminal Law Review*, 13(2): 379–403.

Index